Savannah Lore and More

Tom Coffey

Frederic C. Beil
Savannah

First published in the United States by
Frederic C. Beil, Publisher,
609 Whitaker Street,
Savannah, Georgia 31401.

First edition

Library of Congress Cataloging-in-Publication Data
Coffey, Thomas F., 1923–
Savannah lore and more / by Tom Coffey.
p.   cm.
ISBN 0-913720-92-5
1. Savannah (Ga.)—History—Anecdotes.
2. Savannah (Ga.)—Miscellanea.
I. Title.
F294.S2C644   1997   97-22784
975.8'724—dc21   CIP

Beil website address: http://www.beil.com

This book was typeset by SkidType, Savannah, Georgia;
printed on acid-free paper; and sewn in signatures.

Printed in the United States of America

Savannah Lore and More

In memory of
my newspaper mentors
John L. Sutlive, Jack J. Cook,
Walt Campbell, and Harley Cabaniss,
and with gratitude to many friends

Contents

Contents

Savannah Lore and More

Preface

In the First Book, O Theophilus . . . I'd better pause right here and explain. That opening line is a swipe from Acts of the Apostles, the fifth book of the New Testament, and attributed to Saint Luke, an attribution I would not question, though I understand many calling themselves Bible scholars do. In fact, my thirty-plus years as a Sunday school teacher at St. Michael and All Angels Episcopal Church taught me, in my research, that scholars take delight in mucking up the understanding of the Good Book that we average Joes have been contented with all our lives. Did Paul actually write all those Epistles? Turn loose a scholar on that question, and he's off and running on research to last perhaps several years, likely sustained by a grant from some foundation whose board members couldn't care less who wrote, say, 1 or 2 Corinthians, or Ephesians, or Colossians, or even Titus. Scholars already have convinced many that Paul didn't write Hebrews, although the King James Version tells us that he did. They'd have us believe what Sportin' Life in *Porgy and Bess* contends: "the things that you're liable to read in the Bible ain't necessarily so." Those scholars will have their reward.

I swiped the opening line of Acts for a couple of reasons. First, I doubt that the heirs and assigns of St. Luke (or his literary agent, if he had one, or the agent's heirs and assigns) will sue for plagiarism. Second, I wrote a book titled *Only in Savannah,* published in 1995, and it enjoyed a degree of success on the domestic as well as the remote market (three hardback and one softback printings); and this is its sequel—just as Acts is believed by many of us (including, even, many Bible scholars) to be a sequel to the third Gospel, which is attributed to and bears the title of Luke, the Glorious Physician. Now, you're wondering what Luke (let's concede for the sake of getting to

1

the point that he wrote Acts) meant by "O Theophilus." Just who was the addressee? I did some research on that point, not sustained by any foundation, thinking perhaps that Luke might have omitted an apostrophe and intended to write "O'Theophilus," who could have been an Irishman of that era, more than four centuries before the now-sainted Bishop Patrick began his Christian missionary work in the Emerald Isle, the land of my forebears. I learned that Theophilus might have been a person of that name (perhaps Greek or Roman), and that the literal translation is "lover of God," or "one who loves and fears God." I also learned that Luke might have been addressing any and all of the faithful, and that his salutation was to the God-fearing world in general. Also, I reasoned that most of my friends (and that includes especially all who bought the first book) are God-fearing people—a bold presumption, perhaps, but please accord me and my friends the benefit of doubt. If any atheists or agnostics are among them, I love them as children of God who simply fail to acknowledge their spiritual parentage.

So, to continue my salutation, allow me to say to you readers that in the First Book I attempted to set forth certain bits and pieces of Savannah folklore, be it all true or partly apocryphal, and to blend with the folklore some information I knew positively to be true. This sequel, therefore, will contain some folklore and other factual information that didn't make the first book.

With that, the reason for the title, *Savannah Lore and More,* ought to be obvious. Please recall that my first book on Savannah came out some months after the best-seller *Midnight in the Garden of Good and Evil,* a Peyton Place-ish book about Savannah, full of good stories, some of them juicy, and plots woven around the main plot, which concerned a celebrated killing of a young man of no meaningful repute by an older man of much meaningful repute. The author of *Midnight* is John Berendt, a gentleman I met shortly after my first book came out, and whose work I couldn't put down until I had burned midnight (if you please) oil to read the tome through. His writing style is excellent, and he indeed knows how to weave a main plot with other plots to such a degree of skill and finesse that it's all one readable and gripping story. Ah, talent!

Before *Only in Savannah* came out, Tom Barton of the *Savannah Morning News-Evening Press,* who edits the editorial pages and is a writer high caliber with high readership, read the galleys, interviewed me, and then wrote a preview story about the book and me for *Savannah Magazine.* The magazine referred to my forthcoming (at the time) work as "The Other Book," meaning "other" than Mr. Berendt's, which already had come to be referred to as "the book." And often before publication, friends would stop and ask me, "When's the other book coming out?" So *Only in Savannah* became "the other book," but damned if I want to call this tome *The Other Book: II.*

Little else needs saying in this introduction to a book that's more of the same in some respects and a shade or two different in others. That I could squeeze two such tomes out of this wonderful community I call home attests to the fact that Savannah is, indeed, a remarkable town. My apologies to St. Luke, the Glorious Physician, and to all his heirs and assigns, with the deep and abiding hope and prayer that those who read this work will tell their friends that they simply cannot read the First Book without wanting *More Lore*.

TOM COFFEY

This Is Savannah ... Update

Savannah is a historic city, no question. It is, in fact, the Mother City of Georgia, the place where, on February 12, 1733, James Edward Oglethorpe, representing the Trustees of Georgia, established England's thirteenth colony to serve, among other things, as a buffer between the Spanish in Florida and the twelve other colonies to the north. And to this day, we're proud to say, the Spanish haven't ventured above the St. Mary's River, which separates Georgia and Florida, since General Oglethorpe's soldiers defeated them in the Battle of Bloody Marsh, where Brunswick now flourishes as one of Georgia's active seaports. And as a historic city, Savannah continues to make history.

Savannah made big history on the twenty-eighth day of November 1995, when the quadrennial municipal election came to a climax in the runoff between the two surviving candidates in a four-way race for mayor, and Floyd Adams, Jr., defeated incumbent Mayor Susan Weiner by less than a three hundred-vote margin. Adams, a Democrat, thus became the first black mayor in the city's history, upstaging Mrs. Weiner, a Republican, who only four years previous had made history by becoming Savannah's first woman mayor. She ousted Democrat John P. Rousakis, who had served twenty-one years in the office. Rousakis, trying for a comeback in 1995, was one of the two candidates who failed to make the cut in that 1995 election. Talk about voter-induced affirmative action—first a woman, and next an Afro-American!

Mayor Adams made even more history by drawing the largest crowd ever to attend a Savannah inaugural ceremony—more than three thousand strong. That's because he chose to take the oath of office in the Savannah Civic Center rather than to follow the custom of holding the ceremony either outdoors in front of

4

City Hall or indoors in the municipal building's council chamber. It was a racially mixed audience that cheered the new mayor and his council comprising five white and three black aldermen, and a brand new era in city government was born. Mayor Adams' first act was to name a bipartisan committee of clerics and other citizens to outline a course for improving racial harmony, and to declare vociferously that he intended to be the mayor of all the people.

Otherwise, Savannah remains (as the First Book emphasized) a city that often finds it difficult to take "yes" for an answer. For example, as this writing commenced, the world trade center projected for Hutchinson Island was still being debated and stalled in its implementation. Hutchinson Island is situated just across the Savannah River from River Street, one of the city's most popular strips, along which tourists browse and spend money by shopping and eating in the daytime and by dining and reveling at night. The trade center, when completed, will be an economic and tourist boon to Savannah; and if this book makes publication before its completion—or even before its start—just you wait and see; eventually, it will come to pass, even amid additional bickering and yapping, and home folks one day will wonder how Savannah ever got along without it. Indeed, as publication nears, plans for the project have been agreed upon.

It may be a hidden blessing that Savannah bickers and yaps whenever worthwhile projects begin to take fruition in the minds of movers and shakers. It well may be that the end product, the trade center in this instance, will get off and running because of, as well as in spite of, such widespread debate on the going-in side. The early-on questions were: Which side of the river is better? Won't a trade center on the island create a traffic jam at the foot of the bridge connecting Savannah proper to the island? (And never mind that the bridge is constructed in such a way that an interchange can be affixed to the far side of the bridge. There's also a plan for water taxis, as some other cities have.) Can anyone guarantee that a trade center actually will bring in more visitors to utilize the planned new hotel facilities as an adjunct, or play the golf course, or watch the Indy-car races, the inaugural of which occurred in May 1997, on a mile-long track already built on the island? Will it bring new exhibitors, larger conventions? Will it cut into the convention business of the Savannah Civic Center, which has been enlarged to accommodate more conventioneers? Such questions are illustrative of the many caveats thrown up by doubting-Thomas Savannahians. Who can guarantee anything? Nothing ventured, nothing gained—that's a rebuttal to the doubters advanced by those in county government who are responsible for getting the trade center and its ancillary facilities built. Still, perhaps the skeptics give impetus to a guarantee against mistakes that would prove costly in the future.

Savannah, however, isn't all bad or, to be more precise, all pessimistic; in fact, it's mostly good, in spite of itself. It continues to attract business, two of the most recent start-ups being a large distribution center for Home Depot and a plant to manufacture aircraft parts. It continues to draw tourists from many climes and places, coming to explore the city's famed Historic District, recognized by the Department of the Interior as the largest such preserved section in America, and imprinted "on the map" more indelibly by author John Berendt's *Midnight in the Garden of Good and Evil,* the best-seller that penetrates the facade of Savannah's uppercrust as well as extolls some of its seamy side. Indeed, Berendt's book is credited with bringing in more visitors, and there are guided tours to the places the book features, complete with a special *Midnight* tour map pinpointing those locations. Visitors want to know, for example, where Lee Adler lives. Adler is a prominent Savannahian, long involved in historic-preservation enterprises, to whom the book accords very bad press, but who didn't yield to advice from many of his friends that he "sue the bastard," for reasons, I suppose, best known to himself. The book shocked many old-line Savannahians, especially those in the social swirl, terming it "bad publicity." But it's a sure bet that the shock set in only after they read the book, which means they bought it, as did thousands and thousands of others across America, thousands among whom have made pilgrimages here simply to see Savannah close-up. The book is classified nonfiction, but some old-line Savannahians maintain that it's not all factual, and they thus term it "faction." And if that kind of damnation bothers author Berendt, likely it's when he's on the way to the bank. On the market the book is a smashing success, and it's on its way to becoming a Clint Eastwood–produced movie.

Savannah's tourist influx also has been propelled by the multi–Oscar-winning movie *Forrest Gump*. The movie opens in Savannah, showing much of the city as a feather floats down to a bench on which the title character, portrayed by Tom Hanks, sits and tells his life story to various people who are waiting for a bus. The park bench beside the bus stop is addressed further in this book, but after the film's release and its instant popularity set in, someone here suggested placing a historic marker beside the bench, which in reality was only a movie prop placed in a spot where no bus line actually stops or even passes. But the idea soon died because, Heavens!, you'd have thought someone had suggested painting the sword on General Oglethorpe's statue (right behind the bench in the movie) sky-blue pink; or worse, staging a hootchy-kootch show in historic Colonial Cemetery atop the gravesites of Revolutionary War heroes. Then-Mayor Susan Weiner was all for glorifying the bench, her background as an actress coming to the fore. But alas . . .

Savannah people stood strong, and sometimes so cooperatively that cohesiveness ran to the ridiculous extreme, in preparing for this city's role in the 1976 Olympics, the main show of which was in Atlanta. Savannah drew the host role for the ocean-sailing events, held offshore in the Atlantic Ocean; but the only wrangling and yapping came from afar in the person of a Canadian who headed one of the international sailing organizations. The fellow breezed into town a few times in advance of the competition like a prima donna arriving two minutes before the overture, and complained loudly that not enough was being done to accommodate the ocean sailors who would compete for the Olympic medals. Each time he came complaining, local committee chairman Archie Davis and his group treated him as the gentleman he really wasn't. He got the undeserved red-carpet treatment each time. What he failed to realize was that Savannahians do things in their own way and in their own time, and while their way and time may seem aggravating and slow to outsiders, they do meet their deadlines. The crank, incidentally, was one of those Canadians who tried to land the 1996 Olympic Games for their country, so if a perception of sour grapes existed, one can understand. Even so, whatever wrinkles he imagined were ironed out, the only thing that could have hurt the Olympic sailing events would have been unfair winds.

As noted in the First Book, Savannahians still ask visitors, early on, what they prefer to drink. They're still obsessed with preserving the trees in the lovely urban forest, which has made Savannah famous as well as beautiful. And they still like to eat out. Such restaurants as Williams Seafood and Johnny Harris continue to hold their own in the face of many seafood restaurants that give Williams competition, and Barnes' Restaurant (two locations now) and Carey Hilliard's, both of which feature barbecue. Anna's Little Napoli and Desposito's have in recent years acquired competition from such newer Italian restaurants as Garibaldi's, Bella's, and Il Pasticcio. Eli Karatassos, whose career has spanned politics, banking, and public relations, has brought along nicely a midtown and a downtown deli, both reminiscent of his father Pahno's place on Broughton Street in Savannah's golden days, when downtown was the place to go. Gottlieb's, both the bakery and deli, have closed, but next-generation brothers Alan and Isser hold forth in food and catering. The Pirates' House and the Pink House, both downtown in historic quarters, hold their appeal to visitors and locals alike; and upstairs in the Pirates' House former radio mogul Ben Tucker, a talented musician as well as an entrepreneur, runs Hard-Hearted Hannah's, a successful night spot featuring Emma Kelly at the piano. Elizabeth on Thirty Seventh, in midtown, remains one of the excellent-cuisine "newer" restaurants. For plain good food, and especially hamburgers and home-sliced and -cooked french fries, there's eternally the Crystal Beer Parlor, not to be confused with the chain Krystal and its tiny burgers (Crystal is discussed in another chapter). And as always, there's Mrs. Wilkes' Boarding House on Jones Street, serving breakfast and midday meals, family style, outside which tourists queue up to await their turn inside.

There's still crime in Savannah. Sometimes the crime rate goes up, and at other times it goes down. It remains a prime topic, especially among politicians at election time, when the murder rate gets exploited by the outs, as if any officeholder could prevent an angry person from killing an adversary out of sight and earshot from the authorities. City politics has gone nonpartisan, yet only in the sense that members of both parties compete in the same election, thus eliminating the need for party primaries; it saves money. Otherwise Republicans stump for GOP candidates and Democrats for their own; and yellow-dog Democrats (who'd rather vote for a yellow dog than for a Republican) still maintain that GOP stands for God's Outcast Party.

Savannah's daily newspaper operation is under newer local management, though still a part of the ever-growing, Augusta-based Morris Communications Corporation, headed by William S. Morris III, who prefers to be called Billy. Don Harwood has retired, succeeded by energetic and community-minded publisher Frank T. Anderson. Longtime executive editor Wally Davis has retired, succeeded by Rexanna Lester, a seasoned newspaperwoman promoted from managing editor, and succeeded herself by young Dan Suwyn. Together they restructured the *Savannah Morning News* and *Evening Press*, both in appearance and staff-wise, and then on Halloween 1996 the afternoon paper rather quietly ceased publication. There is now only the *Morning News,* since the sister paper went the way of most afternoon sheets, victim of changing reader habits and television's six o'clock news. Tom Barton holds forth as a bright and aggressive editorial-page editor. Retirees Archie Whitfield and Yours Truly continue to write columns, but as free-lancers (which really means we're unemployed), and there's a brand new crop of "old-timers," some with as few years' service as ten.

But many old-line Savannahians remain creatures of habit,

and frequently call the retirees to comment on what's in the papers or to seek help in getting something into print. I do not regard this as annoying. First, it tickles the ego, but it also keeps a retired editor up on how readers now perceive the daily press. In addition, it's pleasing that most readers who contact me are impressed with Mark Streeter's political cartoons, even those who sometimes criticize him as too liberal. Streeter is a third-generation employee of the company, and the first full-time cartoonist. He has a brilliant future and Pulitzer prize potential.

The Georgia State Port, with ever-improving terminal facilities stretching from the cityside waterfront all the way upstream to Garden City and Port Wentworth, continues as the hub of Savannah's lifeline business—shipping. Definitely, Savannahians do not fume and fuss over outlays for port improvements, probably because the Georgia Ports Authority is a solvent state agency, making a profit and paying its own way. GPA calls upon help from state government only when it needs Georgia's good faith to be pledged on the issuance of revenue bonds to pay for expansions. Savannahians thus appreciate the business the port brings to the city and state. They also appreciate not having to roll local tax dollars into the state port.

But some local squawking did arise when the Savannah Airport Commission built a larger, more handsome, and more utilitarian terminal and closed the old one, even though the airport also is a public facility that pays its own way. The squawkers, mainly through letters to the daily press, contended that the old terminal was sufficient to accommodate business and it was a waste of money to build the new one. The rebuttals conceded that the old terminal would have served Savannah's needs for several more years, but that the new terminal was built with the future in mind. No organized opposition materialized;

in fact, most of the objections arose after the new terminal was completed and in service. One thing both objectors and supporters will agree on is that the new terminal is a wonderful improvement over the old, is fully accessible by interstate highway, and has landscaped grounds capable of accommodating numerous satellite and ancillary businesses. As for the old airport, it's not awfully far from the new terminal and still functions as the base for several private flying services, as well as Gulfstream Aerospace, builder of executive jets, and the Georgia Air National Guard, which maintains a training center used throughout the year by other states' Air Guard units on tactical maneuvers.

Savannah remains . . . well, Savannah. Her people squabble, sometimes every step of the way, into the future they choose to venture slowly and deliberately towards. That's one of our city's peculiarities. But then, we may be a kinfolk-city to the great state of Missouri, nicknamed the Show-me State because of its people's skepticism. Missourians point with pride to that trait of theirs, and I'm convinced that most Savannahians do the same. But what the heck, we've a great city. We love it and, obviously, so do a lot of folks from elsewhere.

Savannah's Effect on People

Savannah has both beauty and charm, not to mention a down-home quality that makes her people ... well, different. We call ourselves a big city, but we really aren't big in the sense that Atlanta, Charlotte, Memphis, and Nashville are big. Atlanta, in fact, would inspire the late Ed Sullivan to say "r-e-a-l-l-y big"; it has progressed far beyond what it once was, and in the progression, lost its old hometown flavor. Indeed, all Georgians once could look upon their capital city, in one way or another, as everybody's hometown because there were different things about Atlanta with which people from Cobbtown, Savannah, Hahira, Macon, Hephzibah, Augusta, you name it, could associate. No more.

I mentioned first Savannah's beauty and charm, which defy description; but visitors pick up on that beauty and charm, and their impressions stick with them. Consider, for example, Pat and Sally Little, two dyed-in-the-wool Savannahians who, like most people living anywhere, have friends living elsewhere. The Littles over the years have been privileged to host some of their friends from other climes and places, including Ron and Carla Lowe, of Longwood, Florida, and Duncan and Lindsay Armstrong, from Charmadean, Worthing, England. At different times the Lowes and the Armstrongs visited, the latter couple having come from abroad to participate in the annual Scottish Games, sponsored by the St. Andrew's Society, of which Pat is a loyal member, proud of his Scottish heritage.

After their visits to Savannah, and neither couple ever having met the other, and not being aware of what the other couple had done, each couple named their new offspring Savannah, after our city. The odds of two of the Littles' acquaintances choosing Savannah as the given name for daughters must be

13

tremendous. But their reasons were the same—both couples were smitten with Savannah's beauty and charm. Any parent of a newborn girl knows how beautiful and charming a little baby seems, lying there in that hospital bassinet. So in faraway England and in down-south Florida live Savannah Jo Armstrong and Savannah Lowe. (And it was flattering to this author when, one bright day, the Littles stopped by the house with the birthday gifts they had chosen for our city's namesakes, asking me to inscribe and autograph copies of *Only in Savannah,* the First Book.)

As for Savannah's down-homedness, it definitely doesn't defy description. Not long ago, friend Malcolm Macnabb mailed me a copy of a column I wrote in the *Morning News* ages ago. He had found it among some of the articles that his late wife, Winifred, had clipped and saved. What inspired the column was an experience I had as a juror, waiting inside the jury room until being summoned back to the courtroom. I related how we members of a six-person jury, seemingly strangers to one another and having time on our hands, found ere long that we really weren't strangers at all. Two of the members discovered that before retirement they had worked for the same large manufacturing plant, and before long they established between themselves a host of mutual friends. The fellow next to me, it turned out, had married a school chum of my daughter, so before long we culled up mutual friends, including the fellow's mother-in-law whom I had known for years, as well as her late husband. The other two jurors turned out to be a daughter and son of people I knew, the lady's dad having been an athlete of no mean ability whom I had written about as a sportswriter. Then, one of the ladies remarked how the barrier of the strangers had been broken, adding: "You know, there's something about Savannah, a certain small-town quality, that I hope it never loses." I concluded the column with these words: "You can mention a random Whatsisname, or the Old Fort, or some of the old jocks, or just someone who's kin to someone else, or who worked for a certain firm during a certain period ... or come up with any kind of loose clue. And Bingo! Suddenly people who have been thrown into a common setting are no longer strangers. A big city, Savannah, but with enough small-townishness to make the living mighty easy and good."

That's Savannah. There's no other place quite like our city. Savannah grows on people, it affects them. Some even make their daughters our town's namesakes.

Savannah Idioms and Locations

Most communities have their own idiomatic words and phrases, which convey to natives and longtimers messages that are immediately understood. Locations within a community also take the form of idioms. Times Square is not only a location in New York City, it's an idiom, and not just "local" but world-wide. Anyway, here are some of Savannah's.

The Brown. If you hear a Savannahian mention "The Brown Farm," you know he or she is a longtime resident; if the term used is merely "The Brown," that means a longer-time Savan-nahian is doing the talking. The Brown Farm is no more, and hasn't existed for nigh on to fifty years, but in days of yore everybody was familiar with it, either through observation or personal experience. Those who personally experienced it were a small minority of minor lawbreakers. The Brown Farm, you see, was where nonviolent prisoners were sent to work off their sentences, and "work" was truly the operative word. And no, it wasn't like a county stockade, for Chatham County had one of those too, situated on the outskirts of town and not too far from the Brown Farm, as well as a county jail downtown where arrestees were incarcerated until their cases were disposed of. But the Brown Farm had character. Moreover, it was a beautiful place, maintaining the landscaping from days when it was a plantation. A double line of huge oaks bordered the drive from the main road to the headquarters building, which stood where, once, the plantation's big house stood.

It was simply a work farm for lawbreakers who drew sen-tences ranging from thirty to ninety days, and for such offenses as public drunkenness and simple assault occasioned by allowing disputes to spill over into fisticuffs. Brown Farm internees weren't shackled. They were quartered in dorms that were quite comfortable by comparison with jail and stockade cells, and they were able-bodied, capable of doing manual labor. It was a farm on which practically every vegetable raised on private farms grew, ostensibly for the purpose of providing food to prisoners in all the places of incarceration. And other beneficiaries of the Brown Farm's largesse were the politicians and county employees. In the days of the Great Depression, when county workers' salaries were meager, no county employee's family ever went hungry. The Brown Farm always was their source of a mess of turnip greens, or corn, or watermelons, or whatever. That was a fringe benefit of county employment. And why not? After all, the Brown Farm produced far more than all the prisoners possibly could eat.

Citizens who worked in the private sector never raised any objection to the way the farm's produce was distributed. That simply was "the way it was," and anyone who harbored personal objections could rationalize the system by the knowledge that the county also allotted surplus produce to agencies providing meals for the homeless. The Brown Farm, named for the family that once owned the land, generally was regarded as a good thing—it exacted human toil from prisoners who otherwise would have cooled their heels in jail cells, sitting around and doing nothing except, perhaps, listening to the radio in pre-television days.

Shortening the term "Brown Farm" to simply "the Brown" or just plain "Brown" is attributed to the late Judges John Schwarz and H. Mercer Jordan, lawyers who successively served as Police Court Recorders. Actually, the name of the tribunal was (and still is) Recorder's Court, but it commonly became Police Court because its location was in city police headquarters. (It's now in the Chatham County Courthouse.) The Recorder hears cases first and determines whether to take jurisdiction and mete out sentences, or to remand the cases to a higher court. All felonies and misdemeanors, of course, go to higher courts, but violations of city and county ordinances are handled at the Recorder's level.

Judges Schwarz and Jordan, taking jurisdiction in such minor cases, would pronounce sentences by saying, "Fifty dollars or thirty days Brown," giving the prisoners a choice of paying a fine or serving time. In Depression days fifty dollars was a lot of money, so most prisoners opted for the Brown Farm. There were several regulars, especially among the inebriates who happened to get arrested for being "drunk on the street." One in particular was a polished gentleman, well educated and skilled in bookkeeping, whose only problem was being an alcoholic with insufficient self-control to do his drinking at home. Invariably he would get drunk in public. So he became virtually a regular employee of the Brown Farm, assigned to do office work during his thirty-day stints. He was such a regular that whenever his case was called in Police Court he merely would nod to the judge, and the judge would nod back and with a wave of the hand say, "Thirty days Brown," knowing already that the fellow hadn't the wherewithal to pay a fine. He was one of the few inmates who never had to work outdoors.

To this day you'll hear old-timers complain that "They never should've done away with the Brown Farm," maintaining that the best punishment for misdeeds is hard labor and not "sitting around and watching TV." When police complain of the "revolving door," whereby criminals they arrest never serve out their sentences, old-timers will say, "We need the Brown again."

Both penal and political reform led partially to the discontinuation of the Brown Farm. Changes in means of punishment came with penal reform. And as political reform set in, reformers decided that the Brown Farm was as much a boondoggle for politicians as it was a means of punishment. Why, they asked, should public workers have the benefit of all those free groceries?

The other factor leading to the dissolution of the Brown Farm was Savannah's population growth and burgeoning development on the southside. Residential subdivisions began to spring up everywhere as home ownership set in as a way of life. The Brown Farm's tract was situated right in the middle of where residential sprawl was occurring. The county sold the land to developers, and now, just east of the Casey Canal and north of Montgomery Crossroad, on what was Brown Farm property, is Mayfair subdivision, a neighborhood of classy houses, beautifully landscaped amid stately oak trees. To the county's credit, it utilized Brown Farm property in such a way as to preserve the trees, and also practiced soil stewardship so well that Mayfair's lawns may well be the greenest and most fertile in town.

The Hawkeye. Not many Savannahians are left who know what "See you in the Hawkeye" means, except as a parting expression similar to "See you around." The idiom remains, however, because it has been passed down from those who knew its meaning full well. And what it means is that you'd better behave yourself or you might get written up in a newspaper called the *Hawkeye,* an earlier-day equivalent of being featured today in the *National Enquirer.*

The *Hawkeye* was a weekly paper edited and published by the late James Robert Miller, who a few years after the turn of the century came to Savannah from Bulloch County and began what Savannahians called a scandal sheet. I'm too young to have seen a copy of the paper, but from the stories passed down I must agree it was indeed a scandal sheet.

Oh, it wasn't entirely devoted to scandal. There was some legitimate news in it, I am told, but editor Miller printed just about any and everything, including a gossip column that minced no words, called a spade a spade; thus, his paper enjoyed a wide circulation because Savannahians, like people everywhere, enjoyed reading juicy items. Which is why the *Enquirer* sells so well from the display racks beside checkout counters at America's supermarkets. And the more prominent the subject of a column was, the better the paper sold. Reputedly, nothing and nobody were sacred to the fearless Mr. Miller.

Editor Miller sired three sons, one of whom was newspaperman Frank Miller, editor and publisher of the *Pembroke Journal*, the official organ of Bryan County. The younger Miller was a firebrand country editor who never backed away from any issue, but who never delved into the personal lives of his fellow citizens. The breed definitely improved with Hawkeye Miller's next generation. But after the elder Miller died, Frank Miller of Pembroke often was referred to as Hawkeye, and a few people confused father and son. The younger Miller never did forswear his inherited nickname, but he would make it clear that the original Hawkeye was his daddy and not himself.

The *Hawkeye*, I have been told by those who recall reading it, would bluntly report, for example, that a certain lawyer (or doctor, or banker, or executive; yea, even minister) was seen at midnight leaving the premises of a certain lady whose husband was out of town on business. Miller would call names—Lawyer So-and-so and Mrs. Such-and-such. Or, he may have learned of some shady business deal, or political chicanery, or anything else amiss or sinful, and right into his column it would go—all to the delight of Savannah readers.

Whether Miller was ever sued for libel, I have no way of knowing for certain; but those who spun lurid tales of the *Hawkeye* stoutly maintained that he never spent a day in court because what he printed was invariably the absolute truth, and any aggrieved subject of his writings who would pose a legal challenge would risk a baring of even more incriminating sordidness because editor Miller never proceeded on hearsay alone but kept indisputable documentation.

Some of the tale-spinners claim that Miller attracted advertisers in his paper because business owners wanted to stay on his good side, fearing that if they didn't advertise he would "get something" on them and print it in the *Hawkeye*—a form of self-imposed blackmail-before-the-fact, you might say. No one ever suggested that he resorted to blackmail in order to obtain advertising, his reason being that he'd rather print juicy stuff and see people squirm than become a millionaire. A genuine iconoclast, Mr. Miller.

The newspaper vanished upon the demise of its editor, much to the relief of any and all Savannahians who were "messing around" or otherwise misbehaving in their personal or business lives. Anyway, the *Hawkeye*'s legacy is the idiomatic expression "See you in the Hawkeye," less in use nowadays, but still heard occasionally.

Lard's Greasy. Savannah is the only place I ever heard someone say, "He don't know lard's greasy." I use the expression often, and have worked it into my newspaper columns, but each time it appears I usually get inquiries about it. The expression may be used elsewhere, but I suspect it's a Savannah idiom.

What it means is that the person to whom it applies must be dumb as hell about the facts staring him or her in the face. For example, a fellow drives the wrong way on one-way Drayton Street and is summoned to the curb for an interview by a traffic policeman. He gets a ticket for the violation, but a week or so later he again heads the wrong way on Drayton. He simply "don't know lard's greasy." In other words, he can't get it through his thick head that a one-way sign at the intersection means exactly what it says.

Another example: It's legal to fish without a license in saltwater streams, but to fish in fresh water a fishing license is required. So, a fisherman puts his boat in at the King's Ferry bridge and proceeds to try his luck on the other side of the Ogeechee River. The fish aren't biting there, so he cranks up his motor and moves upstream, passing beneath the bridge. In local waters the King's Ferry bridge is the point of delineation between salt and fresh water, the river upstream of the bridge being fresh. A game warden spots him and asks to see his license, which he does not possess; he tells the warden he wasn't aware that he needed one. The game warden lets him off with a warning, advising that the fisherman obtain a license if he intends to fish fresh waters in the future. Two weeks later the fisherman ventures upstream again, but still without possessing a license. This time the warden cites him for the violation and the fisherman has to go to court and pay a fine. He's someone who "don't know lard's greasy."

It's a good and meaningful expression, implying not only gross ignorance but also stupidity. Try using it, and remember that Savannahians pronounce the word *greezy*, and not, as you hear it in many climes and places, *greecy*, as in the Hellenic country abroad.

Gottum. What this means, simply is, "got'em," which means in possession of, or in control of. It is found elsewhere in fractured American Indian. You see it in cartoon captions—for example, "Chief Rain-in-Face gottum squaw and papoose." Its peculiarity to Savannah is slightly different. Mostly, it's a sports term.

Likely "gottum" began with the first athletic contest between Benedictine Military School (called Benedictine College, abbreviated B.C., in earlier days) and Savannah High School. Those schools have been competing since right after the turn of the century, and theirs is the oldest continuous prep-school sports rivalry in Georgia, vying even with Georgia Tech and the University of Georgia. The schools play each other in all sports, but football is their biggie. The Other Book briefly mentioned this rivalry.

Each year the pregame hoopla begins long before the football teams actually clash. Partisans of each side are confident way in advance that their team absolutely, positively will emerge victorious. So you hear them say either "B.C. gottum" or "High School gottum," depending of course on who's uttering. That means, of course, that the utterer's favorite team is in control, superior, bound to win, etc.

Geechee. Grammatically it should begin with an apostrophe, the shortened form of Ogeechee, the name of a river bordering Chatham County on the south. It's an Indian word, like Susquehanna and Potomac. The dialect that old-time Savannahians speak is called Geechee. And so, for that matter, are Savannahians referred to as Geechees.

It's an honorable term, though in recent years those given to political correctness have termed it racist because, in former days, Savannah blacks, who speak the dialect well, were referred

23

to as Geechee Negroes, and never mind that whites also were called in those days, and still are, Geechees.

For years Armstrong State College, one of Savannah's institutions of higher learning, nicknamed its athletic teams Geechees, but in a spasm of political correctness made the change to Pirates. Still, people from other parts of Georgia call Savannahians Geechees.

In recent years graduates of the several local high schools, which, until after the 1954 Supreme Court decision, were lily-white, have formed a group called the Happy Geechees, and every October they hold a reunion featuring a Saturday morning coffee and a dinner and dance that evening. Alumni from over a span of about fifteen years participate, and they're proud to be called Geechees.

The Old Fort. Savannahians of all generations know that means the downtown section hard by, and extending through contiguous neighborhoods—old pre-Revolution Fort Wayne. It originally was a predominantly Irish-Catholic section in the shadow of the old gas works, which utilized the Fort Wayne property. The gas works shut down after the pipeline from the West was extended to Savannah, bringing in natural gas. Fancy residential apartments, offices (including the gas company's), and boutiques now occupy Fort Wayne proper; and the Old Fort neighborhoods now comprise some of Savannah's finest historic restoration, the northeastern portion of the broader and famed Historic District. The Old Fort section has evolved from a district where low- and middle-income families lived to an area of sumptuousness.

Lace-Curtain and Billy-Goat. These two terms differentiated between the haves and the have-nots among Savannah's earlier Irish-Catholic families. Those of affluence were called

24

lace-curtain Irish, because they could afford luxurious appointments in their homes. The poorer ones were called billy-goat Irish for two reasons: first, they lived a more Spartan existence; second, many of the families raised goats in their backyards and sold goat's milk, which in earlier days, before formulas were devised, was deemed quite nourishing for babies. While the billy-goat term has fallen into disuse, you still hear, in a derogatory and sometimes envious sense, affluent Irish families referred to as lace-curtain, especially if those families act "uppity," which is a universal idiom for stuck-up.

Bull and Broughton. Until shopping centers and malls came along, Broughton was Savannah's main drag, the principal location of retail businesses—quality men's clothing, stylish ladies' apparel, department stores, hat shops, luggage stores, movie theaters, etc. Broughton Street runs east-west, and Bull Street north and south. The four corners where the two streets intersect once were the most prime real estate locations in town, local government deriving its highest taxes therefrom. Alas, no more.

But in those days one could stand at the corner of Bull and Broughton and, in an hour or two, "every friend you know" would pass by. The intersection teemed with humanity. "Meet me at Bull and Broughton" was Savannahians' by-word. A more base by-word went something like, "If I'm wrong, I'll kiss your ass at Bull and Broughton and give you an hour to draw a crowd." It was, absolutely, the place.

Savannahians now shop mostly elsewhere because the old established and substantial retailers have either retired or died, or they or their progeny have moved their businesses to the malls. Even so, "Bull and Broughton" remains not only a location, but also an expression with meaning. In fact, after

Only in Savannah was published, and good people who bought my book would call and ask if they could bring their copies by the house for this author to autograph, I'd reply: "Come by the house, or I'll meet you someplace—even Bull and Broughton at high noon on Christmas Day."

The Big Park. It's called Forsyth Park. It's bounded by Gaston Street on the north, Park Avenue on the south, and Drayton and Whitaker streets, respectively on the east and west. It's Savannah's Central Park. The northern half is a placid park, beautifully landscaped, and with benches spaced along the walks that converge on a lovely fountain, the design of which was inspired by the fountains at Place de la Concorde in Paris. The southern half is open space, formerly utilized for baseball, football, basketball, softball, and tennis—now for soccer, tennis, basketball, and outdoor theatrical productions, including concerts by the Savannah Symphony and other musical groups.

Only "new" Savannahians, however, refer to it regularly as Forsyth Park. Old-timers still say "the Big Park," and with a degree of reverence. Both kids and adults called it that in days of yore, mainly as a way of differentiating between Forsyth and Colonial parks, the latter being a small playground on the southern tip of Colonial Cemetery, and now named Davant Park in memory of a former chairman of the Park and Tree Commission.

Where would the basketball game between the teams from Troup Square and Washington Square be played? Either Colonial or the Big Park, would be the reply. And after the kids grew up, they'd reminisce with peers on those delightful years in the big park. In fact, there were some Savannahians who, if you mentioned Forsyth Park, wouldn't know what you were talking about. They knew only the Big Park. And to this day, the appellation sticks as old-timers still reminisce, and ignore the fact that the park is named for botanist William Forsyth, for whom the shrub forsythia is namesake.

Thirty-fifth School. Sort of like the Big Park, many Savannahians still refer to Thirty-fifth Junior High when they mean Richard Arnold School. That's because, for years, the junior high school on Bull Street, occupying the entire block between Thirty-fourth and Thirty-fifth streets, was called Thirty-fifth, and why the street on the leading edge of the property was ignored is a mystery.

In the 1930's the school was renamed for Dr. Richard Arnold, who was mayor of Savannah when General William Tecumseh Sherman ended his infamous March to the Sea here, after cutting a swath of destruction and scorched earth from Atlanta (where the Civil War general began the burning) through the heartland of Georgia. In order to spare Savannah from destruction, Dr. Arnold drove his horse and buggy to the edge of town and surrendered the city to Sherman, conceding the hopelessness of putting up a fight since Savannah's militia units were away fighting Yankees elsewhere.

It may be simply habit that impels longtime Savannahians to hang on to the Thirty-fifth reference to the school. On the other hand, there may still linger a modicum of the unreconstructed Southerner in some Savannahians who hang on to the notion that Mayor Arnold should have rallied the civilians to load their muskets and fight Sherman's army to the last man. In retrospective reality, though, Mayor Arnold was one of Savannah's early-on historic preservationists. Try to imagine what our city would look like today if Sherman had stormed in and burned all the beautiful buildings that America's largest historic district still embraces, and which attract tourists from all over the world. One of the buildings, the Green-Meldrim House, where Sherman made his headquarters, is a marvel in architectural design, and a stopping-off place for every conducted tour.

Old Betsy. You hardly ever hear the term now, but for many years Savannahians referred to the *Savannah Morning News* as Old Betsy. It was both derogatory and a term of endearment, depending upon who was talking, but everybody knew what the term meant.

The newspaper—started in 1850, suspended from publication after Savannah fell to the Yankees, but resumed after the Civil War ended—was in many ways like an old lady—staid, sometimes stoic, genteel in both its news coverage and its editorial policy, yet tough and fearless whenever things got so bad that it needed to speak out boldly. Those against whom the *Morning News* spoke out were the ones who used "Old Betsy" in a derogatory sense. Others who relied heavily on the paper to bring them the news and to interpret the burning issues of the day used the term out of respect; the paper reminded them of the all-wise and sage dowager of a family, somebody's Aunt Elizabeth to whom family members would turn for the last word. Betsy, of course, is a derivative of Elizabeth.

Some Savannahians, but very few now, still know what Old Betsy means, even those still-living politicians of the immediate post–World War II days who called the *Morning News* "the old lady of Whitaker Street" and her sister paper, the *Savannah Evening Press,* "her echo."

Pickup. There are pickup trucks. And if you drop something on the ground, you stoop and pick it up (unless you don't want it and are prone to litter). A fellow out cruising, and spotting a young lady who exudes signs of willingness, will pick her up, and she is known as a pickup. UPS and Federal Express will pick up your package and deliver it elsewhere. An athletic team is playing sluggishly, but suddenly one of the players will come to life and start playing vigorously, inspiring teammates to emerge from their state of lethargy and go on to win the game; that player picks up the team.

But ask anyone who grew up in Savannah what Mama meant when she said, "Now pick up, you heah me?" The child will tell you that Mama was giving a direct order: "Clean and straighten your room," or "Get rid of that mess you left on the dining room table," or "Go out side and get that clutter out of the yard."

Somehow that Savannah idiom has a more forceful impact than "clean up" or "straighten up." There's only one answer when such an order comes down: "Yes, ma'am."

Certiorari. This is a legal word, a noun, defined by Webster as "a writ issuing from a superior court calling up a record from an inferior court for review." To repeat—noun. But in days when I covered the courts I cannot recall how many times I heard Savannah lawyers use it as a verb. "We'll certiorari it," they'd say. So I hereby class the verb (?) certiorari as a Savannah idiom, but confined, thank goodness, to the courthouse. And I'm sure the same lawyers tell clients they'll "habeas corpus" their case. Ah, lawyers!

In Bonaventure. The best-selling *Midnight in the Garden of Good and Evil,* by John Berendt, made Savannah's Bonaventure Cemetery super-famous, not only with several references in the story to that historic graveyard, but also with a picture on the jacket of one of Bonaventure's many beautiful statues.

Bonaventure already was well known, but not like it has been since "the book" put it on the map.

Bonaventure commands attention because it is one of the most placid and beautiful graveyards you'll find, especially in springtime when azaleas, dogwood, and wisteria grow in profusion beneath ancient oaks whose spreading upper branches virtually form tunnels above the road paths along which funeral processions move. Perhaps the most attractive part of Bonaventure is the stretch paralleling the Wilmington River, separated from the stream by a sprawl of marsh, whose lush green in the warm months gradually changes to golden brown as autumn succeeds summer and then blends into winter—the change occurring much the way a chameleon makes its costume change. Enhancing this spectacle are the small craft, both private and commercial, moving along the Wilmington, which is a part of the Intracoastal Waterway. Upstream can be seen the magnificent high-level bridge on U.S. 80, connecting the town of Thunderbolt on the mainland to the several barrier islands beyond. Downstream is a view of Bonaventure's Greenwich section, newer and not as populated with departed ones at eternal rest as its antecedent, but whose latter-day statuary rivals in elegance the older, patina-covered grave markers in what is called "Bonaventure proper."

Savannah, however, has more cemeteries than Bonaventure. Ten are listed in the Yellow Pages, but the others dotted here and there, not only in the city but also in the entire Chatham County, aren't listed in BellSouth's directory simply because they do not have telephones. Indeed, Colonial Cemetery, in the heart of the Historic District downtown, dates back to the early days of the Colony of Georgia, and of course is much older than Bonaventure. So also are Laurel Grove and two Jewish cemeteries on Savannah's westside. Resting in Laurel Grove are such famed Savannahians as Juliette Gordon Low, who in her native Savannah founded the Girl Scouts of America; James Pierpont, composer of "Jingle Bells," the Yuletide song that belongs to the ages; Francis S. Bartow, the Civil War officer who fell mortally wounded at First Manassas, a battle his Southern contingent from Savannah won; and many other luminaries of history. Bonaventure, you see, is not Savannah's *only* cemetery of note.

Yet, in Savannah, Bonaventure is synonymous with cemeteries all. For example, a former Savannahian will return after a long absence and ask a friend what ever happened to, say, "Ol' Joe Doakes." The reply: "He's in Bonaventure," which may or may not be true. Ol' Joe might actually be six feet under in one of the four Hillcrests, or Forest Lawn, or Catholic Cemetery. Telling an inquirer that someone's "in Bonaventure" is simply another way of saying that person has gone to his or her reward. Also, an argument may start, and the clincher line likely as not will be, "I'll see you in Bonaventure before I'll admit you're right."

Thus, "in Bonaventure" not only is an idiomatic expression peculiar to Savannah, but it's also a reference to a well-known location. It's so well known that it has attracted tourists for many years, especially in the blooming season; and now, since *Midnight* became such a literary success, many tourists find time to visit the cemetery and seek out the marker pictured on the book's jacket. And tour guides, who bring them to Bonaventure, before leaving will point out the grave of Johnny Mercer, one of Savannah's native sons whose songs from the Depression days until his death in 1976 the world still sings.

The inscription on his modest tombstone is one of his song's titles—"And the Angels Sing."

Streetcars. Many Savannahians are still around who pleasantly recall the trolley cars, the tracks of which interlaced the city, and the clang-clang-clanging, which, while loud, was so commonplace that it was hardly noticeable. They reminisce about the long streetcar rides to such outlying places as Thunderbolt, the Isle of Hope, Port Wentworth, and the Montgomery community. A very few who are still around remember when the E & W (East & West) belt line ran slap-dab through the middle of the old City Market. There was also the popular A & B (Abercorn and Barnard streets) belt; the Mill Haven car that went into the industrial westside; and the streetcar track that ran through the heart of Ardsley Park, an exclusive southside neighborhood whose small lots are so out of proportion to the mansion-sized residences built on them.

Adults tell their grandchildren how they "pulled trolleys" in the dead of night by running behind a streetcar, grabbing the rope on the rear end, and disconnecting the trolley from the overhead power line, bringing the streetcar to a sudden stop and causing the motorman to spout foul language in disgust, even with fine ladies aboard. It was a childish prank that did little harm save put a crimp in the streetcar's schedule, but, in retrospect, hazardous to the trolley-puller. In those days, however, such pranksters ignored such dangers, ranging from a fall and broken limb to the punishment that a motorman might inflict should the culprit fail to make a getaway, not to mention the punishment by parents should they get wind of the misdeed.

Shortly after World War II, the streetcar lines were shut down, and public transportation became all bus. Still, the memory of streetcar days lingers, to the extent that longtime

Savannahians hang on to the "waiting for a streetcar" expression. Example, someone will be standing on a corner, and a friend who recently passed and waved to him will come back along and see him still standing in the same place. "What're ya doing, waiting for a streetcar?" the friend will ask. These days it will be a long wait because the nearest thing in Savannah to a streetcar are the motorized mock-up trolleys hauling tourists around.

The Bag. In 1935 the industry that lifted Savannah from the economic doldrums began operation. It was Union Bag & Paper Corporation, which proffered many new jobs to the community. Union Bag ushered in a new era, one of recovery and eventual prosperity; at its peak the employment was about eight thousand. And so "The Bag" became a byword. "Where do you work?" someone would ask, and the reply was, "The Bag." Oh, a few would say "Union Bag," but mostly it was the short-form reply.

A quarter of a century ago, Union Bag & Paper bought the Camp Corporation, another papermaking giant (they called it a merger, even then), and the company's name changed to Union Camp Corporation—no hyphen between the names, just plain Union Camp. Still, few employees now say they work for Union Camp. "The Bag" remains, passed down from those who long since have retired. As for the olfactory discomfort caused by Union Camp's sulfuric emissions from its smokestacks—not as severely pungent now as in earlier days because of applied better technology—well, that's another story, having little to do with idioms and locations.

Cut Old Touches. Marjorie, whom I married in 1989 after a commuting courtship to Florida, to which she moved after growing up in Ohio, was puzzled when I reported having cut old touches with a fellow I ran into and hadn't seen for years. "Y'all did *wha-a-a-t?*" she asked. I had to explain that the Savannah idiom "cut old touches" is the same as saying "catch up on things" or "brush up" or "talk over old times." In fact, while cutting old touches someone might ask what ever happened to Ol' Joe Doakes, and you might reply that he's in Bonaventure.

Irish Is Up. The Irish, in Savannah and elsewhere, are proud of their reputation as fighters. Some I know allow pride to override their good sense, and will wade into a fight even in the face of bad odds—such odds as a weight differential of fifty or more pounds, not to mention disadvantages in reach, height, and overall stature. Seemingly the Irish "ain't scared of nuttin'," which explains why the Notre Dame football team calls itself the "Fighting Irish," although I must inject that there's seldom a weight, reach, height, or overall stature differential between Notre Dame and its opponents that isn't heavily in that school's favor. Nor, I should add, is every member of the Notre Dame team Irish. Just look at 'em next time they're on TV.

It's the Savannah Irish to whom reference is made here, and they number many. Not all of them carry their fighting instincts to the absolute conclusion of engaging in fisticuffs. Most of those I've known hold fisticuffs only as a last resort, doing most of their fighting verbally. Believe me, they can disagree, with one another as well as with outsiders. Savannahian Tom Dillon, a lawyer of Irish descent and one of Savannah's outstanding citizens, once told me why he had opted not to make a trip to Ireland with a group of his fellow-Irishmen whom he had seen the previous evening at the Knights of Columbus hall to discuss flight arrangements, itinerary, etc. They argued, Tom related, from the time the meeting started until it ended, and then little peel-off groups continued to argue after the meeting. "That whole trip will be an argument, from the time they board the plane here until they return," Tom said, adding that he simply was not up to it. Tom, while harboring all the good Irish instincts and traits, apparently is more genteel than the others. Or perhaps he had argued enough in younger years and decided he wanted no more.

In younger days, when I stopped by Gildea's bar for refreshment on the way home, I'd watch in amazement as an Irish friend or two would engage in verbal disagreement over one topic or another, often a sports topic, and more often comparing the skills and attributes of certain athletes—such as, which quarterback could throw a pass the farthest, or whose lifetime batting average was higher, or who stole the most bases. Once I saw a couple of them step outside to settle a question that more easily could have been settled with a consultation of the record book. Another time (I came in late and thus never knew what the argument was all about) I saw a little guy and a bigger guy (Irishmen, both) step outside; and the little guy, though loser of the fight, acquitted himself well, sparring and using fancy footwork, and getting in a blow or two, before the bigger fellow landed a punch squarely on his adversary's jaw and knocked him to the ground. The little guy would have come back for more had not the spectators who had spilled out of the bar decided that the fight was over and stepped between the two. Also, they made the two shake hands and come back into Gildea's for another drink.

So the idiom of Savannah, applied to Irishmen who like to disagree with one another, is that they "get their Irish up." Which means, as they reach a limit of tolerance, they become belligerent. The term applies not solely to Savannah Irish males.

Female Irish, while seldom if ever resorting to physical encounters, also can get their Irish up, and thereby spew more acrimonious invective in such a colorful way as to put their male counterparts in the proverbial shade. The moral of this discourse, I guess—never cross an Irishman or an Irishwoman, especially if he or she already has his or her "Irish up."

What's Yours, Sir?

By now you have heard—no doubt, experienced!—that Savannah is noted for asking a visitor "What would you like to drink?" The question is propounded not as a matter of subsequent course, following the customary amenities, but as a matter of priority. It's usually the first question a visitor gets, which exemplifies the hospitable nature of Savannahians. They simply want to make folks feel right at home; in fact, Savannahians ask *one another* that question ere they meet in a social setting. Heck, it doesn't have to be social; the question will come even at a serious business lunch, when under discussion are matters involving thousands of dollars. There is, in fact, a Baptist preacher of my acquaintance who took the pledge of abstinence as a requirement for ordination, and whose parishioners are well aware that he did. He tells me that even he, when taken by a certain member of his flock to lunch, will be asked, "What would you like to drink?" He always replies "iced tea," but he suspects, actually *knows*, that this certain parishioner keeps hoping that one day the pastor will slip and say "vodka on the rocks" or "Scotch and water" or "Bud light," and then feel free to order a stronger drink for himself. The pastor enjoys holding the upper hand, and he allows that the entire community derives a side benefit because, by holding the parishioner to the soft stuff, the pastor keeps one less drinking driver off the streets.

There aren't enough such pastors to protect the entire community, however; indeed, the clergy of some faiths see nothing wrong with "libation in moderation," as they phrase it in their rationalization. But Baptists are different. Conscientious ones, both clergy and lay, regard Demon Rum as an extension of Satan's long arm, and it's difficult to argue with them as one ponders the misery resulting from substance abuse. Those who indulge in drinking, therefore, should respect the sentiments of those who abstain, and by no means poke fun at others' deep-seated convictions.

Still, I am certain that a major portion of Savannah's population comprises those who do not abstain. Proof lies in the fact that seldom, if ever, does a liquor store go out of business. My friend and neighbor, Buster White, did shut down his package shop and bar on West Broad Street, near Broughton, but not for lack of patronage. Instead, an urban renewal project forced him to close, as his location was a small part of the property needed for building a new Chatham County courthouse. White did not relocate his business because he was at or near the age of retirement, and dispensing spirits, wine, and beer was not his main line of work. He was also an entertainment promoter who over a span of more than a half-century brought many top-flight attractions to Savannah, ranging from classical ballet to Broadway shows to boxing and wrestling. Many luminaries of show business graced Savannah's stages under the auspices of Charles J. "Buster" White and Famous Artists, a business in which he and Atlantan Ralph Bridges were partners. If White had not been engaged in other more lucrative business pursuits, however, it's a sure bet he'd have opened a package shop somewhere near the new courthouse. It's also a sure bet that such a business at an alternative location would have succeeded, given the priority that Savannahians place on the stuff from which libations are mixed.

By illustration, take the case of the late Ephriam Cooper, who operated the Decanter, a beverage shop on DeRenne Avenue, between Bull and Abercorn streets, until he retired and sold the business five or six years before his death. Cooper was living proof that free enterprise works. A member of a Jewish family of moderate means, he learned the retail beverage business as an employee of another package store, floated a bank loan, commingled his own savings, and bought the Decanter; and as business increased he expanded the package shop into two adjacent storefronts.

About the time Cooper's expansion was in progress, however, the city decided to widen DeRenne Avenue to accommodate increasing traffic. This project entailed a temporary detour that was intended to be in effect about a month. But alas, the road builders encountered a deep layer of muck beneath DeRenne, and thus had to bring in much heavy excavation equipment to scoop out thousands of yards of the gooey stuff. Logically that meant the detour would have to stay in effect much longer. Would you believe, almost a year? And logically that longer period of time had a serious impact on the businesses fronting on DeRenne, simply because customers opted to go elsewhere rather than fight the snarled traffic along the detour. During that period, four of the businesses closed, two moved elsewhere, and the other two just closed forever.

But not the Decanter. Sure, Ephriam Cooper said, his customers were grossly inconvenienced, not being able to drive to his front door, park, and come inside to buy their packaged goods. But that didn't deter them. They merely parked their cars a block or two away and walked to the Decanter. You see, Cooper offered attractive prices, and he also was an expert on wines. Fine ladies from all over town consulted him on wine choices as they prepared for dinner parties. He spent most of his adult life reading up on wines. He could tell you, for instance, whether 1976 was a "good year" for cabernet sauvignon, or a bad year. He knew which wines went with which entrées, and the reputation of his expertise spread. And of course he knew his whiskies, liqueurs, brandies, etc., and could offer reasonable explanations why one brand of bourbon cost more than another, the difference between red label and black label. He was one of the most customer-oriented retailers in town. His was personal service.

So it's understandable that neither rain, nor snow, nor muck, nor detour could keep his customers away, even though there were other package shops not too far from his to which they could have turned during those days when DeRenne Avenue was a deep hole in the ground. Seldom if ever does a liquor store in Savannah go out of business, and this narrative illustrates the point very well. It also proves, as an aside, that aiming to please customers is a good way to stay in business.

Same Ol', Same Ol' Name

If you read the First Book, and have been out of town (our town, of course) ever since, you are not aware that the sparkling, lofty, and marvelous four-lane bridge linking downtown Savannah with South Carolina and other northward climes and places finally has a name. You will recall the First Book's account of how the high-level bridge, built to replace a lower high-level bridge that the incoming cargo ships began to scrape as they passed beneath, remained unnamed.

You see, the previous bridge had been named for the late Governor Eugene Talmadge, Georgia's gallus-snapping firebrand, and segregationist, politician, who was elected three times to that high office in the prewar Great Depression, and for a fourth time the year after Germany and Japan had capitulated. Desegregation had not arrived when that first bridge was completed; but our city, county, and state were very much desegregated in 1991, the year the new bridge was finished. Community leaders thought it best to name the new bridge for someone else, rather than to perpetuate a reminder of the Jim Crow days of yore. The local newspapers invited readers to suggest a name, and the mail-in response was overwhelming. Suggested names ranged from Tomochichi, the Indian chief who had greeted General Oglethorpe in 1733, the year that Englishman founded the Colony of Georgia here, to Jimmy Carter, the only Georgian to be elected president of the United States. This author, in his newspaper column, favored Carter, which required some soul-searching laying aside of personal feelings about a Georgian who wasn't our greatest governor, and by no means our greatest president, but who nevertheless deserved recognition for having attained the nation's highest office.

In the autumn of 1995 Chatham County Commission

Chairman Joe Mahany took matters into his own hand. He instructed county workers to fashion and erect "Jimmy Carter Bridge" signs at each end of the span towering above the Savannah River. Okay, that was it, everyone sighed, but that was not it. Tom Murphy, veteran speaker of the Georgia House of Representatives and Georgia's most powerful politician, crashed the party. "It's not his bridge to name," Murphy said from his Atlanta office, the pronoun "his" referring to Mahany. Murphy contended that only the legislature or the highway board held authority to name a bridge, and just a week or so later the Department of Transportation's board, at one of its regular meetings in Atlanta, voted to name the new structure for—the late Governor Eugene Talmadge! Just like that, the bridge had a name, but not a new one.

Mahany did not take the sudden resolution of the bridge-naming problem lying down. He appealed to the local legislative delegation to drive through a bill to name the bridge for Jimmy Carter, and Murphy be damned for his interference. "It's not his bridge, either," Mahany contended, the pronoun "his" applying to Murphy. Yet it seems at this writing that the Talmadge name will stick, at least for the lifetime of Speaker Murphy, who has served in the General Assembly seemingly for a hundred or so terms and who can cash in political chips even from the theoretically independent highway board.

There is another "lifetime" to be taken into consideration, and that's Herman Talmadge's. Herman, the son of the late Gene Talmadge, is a former governor and a former United States senator. Herman too rode the segregationist-politician wave when it was politically advantageous to do so, but mellowed considerably through his years of public service and became, at least outwardly (and who can tell about inwardly?), truly a reconstructed Southerner. Murphy and older Georgia politicians felt that out of respect for Herman Talmadge the new bridge should carry forth the old bridge's name.

And, surprisingly, the decision on the Talmadge name did not draw an outpouring of protests from black citizens, or white liberals, or black or white conservatives who eschew Gene Talmadgeism. Apparently more important things now occupy the minds of Georgians. In fact, bands, more and more, are playing "Dixie" again, and the protests over inclusion of the Confederate flag as a part of Georgia's state banner have simmered down. Sic transit . . . whatever.

A New Old Name

The nicknaming of Savannah's professional baseball team the "Sand Gnats" in 1996 didn't take nearly as long as naming the new Savannah River bridge, and it was a lot more fun. In fact, the name was settled upon within a span of about six weeks, the reason being a deadline as baseball season approached. When time is of the essence, things in Savannah can move.

Had the status remained quo, Savannah's entry in the Class-A South Atlantic (nicknamed Sally) League would have borne the name Cardinals, after the parent National League club in St. Louis. For nine years the team had been the Cardinals, and seemingly the local farm club's affiliation with St. Louis was as solid as the Rock of Gibraltar. The local 1995 club had been mediocre, but Savannah had won back-to-back Sally League pennants in the 1993 and 1994 seasons. Attendance was high, and so was enthusiasm, even in the losing 1995 season. St. Louis and Savannah made for a good baseball marriage.

Suddenly, however, the St. Louis Cardinals' management went to baseball's winter meetings in early 1996 after having gone through a major front-office shakeup. Augustus Busch, scion of the beer-baron family that had owned the organization for years, decided to get out of baseball. The new owners decreed many changes, one of which was to pare down the club's number of farm teams. It was just by happenstance, and lucky coincidence, that the Los Angeles Dodgers were shopping around for a place to locate a Class-A affiliate, and there was Savannah—available. New Yorker Ken Silver, owner of the Savannah franchise, was approached, and he agreed to shift the remaining year on his affiliation contract with the Cardinals to the Dodgers.

But what to call the team? Dodgers would be an easy choice,

after the new parent club. But then, suppose that after the contract expired the Dodgers would shift their farm team elsewhere? That would mean finding another name for the local club, which has had many names since the early 1950's, when the longtime Savannah Indians name was cast off in favor of the Athletics, after the then-parent club. Subsequent names included Reds (Cincinnati), Pirates (Pittsburgh), Senators (Washington), White Sox (Chicago), Indians (Cleveland), Braves (Atlanta), and, of course, Cardinals. With each change came also a change in decor—uniforms, signs, scoreboard, letterheads, scorecard programs, souvenirs, advertisements, anything else related to the ball club. And at the time of the switch from Cardinals to Dodgers, general manager Ric Sisler had a big inventory of items related to the Cardinals—the *Savannah* Cardinals, meaning that such items could not be returned to the St. Louis club and that Silver and Sisler were stuck with unmarketable merchandise. Also, everything in Grayson Stadium was painted Cardinal red.

Silver noted that many minor league teams across the country had been adopting individual nicknames as a cushion against unnecessary conversion expenses when and if an affiliation with a club in the big leagues should change. In the Sally League such names as Mudcats, Riverdawgs, Redstixx, and Polecats had surfaced. So Silver and Sisler appointed a committee of baseball fans to find a new nickname, one that would stick, no matter which organization Savannah might hook up with at a future time. The local committee came up with dozens of suggestions from the public. Some wanted "Geechees," which Savannah people are called. There was "Steamers," because Savannah is a seaport. There was "Shadow," for some unclear reason. There was one suggestion after another; and the committee, voting several times, pared the possibilities down to five, after which Sisler persuaded radio and television stations to sound out the public's opinion. An overwhelming choice, by more than sixty percent, was Sand Gnats.

The name brought out critics, however, but only a few. Since pesky sand gnats are so very much indigenous to Savannah, it seemed appropriate to most, especially to regular fans who swat gnats at the ball park. One critic remarked, "Hell, it's bad enough that the gnats come out and bite whenever they take a notion, but if you name the team for them, and put their name in the paper, the bastards'll be out there biting us every home game." A valid criticism, but it didn't change the selection.

But what about the team's logo? Just what, pray tell, does a sand gnat look like? They're so small, and so elusive, it's doubtful that anyone has ever seen one in such detail as to be able to give an accurate description. In fact, victims of sand gnats refer to them as "no-see-ums" while angrily fanning them away. But the fact that a sand gnat defies description was a plus for commercial artist Jeff Wilkerson, who designed the logo. He could rely solely on imagination, and he did in producing a cute, vicious-looking insect, long fang bared, and swinging a baseball bat. It well could be the most eye-catching logo in all baseball, major and minor leagues. As for the name, it's new to the ball club but rather old around Savannah.

Even so, in reality, you must be made aware that there is no such thing as a sand gnat. It's not listed in dictionaries or encyclopedias. Actually, what locals in recent years have called the sand gnat is a sand fly. They've become known as gnats because they are even smaller than actual gnats; and unlike actual gnats, they bite. Older generations, however, grew up calling them sand flies, and only a short distance beyond Savannah's city limits, near the Isle of Hope, is a community called Sandfly. It's called that because the critters abound there in the hot months, and baseball fans wouldn't dispute it if someone should say that Sandfly is home base for the sand gnats pestering spectators on nights when wind and climate are in proper confluence for prompting the bugs to fly out in search of unprotected human skins. Lord knows, they've got to come from somewhere.

Some Little Stories

The Butt-biters. Athletes engage in all kinds of pranks against one another. For example, on road trips they short-sheet teammates, a prank I originally encountered in World War II military days. It works this way. A prankster will loosen the bottom sheet of another's bunk, folding it neatly across the blanket's top. When the unsuspecting dupe retires and hops into bed, he gets the surprise of his life as his feet reach the halved part of the folded-back bottom sheet. Athletes do such other things as pour salt into a teammate's coffee or tie someone's shoe laces together while another teammate diverts the patsy's attention. Pranks are plentiful and varied, and most athletes take them good-naturedly.

Some athletes become coaches, but they hang on to many of the customs they learned in playing days, especially the pranks. Coaches never seem to grow up entirely, and that accounts for the way they can relate to their younger charges. As a sports-writer, I always marveled at the rapport, the esprit de corps, the good-natured relationships between coaches and those under their tutelage. I also marveled at the cheery rapport coaches enjoyed among themselves, especially when members of the opposite sex were present. For instance, take a certain set of coaches who came to Savannah about the same time and were assigned to Savannah High School and the now-defunct Commercial High School, all brought here by Fred G. "Buddy" McCollum, who in the 1950's left the head coaching job at Troy State College in Alabama to become the first athletic director of Savannah's public schools. Until McCollum's arrival, the schools had their own separate athletic departments. The idea of a central athletic office was to coordinate matters common to all schools, such as equipment purchases and scheduling, which became even more important because Savannah was on the verge of forming several new high schools.

Buddy McCollum, an Auburn alumnus and former assistant coach at his alma mater, imported several coaches who had played for colleges in Alabama—Ralph Pyburn as Savannah High's head coach, with Jim Reynolds, Carlos Bassett, Jack Wynne, Lamar "Turp" Spear, and Lamar Leachman as assistants. He brought back to Savannah from Clearwater, Florida, native son M. A. Spellman, and approved Spellman's choice of Chan Highsmith, one of Spellman's teammates at the University of North Carolina, as his chief assistant. McCollum was pleased with his choices; and hoping to build morale, he encouraged the coaches and their wives to socialize. Some of them did one afternoon at the swimming pool of the old DeSoto Hotel. It was one of those swim, sit around, and get-acquainted affairs.

Suddenly, while most were in the pool, a shriek sounded as one of the girls leapt high out of the water. Then another. Then still another. Chan Highsmith, who had been swimming underwater, surfaced with a big laugh. The girls were looking astonished. Back underwater Highsmith submerged, and there were more shrieks. The other coaches began to submerge, and the shrieks continued. Shrieks and laughter. Not that much collective fun had anyone witnessed in ages. Finally Coach Spellman explained what was happening: "Chan's initiating the girls into the Butt-biters Club."

Highsmith had started it, and the other coaches had joined in. What they were doing was swimming underwater and biting the posteriors of the females, all of whom, once they got past their astonishment, seemed to be enjoying this immensely. Some of them began to engage in turnabout, biting the rear ends of the male coaches. Spellman further explained that it was a prank Highsmith brought to Savannah from his days as a player for the North Carolina Tar Heels, back when players, whenever they got into a pool together, would bite one another's butts. To Spellman's knowledge, that was the first time Highsmith had crossed the gender line. It happened in Savannah. Whether the practice has endured—who knows?

Acceptable Nomenclature. In the mid-1950's Savannah was growing southward. Subdivisions were springing up everywhere, bucolic settings becoming urbanized about as fast as developers could borrow the money and build houses for sale. In order to encourage the growth, the City of Savannah extended its water mains beyond the corporate limits into the developing areas, finding a lucrative market for water—and of course with an eye toward future annexation of those areas into the city limits. But water-line extensions also meant that sewerage had to be provided, and that naturally created the problem of wastewater and sewage disposal. The solution: oxidation ponds.

In order to establish the oxidation ponds, however, the city government needed the Chatham County government's approval. So one day the city's engineers appeared before the county commission with a formal petition. They brought along an expert from out of town, since oxidation ponds were new to the area. The expert did the presenting and the talking. He pointed out that oxidation ponds performed the same function as the more elaborate sewage disposal plants. The main difference, he said, was that oxidation ponds served smaller areas, relying on oxygen from the air above a pond's surface to mix with certain chemicals and to dispense with the bacteria accompanying the waste, thereby rendering safe the effluent discharged from the pond, which would be piped away to a nearby stream.

The word "biodegradable" hadn't come into common usage then, but the expert was saying that wastewater, properly treated, was rendered biodegradable. In those days not everyone understood much about disposing of raw sewage, because for years Chatham County's septic outfall had been discharged untreated into the many streams of the Savannah and Ogeechee rivers' estuaries. Only in recent years had Savannah's first disposal plant been built, and it served only a small part of town.

The expert admirably made his pitch to the county commissioners, mixing scientific and technical terms with everyday language in such a way as to befuddle some of them. One such befuddled commissioner was Kirk Sutlive, probably the most sophisticated member of the governing body. Sutlive's sophistication came from his experience as public relations manager of Union Camp's huge papermaking plant, the largest of its kind in the world. He was, by profession, a journalist in one of Georgia journalism's most noted families. He was a speechmaker and master of ceremonies par excellence. He emceed far beyond Savannah's borders, notably at the Eggs & Issues breakfasts the state chamber of commerce sponsored weekly in Atlanta when the legislature was in session. He lobbied for the paper industry with lawmakers, and in speeches in large and small communities he also lobbied rank-and-file citizens, convincing them that paper mills really didn't smell as bad as they seemed to, and—with one of his classic lines—that "those pulpwood trucks on the road aren't as dangerous as they look." Listen to Kirk Sutlive, and you would come away half-believing that odors emanating from pulp mills were like those from a perfume factory. Sutlive was that convincing and persuasive. He was smooth, all right, and he spoke in a pleasant singsong manner that wasn't so singsongy as to grate on one's nerves. It was Kirk Sutlive who became the county commission's point man in quizzing the expert shilling for the oxidation ponds.

"The way you've described this," Sutlive said after listening to answers to several of his questions, "an oxidation pond sort of purifies the waste that comes from people's toilets and kitchen sinks, then sends the purified stuff through pipes to streams. Right?" Absolutely, the expert answered. "Well," Sutlive pressed, "you keep calling it an oxidation pond. Isn't that about the same thing as a sewage disposal plant?" That was about it, the expert replied. "So couldn't we simply call ours sewage disposal plants?" Sutlive asked. The expert said he guessed that would be all right, but "oxidation pond" sounded a whole lot better, and didn't the gentlemen of the commission agree? Kirk Sutlive pondered for a moment, looked at his fellow commissioners, and then, with an impish smile mirroring his well-known wit, allowed: "I guess you're right. In fact, I'd much rather live next door to an oxidation pond than a sewage disposal plant. Gentlemen, my fellow commissioners, I move that we approve the application of the City of Savannah to construct oxidation ponds—and not sewage disposal plants—on the southside tracts in question." The motion carried unanimously.

Our Man in Radioland. Paschal N. Strong, of a well-known Savannah family, won an appointment to West Point in the late 1920's; and before graduation he had distinguished himself by writing and publishing a series of adventure novels appealing to boys. *West Point Wins* was one of them, *West Point Over the Top* was another. Strong, if he couldn't make it as a professional soldier, definitely would as a writer, his hometowners agreed. He made it, fortunately, as both. After receiving his Army commission, he dreamed up, wrote, and sold to a radio syndicate what would become one of the longest-running afternoon adventure series—*Jack Armstrong, All-American Boy.* The hero got into and out of more scrapes and tight places than even Pearl White, the movie heroine of *The Perils of Pauline*.

Army officer Paschal Strong, called "Pat" by his friends, had a vivid imagination, and during the days of the Great Depression he supplemented his meager military salary with income from his radio show. But Pat Strong seemed to downplay himself. Once over lunch, after he had retired as a brigadier general, he told me he had been only a "mediocre soldier and a mediocre writer—mediocre but adequate." He pointed out that he was possibly the only general officer who had never been tapped to attend the Army War College or the Command and General Staff School, and reasoned that he never would have attained flag rank if the Korean War hadn't come along and kept him in the Army beyond what would have been a routine retirement. As for the Jack Armstrong radio series, Strong acknowledged that his series attained a degree of popularity, but never "anything great," like some of the other series and soap operas.

I wished that Strong hadn't been so modest, because I always regarded him as a Savannah hero, which I still do years after his death. For example, one of his military assignments took him to the Philippines; and as an engineer he was posted to the island of Corregidor, guarding Manila Bay, to supervise a strengthening of the defenses on what had become known as "the Rock." He was a leader on the project to design the tunnels in that offshore fortress, and although the Army high command approved the plans, it could not fund them because the money simply wasn't available to the peacetime Army. Strong, by then a captain, obtained permission to raise the needed funds from private sources, and with other officers began calling on the businessmen in the Philippines, reminding them that their islands were vulnerable to assault, and that the Rock, in case of attack, would be the main protection of their business interests. The businessmen listened, heeded the warnings, and donated funds needed to build the tunnels on Corregidor. Some of them, he recalled that day over lunch, actually donated gold bullion from their stashes. The Philippines did not fall to the Japanese in 1942 until Corregidor fell, and it is significant that Paschal Strong was among the military officers who first predicted that air power eventually would neutralize land fortresses—which is precisely why Corregidor fell. The tunnels afforded American and Filipino defenders the protection they needed to forestall the Japanese onslaught as long as they did.

Anyway, long after World War II ended, and Corregidor was avenged, Pat Strong's Jack Armstrong series continued on afternoon radio. Before going to Korea, Colonel Strong served a couple of years as Army district engineer in Savannah, his hometown, and would have retired when that assignment was up but for the Korean conflict. While Strong was stationed in Savannah, his friends learned how he had written his radio series on a portable typewriter he carried with him always. Whenever there was a lull in his military work, he'd pull out the old portable and knock off an episode. He even wrote, with the portable on his lap, while traveling in a staff car between locations in the sprawling engineering district he commanded. He knew how to budget his time.

And the Jack Armstrong episode that amused its author the most was the one in which Pat Strong said he simply couldn't figure a way to extricate his hero from grave danger. As one episode closed, the hero was in a predicament so compounded as to be highly, deeply, and widely confounded. The Friday episode advised listeners to tune in on Monday. Thank goodness,

Strong recollected gratefully and with a witty smile, listeners had an entire weekend, and perhaps by Monday they'd have forgotten some of the perils. As the story resumed on Monday, the announcer said something to the effect that: "After Jack Armstrong escaped from the pit, he . . ." Listeners never learned how the hero escaped, but they had sufficient faith in him to know that he would never succumb to the dastardly wiles of any villain.

Another Engineer. Robert S. Bahr was one of the successors to the aforementioned Paschal N. Strong as commander of the Savannah District, U.S. Army Corps of Engineers. He was a dedicated engineer, with a flair for showmanship and the dramatic. Bahr was intimately involved with the Savannah River's flood control projects, as well as considerable other construction, both military and civilian, in the far-flung district. Whenever he planned to announce something, he'd set up a news conference and invite both the news media and the movers and shakers of the affected communities. He always had the right props—charts, graphs, maps, slides, and sometimes movies.

Bob Bahr, a colonel, was a West Point graduate, but not a ring-knocker. (By way of explanation, non–West Pointers call graduates of the U.S. Military Academy ring-knockers, asserting that in an officers' club the West Pointers send out the message that they are such by subtly tapping their class rings on the table—a sort of elitist affectation.) Bob Bahr was not one of those, I discerned while covering his office as a television newsman in the 1950's, and after returning to newspapering. Upon retirement, after filling two other assignments elsewhere, he settled in Savannah, assumed several roles of civic leadership, became an anticrime activist who kept elected officials sitting up and listening, and once ran unsuccessfully for public office. He and I became close friends, although my own wartime military experience had taken me to only the rank of staff sergeant. He even invited me to be guest speaker at an annual banquet of the local West Point Association. When I reminded him of my meager military rank, he replied, "It's not what anyone was, but what he is—and *you* is the one I want to be our speaker." (Bad grammar for emphasis.) "Yassuh," I replied, and the night I spoke I advised my listeners that no former sergeant ever could wish for such an opportunity to hold captive a room full of officers, active and retired, especially Knights of the Hudson, which West Pointers also are called.

My Bob Bahr story, however, is one of an enlisted man on active duty finally getting the upper hand over a full colonel on active duty, and in a different branch of the service! I witnessed it: I was in television news, and one day I received a call from Colonel Bahr, advising that the Chief of Engineers of the Army would be coming in from Washington the next day, and the colonel wanted to give me and WSAV-TV an exclusive on filming the arrival of his boss. Thankful that the colonel didn't like the other station anyway, I met him at the appointed hour the next morning, and we proceeded in a staff car to Hunter Air Force Base, where the Chief of Engineers' plane would land. Hunter, located on the south side of Savannah, was then a Strategic Air Command base.

About an hour before the general's scheduled arrival, rain began to fall; actually, the bottom dropped out, and it seemed there would be no letup. When the Army staff car arrived at the gate of the Air Force installation, an Air Police corporal on duty there was about to salute and allow the staff car to pass through, but suddenly a siren began wailing. It was an alert, which military posts stage from time to time as a drill for security. (It is significant that atomic weapons were stored at Hunter Air Force Base, making security a high priority at all times.) The corporal, who just a minute or so earlier would have allowed us through the gate perfunctorily, went into his on-the-alert mode as the siren sounded. Politely, but firmly, he requested that Colonel Bahr, his driver, and "the civilian" (myself) dismount. Remember, it was raining cats and dogs. The following dialogue, as best I can recall, ensued:

Colonel Bahr: Corporal, I am the Savannah district engineer, here to meet the Army Chief of Engineers. His plane is due to land about now. Please let us proceed.

Corporal: Sir, we are under alert, and I ask you once again to please dismount—you, your driver, and the civilian. I also must see your ID.

Bahr: But, corporal, it's raining like hell, and my civilian passenger doesn't even have a raincoat.

Corporal: Sorry about that, sir, but I am following the alert procedures. Please now, dismount, all of you.

The three of us dismounted. Bahr did have on a raincoat, and so did his driver. I had to get my fanny soaked as we stood there, showing ID, while another airman searched the staff car, thoroughly inspected my movie camera on the back seat, opened the trunk of the car, and thoroughly searched it. The corporal went into the gatehouse and made a telephone call to the control tower to verify that, in fact, a plane bearing the Army Chief of Engineers was due. Finally satisfied, the corporal motioned us back into the car, returned our ID's, then saluted the colonel, and waved us through the gate. Headed toward the terminal, Bob Bahr was fuming. Of course, he said, the corporal was following procedures. Of course, there was an alert. Of

57

course, you can't fault a serviceman for doing his duty. But dammit, that corporal was so deliberate, so damned slow, and even in his raincoat the colonel got about as wet as I did. Why, he wondered out loud, was that corporal so damned high-handed?

"Let me tell you, Bob," I began to tell him. "You don't know the thrill a corporal can get, having a field officer at his mercy. He was getting even for all the times some colonel, or major, or captain, or lieutenant jerked him around. And for a corporal in the Air Force to have an Army colonel in submission . . . hell, man, you made his day."

As we pulled up to the terminal, and while the general from Washington's plane taxied up, Robert S. Bahr, Colonel, United States Army, suddenly burst out laughing. "Tom, old friend, you've got this thing figured right. That guy was in hog heaven." Since he and his boss from Washington were old buddies, Bob related his recent experience to the general, who enjoyed a hearty laugh.

Politics: It's Still Politics

The demise of political bossism in Savannah and Chatham County came gradually but ever so steadily with the post–World War II reform movements—several of them, one at a time, but each gnawing at the political machine that had been entrenched for decades. The late John J. Bouhan, a red-haired Irish lawyer and a partner in one of the city's biggest law firms, was the last of the bosses, who fought every step of the way as his faction retreated to the point where finally it had no presence on the city council, the county commission, the school board, or the legislative delegation. The erosion of bossism came in a period that spanned about twenty years.

Local politics, however, is just about as interesting these days (but a tad more genteel) as it was in the past, the difference being that there is no central control—over anything. Joe Mahany, the former county commission chairman, probably would have been a Bouhanite had his political star risen in that era, mainly because Irish-Catholics (Bouhan was one) stuck together in those days. But Mahany, an independent Irish-Catholic, didn't need a political machine in winning his post virtually on his own, and startling old-line politicians, especially longtime commissioner Bob McCorkle, whom he ousted from the chairmanship after a low-key Democratic primary campaign in which he went, one-on-one, to citizens and charmed them with his forthrightness and white hair, which never seemed trained for anything except blowing in the wind. Operating on a low budget (but after the primary getting some help from the local Democratic Party), Mahany then defeated Republican Julie Backus Smith in the general election. Popular, charming, and beautiful, Mrs. Smith was completing a term as a district commissioner. She enjoyed a healthy campaign war chest, about three times larger than Mahany's; and she had an overwhelming coterie of supporters out stumping for her, including devotees of the fast-growing Republican Party. But when the votes were counted, she stood loser.

That's just one example of how lone candidates have been able to win without the aid of a boss-led political machine, but there have been many such examples. Such winners have been the beneficiaries of districting, which came about in the wake of the Supreme Court's one man–one vote ruling—a ruling that affected city, county, school-board, and legislative races. Districting eliminated political "tickets," whereby a strong leader would assemble a group of candidates to run with him, and all would get elected together, even though voters had to cast ballots for the individual candidates. When candidates ran as tickets, the team concept was prevalent. The head of a ticket would appeal for voters to "elect me and my team, and we'll run things right." Voters went for the team concept, and only occasionally did split-ticket voting produce a winner. Voting was citywide and countywide, every voter voting on each office.

After the city and county were districted, however, the opportunity was present for individuals to run independently, either as Republicans or Democrats, first in party primaries and then, if first-round winners, in the general elections. That gave rise to the emergence of candidates who held absolutely no political allegiance to any other candidates, factions, or parties, and the races were within districts, not citywide or countywide.

John Rousakis, who served two decades as mayor, came into office, as all mayors before him had, as head of a ticket, and he won his second term that way. But then, districting set in (by legislative fiat), and Rousakis' last three terms he won individually. In districting the city, legislators left two at-large aldermanic seats, but the six other city council members come from separate districts. Districting has made possible the election of more minority members to public office because some districts are majority-black; thus, the primaries and general elections have pitted blacks against blacks in those districts.

Floyd Adams, the current mayor and the first black person to win that office, got his start in public service by winning a district aldermanic seat, which he held for two four-year terms before running for, and winning, one of the at-large seats. With that success in winning citywide, and against a white opponent, Adams decided in 1995 to run for mayor in the city's first nonpartisan (no primaries) election. He and incumbent Susan Weiner, who was Savannah's first woman mayor and only the second Republican to hold that office, won the most votes in a four-way race; and Adams defeated her by fewer than three hundred votes in the runoff required by law whenever no candidate receives more than half of the votes cast in a general election.

Although districting definitely has helped the political cause of blacks, the black community has also helped itself by becoming involved more up-front in politics. Until districting, the only black city aldermen had been Bowles Ford and Roy Jackson, each selected by Rousakis to run as members of his ticket. Although blacks had been enfranchised for generations, always since Reconstruction eligible to vote in general elections, they were barred for years from the so-called "white primaries" of the Democratic Party, in which elections actually occurred, with the general elections in a state where Republicans were merely token in number serving merely as perfunctory endorsements of those Democrats chosen in the primaries. After court rulings let blacks participate in Democratic primaries, their participation amounted merely to endorsements of the white candidates. The black bloc became a formidable force, and candidates courted it; but blacks remained mostly sideliners, whose votes were cherished, rather than active candidates. So districting and equal-opportunity involvement by blacks as candidates, rather than as mere supporters, have radically changed the nature of local politics.

Also changed are the methods of political campaigning. In pre-district days, those on the various tickets concentrated their methods of appeal to voters on newspaper, radio, and television advertising. Their newspaper ads were classically priceless in their snideness, sarcasm, innuendo, and plain-out name-calling directed at opposing tickets. Caricatures and photographs would depict opponents in the most unfavorable light. Nearly every one of the ads bordered on libel, to such an extent that the local newspaper's advertising department would buck proofs of the ads to an editor for a libel check, and often the editor would buck them to the newspaper's attorney. Some ads had to be sent back to the politicians for revisions because, when libel is present, it is usually the newspaper and not the advertiser that winds up in court.

The radio ads were terse and to the point, calling a spade a spade and defining opponents as the bad guys who not only shouldn't get elected but also shouldn't even be allowed to run. And the television ads took the form of half-hour live productions, candidates seated behind desks, extolling their own virtues, and viewing with alarm their foes. The live telecasts were somewhat hazardous because the candidates were liable to say anything that hindsight would tell them they shouldn't have said. A cuss word now and then, a blatant misstatement of fact—often they got carried away, not to mention heated.

The advertising techniques are different now. Seldom does a candidate run a full-page ad, opting instead for smaller space, as well as endorsement ads from various citizens, scattered through an issue in two-column-by-two-inch spaces. The radio spots run quick-and-to-the-point, and all of the television spots are pretaped, thus open to editing and revision, and sometimes redoing entirely. The live TV programs are now forums, sponsored either by the individual stations' news departments or by a civic organization such as the League of Women Voters, with representatives of the electronic and print media quizzing the candidates. That's an expense spared the candidates.

One of the main advertising thrusts is signs, including outdoor billboards, but the most common are the yard signs affixed to short wooden sticks that can be driven into the surface of a lawn. Ride through a neighborhood and count yard signs— you can just about gauge how that particular precinct will go come election day. Billboards are expensive, but yard signs cost about a dollar or less each.

It's doubtful that any of the materials now used in political advertisements border on libel. For one thing, even the most vicious of all candidates is a pussy cat by comparison with those of yore. There are a few exceptions, of course. Now and then a television worker will tell friends about fisticuffs or near-fights—in or outside the studio—on a certain night when a forum was held. One young political activist told me that, as he was standing off-camera while the candidate he was supporting was being quizzed on-camera, a partisan from the other side sidled up to him and addressed him by the m-f word. Even in campaigns that seem civilized on the surface, deep-seated acrimony can abide. Politics usually brings out the worst in people, especially those who habitually harbor the worst yet keep it under control most of the time. And those who outwardly exude acrimony, either in televised or town hall forums, make no apologies, justifying actions with the adage: "You can't fight sumbitches by the Marquis of Queensberry Rules."

("Sumbitch" is a word used often now in politics and other forums and environments, and it means what it sounds like— son of a bitch. It was popularized by the late Lewis Grizzard, a humorist and arguably the best of the South's latter-day columnists. Drawling sons and daughters of the South usually do not say their words fast, but parental training insists that they not be profane, so whenever they feel the need of profanity, they say their selected term fast. Say "sons of bitches" fast, and it comes out "sumbitches"—which, in politics, represents a figurative going with the flow, because we now hear cussing everywhere, even on network TV in before-bedtime slots. In earlier days Governor Marvin Griffin tagged his opponents "peckerwoods" and "jorees," and that was about as strong as he ever got, at least publicly. The late governor explained the terms as names of birds, the former as merely a flip-flop way of saying "woodpeckers," implying that opponents were pecking away at him the way that Hollywood-fabled bird attacks a tree. Still, his voice inflection stressed "Pecker," and listeners assumed that was a more polite way of branding an opponent a plain-out prick. I should add that Governor Griffin was entirely safe in his explanation because country fellows of the South often flip-flop two-syllable words, mainly for effect. Coming to mind, from having lived in rural Screven County three of my childhood years: bo-flam for flambeau, and flow-air for Airflow, which in the 1930's was a model name for one of the Chrysler automobiles.)

Political dirty tricks remain as current as ever. Not surprisingly, during the course of a campaign someone will circulate an unsigned letter recalling something from a candidate's past that the candidate would just as soon forget about. And in primary elections, whenever a candidate in one party seems a shoo-in for nomination, either because of a weak opponent or no opponent at all, voters loyal to one party will vote, instead, in the other party's primary, and for the candidate in the other party's primary who seems more likely to be vulnerable to defeat in the general election. Georgians aren't required to register by party affiliation, so the so-called crossover vote isn't crossover per se. Another dirty trick is to alter an opponent's outside signs, or simply to tear down an opponent's posted signs, or to stick a bumper sticker favoring one candidate over an opponent's sign. Whisper campaigns also are conducted during election seasons, as well as phony opinion polls conducted over the telephone by groups of partisans attempting to confuse voters.

Political campaigns still arouse the voters, some of them to the extent of staying away from the polls, having concluded that no one on the ballot is worth voting for. Voter turnout generally runs fifty percent of the electorate or less, and usually nudges the sixty-percent mark in years when the office of the President of the United States is being voted on. Georgia's gubernatorial elections are always held on the off-year, when the presidency isn't up for grabs and voter participation invariably is lower than during a presidential election.

Districting, as alluded to above, also has changed the character of the races for county commission, school board, and legislative seats. No longer are any of the offices, with the exception of county commission chairman and school board president, voted on by the entire electorate. District-office voting is confined within the several districts, and no legislative seat is voted on countywide, which accounts for the increased number of black county commissioners, school board members, and lawmakers. Thus the black-white issue is seldom injected in local elections. A white voter in, say, District Four, couldn't care less which of the black candidates in, say, District One, is victorious. The white voter goes into the booth knowing there is absolutely nothing he can do about the races in districts other than his own. And that makes for a fairly harmonious situation in local government.

This does not suggest, however, that it's all harmony, especially aboard the various governing bodies and the legislative delegation. For example, Chatham County's legislative delegation of House and Senate members in Georgia's General Assembly for years observed the custom of designating a "dean," basing the selection upon seniority among the members. The dean's purpose was to serve as a spokesperson for the delegation on local issues coming before the legislature, as well as a contact person for citizens desiring to lobby for certain bills and resolutions pertaining to Chatham County. State Senator Tom Coleman served as dean for many sessions, but after he decided to retire from politics it seemed automatic that long-time state Representative Anne Mueller would become dean. It didn't work out that way. State Senator Diane Harvey Johnson, a former member of the House delegation, but whose legislative service was broken when she sat out a two-year term, laid claim to the deanship, and for a week or two there was no dean. Finally the impasse was resolved and the dean "title" passed to Mrs. Mueller, a dubious blessing perhaps because the dean draws no more pay than the rest of the legislators, yet voluntarily assumes a heavier responsibility.

Nor does harmony prevail at all times in city or county government, or on the board of education. For example, former county commission chairman Bob McCorkle was often at odds with fellow commissioners; and one meeting ran for an extra couple of hours because the other members of the commission sat in dead silence in protest against a stance McCorkle had taken on an issue. They just sat there, not a soul saying a word, as if they had all day—which, definitely, they did that day.

Under the leadership of former Chairman Joe Mahany, the county's governing board continued to squabble at times, but somehow the squabbling didn't override accomplishments in such matters as roadways, expanded recreational facilities, and hold-the-line taxation. Mahany was a leader who made it known where he stood, and fellow commissioners, while not always agreeing, respected that. There wasn't the same kind of friction between Mahany and other commissioners as when McCorkle reigned. Mahany was defeated in 1996 by Republican Billy Hair. So far, little friction.

Former Mayor Susan Weiner often experienced an absence of harmony with the other members of City Council. It was mostly a partisan thing, she being a Republican and, with fellow-Republicans, outnumbered by Democrats on the city's governing body. This condition irked her so much that she unloaded her frustrations in a speech to a civic club, maintaining that she too often was stymied by the Democratic aldermen.

Even one of the Republican aldermen, Ellis Cook, annoyed her whenever he voted favorably or unfavorably on an issue she either opposed or favored. She and her husband, Al Weiner, regarded by many in politics and the community as the power behind the throne because of his outspokenness from the sideline, dubbed Alderman Cook a RINO, explaining that the term was an acronym for "Republican in Name Only," exuding bitter disrespect for an alderman who sometimes deemed it best to vote independently. So strong was Mayor Weiner's disrespect for Alderman Cook that she persuaded a former county commissioner to oppose Cook's bid for reelection in 1995; she lost her race and Cook won his.

Al Weiner, incidentally, became perhaps the most controversial nonelected political figure since the late Boss John Bouhan. After his retirement from academia, the Weiner couple came to Savannah from New York, where he had been a professor of dramatics in a university and she had been one of his students. They started a consultant business in Savannah, and she soon became active in civic matters, to the point of getting interested in politics and running for mayor. She defeated Mayor John Rousakis after he had served two decades in City Hall. On the night of her election, when the Weiner victory party was beginning, Al Weiner stepped to the microphone ahead of her and referred to the mayor she had just defeated as a "pig." The remark became the shot heard round Savannah. In such a moment of jubilation it shocked the celebrating Republicans and dampened the spirit of the occasion. From then on Al Weiner was a definite presence on the political scene. Rightly or wrongly, for the next four years Savannahians accused Al Weiner of calling all of his wife's shots, and the accusation was enhanced by his intermittent utterances in condemnation of the holdovers in City Hall, particularly City Manager Arthur A. "Don" Mendonsa. Unsigned letters critical of Mendonsa were attributed, rightly or wrongly, to Savannah's First Spouse (hardly anyone ever referred to him as "First Gentleman").

Mayor Weiner tried desperately to rally sufficient votes on City Council to get Mendonsa fired, but to no avail. She was nearly three years into her four-year term before Mendonsa sent a letter to the mayor and aldermen stating his intention to retire. Thus, with a stroke of his pen, Mendonsa accomplished what Susan Weiner could not do with persuasion. Adding irony to the situation was City Council's hiring of Michael Brown, city manager of Columbus, Georgia, to succeed Mendonsa, and with Mayor Weiner's glowing tribute to Brown as just the fellow they were looking for. The irony lay in the fact that Michael Brown, before going to Columbus, had served five years under Mendonsa as Savannah's assistant city manager. Brown, in fact, was Don Mendonsa's protégé, and Mayor Weiner strongly wanted him to be the one City Council chose. Ah, politics!

The school board, while relatively placid of late, in recent years went through one phase after another of disharmony, firing a string of superintendents amid tumult and shouting. To the current board's credit, however, the school system finally has been dismissed by the U.S. District Court from a desegregation lawsuit dating back to the 1960's. It was one of the longest-running lawsuits on record, in which a federal judge, rather than the elected school board, made most decisions that led to a unitary school system. The board now is on its own in keeping racial balance in the schools, and board members seemingly get along with one another better than in the past.

Yet, because Savannahians historically have jawed and argued over many and varied matters, it's not out of character that its politicians should jaw and argue from time to time, now and then seemingly *all* the time. It's simply Savannah's nature, and citizens seem to enjoy it, often with a shrug and the comment: "That's politics."

The City Managers

Most Savannahians thought that Don Mendonsa, who was city manager of Savannah longer than anyone else, extracted his familiar first name from the middle syllable of his surname. Not so. His formal name is Arthur Adonel Mendonsa; the "Don" comes from the second, third, and fourth letters of his middle name. Also, because Mendonsa was arguably the sternest and most demanding manager among all who held the job in Savannah, his nickname was appropriate. Most city employees referred to him (behind his back, of course) as "The Don," an oblique allusion to the *Godfather* movie's influence.

Savannah converted from the modified and much-eroded "strong mayor" form of government in 1954, after the citizens voted, in order to save the city from bankruptcy, to change to the council-manager form; and the entrenched political machine went into the new form of government kicking and screaming before being supplanted by reformers in the municipal election following the special council-manager election. Reform-minded citizens feared the worst—that the machine would find someone with administrative qualifications, but not too familiar with local government, and that in a year or two the council-manager form of government would fall flat on its face, and things would revert to the old ways. Mayor Olin F. Fulmer, however, was never really a part of the machine, although he held office under the machine's aegis. He therefore outsmarted the machine by going out and finding a *real* city manager in the person of Frank A. Jacocks, then in Spartanburg, South Carolina. Fulmer, a wealthy retired insurance executive, didn't need the job as mayor anyway, and didn't plan to run for reelection, so he had no qualms about acting independently. Moreover, to get his reluctant council's approval of Jacocks, Fulmer touted him so highly publicly that his colleagues had little choice but to rubber-stamp Fulmer's choice. No lame-duck mayor ever stood taller.

So Jacocks was already in office when the reform Citizens Committee's Mayor Lee Mingledorff was elected to succeed Fulmer. Within Mingledorff's first year, Jacocks had wrought so many changes, by instituting a more professional operation, that the city ventured off the red-ink side of the ledger onto the black, albeit only by a few thousand dollars. It was the city's huge deficit that spurred citizens to vote for council-manager in the first place, especially after local banks drew the line on extending additional credit to the city. Jacocks proved the banks and the citizens right, and Savannah's fiscal affairs were in excellent shape. An urban renewal program was off and running, when, in mid-1959, he left for another job, to be succeeded by John O. Hall, who came aboard in September of that year.

Hall, who had previous experience in local government, came to Savannah from a job with private industry in the Middle East. He continued to build upon the foundation Jacocks had laid, enhancing the city's solvency; but what seemed on the surface to be a good marriage between him and the council came to an abrupt end during his third year on the job when he high-handedly presented the elected officials with an unbalanced budget, told them he had made all the cuts he deemed necessary, and said it was their job to make further cuts of their choosing and bring the proposed budget into balance. That was the municipal-governmental equivalent of a colonel spitting in the general's face, and the most angered of all the officials was Mayor Malcolm Maclean, who had succeeded Mingledorff in early 1962. Besides, Maclean and Hall never got along very well personally, observers blaming that on the air of aloofness Hall sometimes displayed to his superiors. He appeared especially aloof to Maclean, almost from the beginning, when the latter was a member of the aldermanic board, prior to his succeeding Mayor Mingledorff. Hall resigned, of course by request. The date was July 11, 1962, which some of Maclean's friends still refer to as his—and Savannah's—"lucky seven-eleven day."

Enter Don Mendonsa, a Florida native with a master's degree in city planning from Georgia Tech. Mendonsa, when Hall departed, was director of the Savannah-Chatham County Metropolitan Planning Commission, and he was excellent in his work. Almost immediately upon Hall's resignation, Maclean and his council offered Mendonsa the city manager's job. He accepted, took office the very day Hall's resignation became effective (seven-eleven-sixty-two), and functioned admirably. And one thing he never did was challenge his superiors to balance a proposed budget themselves. That's the manager's job in a system wherein "manager proposes, council disposes." It is the elected officials' role to set policy; and the manager's role to devise programs for implementing that policy and then run the programs by council for approval, suggestions for amendment, or rejection, and also with a budget proposal containing anticipated revenues to pay for all programs. The system works well, and particularly did it work well with Mendonsa in the manager's office.

Mendonsa instituted even more professionalism into local government, utilizing talent already on board as best he could but never hesitating to bring aboard outsiders with experience and qualifications in their particular disciplines. For example, he recruited a budget director and a personnel chief from outside, while filling police chief and fire chief positions from within. More than either manager before him, he enhanced public

perception of the delineation of authority, and some Savannahians were critical of "this guy who brings in sons-of-bitches
from out of town" to help run the city. Such criticisms never
daunted the mayor and aldermen, or Mendonsa, and the
effectiveness of city government in delivering services to the
people, without according favoritism or punishment to citizens,
increased. It was Mendonsa who began implementation of the
Maclean administration's decision to desegregate Savannah after
the 1964 public-accommodations law went into force, and also
to open more avenues for public employment to minorities.
Desegregation, which occurred at a fast clip, is what doomed
the Maclean administration.

So Mendonsa proved to be "too professional" after Republican businessman J. Curtis Lewis and an aldermanic ticket of his
choosing defeated the Maclean administration in 1966. The
Republican Party, long occupying a back seat in Georgia politics, had begun to emerge and catch on, and that fact, coupled
with a white backlash against City Hall–sanctioned desegregation, gave the Lewis slate its victory. The Lewis council took
office and, while accepting the council-manager form of
government, felt unduly constrained under a city charter clearly
defining the separation of powers between council and manager.
The breaking point occurred when the fire chief announced his
intention to retire.

Lewis and the aldermen told Mendonsa to appoint as the new
fire chief one of the battalion chiefs favored by some of their
political supporters. Mendonsa instead wanted to appoint the
assistant chief, whom he deemed eminently qualified and who
also outranked the battalion chief. Mendonsa made it clear that
the city charter gave him, and not the council, the authority to
appoint department heads. Charter be damned, said the

aldermen, and after days of confrontation over that issue, Mendonsa resigned, effective May 1, 1967.

Lewis and the aldermen then announced that they would make a search for a new city manager, someone they hoped would be more attuned to local customs and preferences; and finally they did hire a native son in the person of Picot B. Floyd. The selection surprised many Savannahians, most of whom knew who Floyd was but were of the opinion that he was comfortably ensconced as a member of the faculty of the University of Georgia's Institute of Government. Surprise lay in the fact that someone would want to leave campus life and jump into the cauldron of municipal government, especially someone who had already experienced municipal government and knew that it was not always a pleasant environment.

Floyd's past experience was in Savannah, as an assistant city manager under John Hall, and then in a similar post in Alexandria, Virginia. Earlier he had been the first executive director of the Historic Savannah Foundation, the private-sector organization that has been responsible for the reclamation and preservation of Savannah's historic buildings. Floyd even earlier, after completing a tour of duty as a Coast Guard officer during the Korean War, was a reporter for the *Savannah Morning News*, and then taught at the local Benedictine Military School, his alma mater. The Lewis administration felt that Floyd, who had grown up here, was a member of a respected family, and was married to a local girl also of a respected family, had more than sufficient familiarity with Savannah and its peculiarities to be an ideal city manager. With pride, Mayor Lewis announced the appointment of a hometown boy.

Although more liberal than the Republican elected officials who hired him, Floyd worked amicably with the council, as well as with the professionals who had been on Mendonsa's staff. Ironically, one of Floyd's first acts was to fill the vacant fire chief's position—with the same person, Arthur Register, whom predecessor Mendonsa had tapped for the job, and to whom the Lewis administration now voiced no objections. He did yield in a few instances on appointments. One of his hirings was longtime Savannahian Henry Jenkins as ombudsman, who had been Mayor Lewis' campaign manager. Floyd rationalized that decision by saying he was convinced that the man was qualified for the job in question—which he indeed was—and later Floyd promoted Jenkins to head public works. In another instance Floyd hired retired Army Lieutenant Colonel Tom Sears to head the new Model Cities program, financed by a federal grant under President Lyndon B. Johnson's Great Society war on poverty. Sears became the first black department head in Savannah's history. Yet, before Sears came aboard, a hassle between Floyd and the council arose. The council maintained that it had the authority to hire Sears because the job involved a special federal program. Floyd said the prerogative was his as city manager. Ironically, both sides were arguing not over Sears versus someone else, but over who called the shot. That marked the first breach of any kind between Floyd and his bosses.

Together, though, Floyd and the council made some accomplishments. One was winning an All-American City award for a widespread community cleanup campaign, aimed especially at the poor neighborhoods where tons of junk and debris had accumulated over the years. By the end of the campaign, Savannah was clean as a new baby's backside. A street-lighting program was begun as a means of brightening neighborhoods in order to reduce crime. The Lewis administration and Floyd also attacked the burgeoning drug problem by setting up a special unit within the Police Department, a sort of "Untouch-ables" kind of force. Progress also was made toward abatement of Savannah's serious water pollution, a program that remains ongoing and at a high cost for overcoming many years of neglect during the era of political bossism, when hardly any-thing was accomplished toward improving the infrastructure.

Not always during the four years of the Lewis administration were Floyd and the elected officials in harmony, but most of the time they were, and during those four years two major projects—the building of the Savannah Civic Center and prelim-inary work on the Riverfront Urban Renewal program—got under way in earnest.

Floyd was in office when a Democratic Party slate, headed by former County Commissioner John P. Rousakis, defeated the Lewis slate at the polls. During the transition period—between the election in July and the new administration's taking office in October—Floyd and the outgoing administration experienced a definite break in relations. Under the city's charter, a city manager works at the pleasure of City Council. He is not required to submit a perfunctory resignation upon an adminis-tration change, the rationale being that the professional side of government remain constant. So he and the defeated adminis-tration tolerated each other through August, during which time the council made a sincere effort to spend the city's surplus on street resurfacing, which Floyd stoutly resisted. So in Septem-ber, the last month of the transition period, Floyd took a vacation, and virtually hid out from everyone, not returning to City Hall until noon, the first Monday of October 1969, which was inauguration day.

With the Rousakis administration, Floyd worked compatibly, played the federal grant game well, and continued to shepherd the two major carryover projects, the Civic Center and pollution abatement. A month or so after Rousakis was in office, Floyd did fire Henry Jenkins from the public works job, contending that Jenkins had been too political during the recent election campaign. Floyd was imaginative and introduced several new programs and improvements in existing programs, including zoning regulations, particularly those that helped to lay the groundwork for special zoning regulations protecting the Historic District. His imaginative nature included, even, a proposal for pigeon control—place ground-up birth control pills in pigeon feed, scatter the feed through the downtown section, and sit back and wait for pigeons to stop reproducing. Alas, it turned out to be only a proposal, never implemented lest animal-rights buffs vent their wrath upon City Hall. The notion, however, made the national news, but there is no record of the method having been tried in other municipalities plagued with pigeons.

In May 1971, nearly two years after the Rousakis administration took office, Floyd resigned to take a job with Public Technology, a new offshoot of the International City Management Association. He later became city manager of Clearwater, Florida, then county manager of Hillsborough County (Tampa), and finally returned to academia and earned a doctorate. He was teaching abroad when sidelined in 1989 by a brain tumor, which took his life in the autumn of that year.

With Floyd's departure from Savannah in 1971, Don Mendonsa returned to Savannah as city manager. When brought back by the Rousakis administration, Mendonsa was administrator of DeKalb County (Decatur), Georgia, and had gained prominence for having restored order to what had been a chaotic county governmental mess. Back in Savannah, he sat behind the same desk he had left in 1967, but he rearranged the office.

After settling in, Mendonsa proved to be the same Machiavellian kind of manager he had been before—a taskmaster who demanded hard work by his subordinates, but who worked harder himself than anyone else. He was never a "Mr. Personality," and his subordinates swore that ice water ran through his veins. He smiled occasionally, but most of the time he was grim-faced while managing a city government that became noted nationwide as one of America's best-run. Three times he was chosen among the top ten city managers in the country.

The city completed and opened the Savannah Civic Center, as well as the $30-million pollution-abatement program, which included construction of a sewage-treatment plant, which now serves the nearby town of Thunderbolt, and miles of new sewerage. He streamlined trash and garbage pickup, instituted a garbage-incineration program, and oversaw completion of the Riverfront Urban Renewal project. The project resulted in the handsome Rousakis Riverfront Plaza, alongside which old cotton warehouses facing the Savannah River have been converted into shops, saloons, restaurants, and small hotels as well as the large Hyatt Regency and, at the end of River Street, the new Marriott Hotel, which served as Savannah's Olympic Village in 1996. Under Mendonsa's leadership, the street-lighting program was enlarged, most dirt streets were paved, and the police and fire departments became more efficient with the application of new technology and higher employment standards, and with the acquisition of updated equipment overall.

Mendonsa, Savannah's third and fifth city manager, stayed twenty-three years on the job during his last stint, and survived an embittered attempt by Mayor Susan Weiner, who had defeated twenty-one-year Mayor Rousakis in 1995, to persuade the council to fire him. She could never muster the necessary number of votes to bring that off. Having amassed the required time in service in both of his stints as city manager, Mendonsa resigned at the end of 1994.

In 1954, out of desperation lest the city go bankrupt, Savannah switched to the council-manager form of government. The system, even with managers from time to time coming under public criticism, has worked, and criticism has never reached such a crescendo as to bring on a public demand for changing the system. It seems here to stay, and deservedly so.

Postscript. The author, who from 1969 to 1974 took a break from newspapering, became assistant city manager of Savannah under Picot Floyd and remained in place under Mendonsa. Twice in those five years I was acting manager—first during that month when Floyd "hid out" from the departing Lewis administration, and again during the three months between Floyd's departure and Mendonsa's arrival. I learned, firsthand, that the job is arguably the most demanding position in Savannah, with daily problems in serving the public mounting upon problems from previous days. I admire anyone who has the stamina for city managing, and particularly Michael Brown, who succeeded Mendonsa (whom he had served as an assistant before becoming city manager of Columbus, Georgia), and who is in office at this writing. Brown's challenge—following one of the country's best managers—has to be overwhelming.

Building the Civic Center

It was a dream come true, and Johnny Mercer was here to share in the realization. So was Hal Kanter. Not every Savannahian can readily tell you who Hal Kanter is, but Johnny Mercer's name is as familiar in his hometown as Bull Street. Kanter, though, is as well known in Hollywood as was the late Mercer, his fellow-hometowner. Both grew up here. Mercer departed for Broadway as a somewhat actor, but hit it big as a songwriter. Kanter, a talented word-spinner with a wit rivaling Jack Benny's or any of the other great comedians, determined to make it big writing for Hollywood productions, and he did. His name usually appears on the credits of the annual Academy Award telecasts, many of the funny lines viewers hear being Kanter's brainchildren. That he is not as famous in his hometown as Mercer bothers him very little if at all.

The dream-come-true that brought both show-biz luminaries home was the grand opening of the Savannah Civic Center in 1971. Ah, the Civic Center, the planning and construction of which spanned three city administrations—Mayor Malcolm Maclean's, Mayor Curtis Lewis', Mayor John Rousakis'! Long before the project got underway, a civic center was definitely in the public's mind as citizens clamored for a bigger and better-appointed place than the old Municipal Auditorium for attending shows and other attractions. The old auditorium faced downtown Orleans Square on Barnard Street and backed up to Jefferson Street. Nice place, but outmoded.

Among the clamorers were Charles J. "Buster" White, Savannah's main entrepreneur in show business, and Mills B. Lane, the Savannah native who headed the Citizens & Southern National Bank, Georgia's largest financial institution, now called NationsBank. Lane lived in Atlanta, where the bank was headquartered, but also maintained a domicile in Savannah; he wanted, always, the very best for his native city. Also among the clamorers were the politicians, especially during election campaigns; the daily *Morning News* and *Evening Press*; the Savannah Symphony Society, desperately wanting to move away from playing Cadillac concerts in a Model-T hall; itinerant promoters; rock music fans; sports enthusiasts envisioning world-class events in a space capable of accommodating decent-sized crowds; rasslin' fans (as differentiated from *wrestling* fans—the latter being a legitimate sport by comparison with show-biz passing as a sport). Practically every mother's son and daughter, the mothers themselves, the daddies, their sisters, cousins, and aunts—all clamored for a civic center.

The Maclean administration commissioned architects—Savannahian Henry Levy among them—and a set of plans came forward around 1964 or 1965. After Curtis Lewis defeated Malcolm Maclean in 1966, the ball was in his administration's court. The Lewis administration didn't like Levy's plans, paid him for his services, hired Savannah architects Ben Ritzert and Vernon Nowell to draw new plans, and determined that at least seven million dollars would be needed for the project. Lewis & Company put the question to the voters in the form of a bond referendum in that amount. Voters overwhelmingly said Okay, the clamorers putting their tax money where their vocal cords had been, and it was, at last, "Go!"

The design became the product of architects Ritzert and Nowell's detailed research. They visited facilities in several other cities, noted the best and the worst features as they went along, and came up with plans embracing the good features they had noted, with some of their own nuances thrown in. Before deciding to build the facility facing Orleans Square, where the old Municipal Auditorium stood, the Lewis administration appointed some citizens to explore several other locations as possible sites. They deemed the downtown site best, enlarging the old building's location to a full city block, bounded by Barnard Street on the east, Oglethorpe Avenue on the north, Montgomery Street on the west, and Liberty Street on the south, acquiring the extra property through urban renewal. The enlargement required closing Jefferson Street between Oglethorpe and Liberty.

Coit Somers, a contractor in neighboring Vidalia, won the construction bid, and brought his experience of having built large structures in many cities. The Lewis administration insisted that he hire union labor, a political concession to the Building Trades Council. Somers wasn't accustomed to working with union labor, but he agreed to on this project, and later deemed it the "biggest mistake" he ever made. One of several examples he cited in arriving at that conclusion was a work stoppage that began one day when his project manager happened to pick up a hammer to tamp down a protruding nailhead. The stoppage didn't end until the manager put the hammer down and held a pow-wow with the unionists, who explained that hammering was a privilege reserved only to those who carried union cards. Somers cited other examples, most of them union-jurisdictional in nature. A mild-natured Southerner, Somers never (well, hardly ever) swore, but one of his sub-bosses did, and when the construction was over the sub-boss sounded off on how the best way to describe working with unions was a "royal pain in the ass." Somers nodded in agreement. Yet the project came in reasonably on schedule, though a couple of months late, much of the lateness due to city-instigated change orders and bad weather.

The fate of the old auditorium came into dispute during the construction. Promoter Buster White asked that the building be kept in place until the new facility was completed because, after all, the part of the land on which the old building stood was designated to be only a grassed plaza leading from Barnard Street to the new building's entrance. White had a season of shows booked, but he lost his plea and had to cancel them. Fortunately White and his Atlanta partner, Ralph Bridges, promoted entertainment in several states; otherwise his loss of a season's bookings in Savannah would have been more of a financial blow than it was.

The old auditorium had hosted all kinds of attractions, from grand opera and symphony concerts to Broadway musicals and serious dramas from the legitimate stage. Stars who performed there included, to mention just a few, actors Bette Davis, Tallulah Bankhead, Tyrone Power, and Raymond Massey; opera singers Lauritz Melchoir, Lawrence Tibbett, and Helen Traubel; concert violinist Yehudi Menhuin; pianist Roger Williams, who played one of his early concerts there; the piano duo of Ferrante and Teicher, who returned often; Fred Waring and the Pennsylvanians, every other year; Spike Jones and his City Slickers, who always packed the house. Pianist Liberace was a favorite, and returned several times. The list is long, and many who trod the old boards would return to play the new Civic Center. Harboring memories of so many stellar performances, nostalgic Savannahians came to watch as the wrecking ball began to pound the old auditorium; one man actually removed his hat and placed it over his heart. *Sic transit gloria mundi!*

Construction of the Civic Center was near its halfway point when I left the managing editorship of the *Savannah Morning News* to become assistant city manager of Savannah, beginning a five-year break in my journalism career, which began in 1940 and would resume upon my return to newspapering in 1974. One of my many duties in the new job was to work with city engineer Chester Steadman as City Hall's liaison with the project, an assignment that took me to the job site almost daily. Steadman and I had many a laugh in days after the building opened, reflecting on the odd things that happened during and right after construction. The general foreman's brush with union labor and its resultant work stoppage provided one reflective laugh. There were others:

- As we entered the building from its south end one day, we passed a certain workman hunkered down near the door, obviously taking a rest; and a half-hour later as we were leaving, we passed that same workman, still squatting in that same spot. An extra long rest period, we concluded.

- The pigeons, which inevitably will appear at any large construction site, were somewhat encouraged by workmen on lunch break throwing them bread crusts. They began nesting beneath the first steel beams to be erected, and progressively moved higher up as new structure was added. As roof and ceiling took form, they perched and flew around amidst the uppermost beams, and continued to roost topside after mercury-vapor ceiling lights were installed in the lofty reaches of the arena.

  How to get rid of the pigeons—that was the question. The suggestion of BB guns was nixed because errant pellets might break the expensive lights. The solution came in several ways. Swatting and stunning them with brooms wielded from high catwalks proved somewhat effective, but there were more pigeons than swatters. Fogging also worked, sending the birds scampering. Other imaginative methods worked to an extent, shooing out most of the birds. But when Buster White brought Holiday on Ice for the very first attraction, three or four pigeons remained, drawing occasional applause from amused patrons as the birds swooped downward into view, above the heads of the skaters, none of whom ever complained about droppings. Ultimately, though, they disappeared from the arena side of the building.

On the theater side of the building, separated from the arena by a common lobby, only a few pigeons remained at construction's end. They were dispatched similarly, until one lone bird remained. That pigeon doggedly determined to stay. It would fly from one side of the theater to the other, but never close enough to floor level for anyone to draw near it. Finally, building engineer Roland Walls and stage manager Vic Scalisi positioned themselves on each side of the loge after noticing that the bird often flew close to the railing in front of the first row of seats. Each held a broom, and each would swing mightily at the bird as it flew near. One of them finally made contact, swatting the bird, home-run style, all the way to the orchestra pit below and down front. Charlie McGirt, the do-everything member of the staff, speedily retrieved the fallen bird and took it outside, much to the relief of building manager Mike Finocchiaro. The pigeon, a tough varmint, survived the ordeal and flew off, likely seeking a new construction site elsewhere.

● The missing hatch cover on the roof provided another chuckle in retrospect. Daily, Steadman and I would check to determine whether it had been located and set in place. Daily, the answer was no. We must have reported that open hatch, through which rain would come into the building and onto a stairwell, seven or eight times. Daily, the foreman would make a note of it. One day, while making our regular check, Steadman spotted a hatch cover in a dark corner beneath the stairway, and how we missed seeing it before remains a mystery. "Give it to me," Steadman said, and then took the cover, climbed a short ladder to the roof, and set it in place. Next day, one of the sub-foremen saw us, walked over, and said, victoriously, "I checked the roof this morning and couldn't find any open hatches." Steadman, smug and smiling, simply said, "Thanks," and we never bothered to tell him how the missing-hatch mystery was solved.

• The electrical service into the building was a big headache, but in retrospect it became funny. For the theater stage, so many amps were required; for the arena, so many additional amps were needed, about twice the intensity of power than in the theater. We were unaware that the arena side was under-ampered until just a few days before the arrival of Holiday on Ice, which would set up for a week of performances. Holiday sent ahead its specifications for various needs, and manager Finocchiaro ran them by Steadman. "Good Lord," Steadman lamented, "we've only half the service they need in the arena." Complicating the problem was the fact that all the electrical equipment by then was firmly in place.

The electrical engineer on the project, through no fault of his own, had prescribed lower amperage for the arena, based on his inquiries of both the ice show and the Ringling Bros. & Barnum and Bailey Circus, which was booked for later. Apparently, in his checks, he had talked with the wrong persons, because the technical people for both attractions couldn't recall ever having spoken with the engineer in Savannah, who probably had talked with some clerk who didn't know an ampere from third base. But, as they say, all's well that ends well, and with the cooperation of the Savannah Electric and Power Company and the electrical contractor, sufficient temporary service was fed into the building to accommodate both the ice show and the circus. It was, however, touch-and-go because the accelerated supply of electricity was not in place until the day before the ice-show crews arrived. Talk about a unanimous "Whew!" Since Buster White, a promoter who insisted on everything being just right, was bringing in the ice show, I hesitate to contemplate the explosion that would have resulted had the ice show arrived and no adjustment had been made for electrical service. White would have been forced to cancel the show and pay it off, and the city likely would have ended up in court. Still, Buster White experienced another problem with the ice show, and definitely it was the fault of Holiday on Ice.

●The other problem was the seating arrangement, and no entrepreneur bringing in a major attraction wants to have an insufficient number of seats for a sold-out attraction, which the ice show definitely was for the first three days of its week's engagement. It was sold out because ice skating was a novelty in Savannah, although ice shows had performed in the past—on a portable rink on the stage of the old auditorium as well as in a smaller rink across town owned by Aaron Newman. But this one, in the new building, would be the biggest and most spectacular ice show Savannahians had ever seen.

Promoter White had received from the forthcoming show, and passed on to manager Finocchiaro, the show's prescribed dimensions for the rink. That left, according to calculations made by the two, sufficient space for setting up two rows of extra seats, on each side of the arena and on top of the ice, just behind the protective barricade. These would be prime seats—ringside. The Civic Center owned an ample supply of thick slabs, made for the purpose of insulating patrons' feet from the coldness of the ice rink—an ideal opportunity to accommodate more patrons and for the promoter to gain additional revenue. White first considered putting a premium price on those down-front seats, but then decided to sell them on a first-come basis. About two hundred in number, those seats definitely did sell first.

Then the show arrived, and set up on the entire rink, summarily eliminating those windfall seats White thought he had and had sold. Protest all he might, White couldn't budge the show's stage manager, whose explanation for the widened rink dimensions was that for an arena Savannah's size, larger than many older arenas, the performers demanded a larger space in which to skate. So, in order to accommodate those who had bought the down-front seats, White and Finocchiaro had to set up extra chairs along the walkway behind the first tier of permanent seats. This was an easy solution where seating space was concerned, but try explaining that to eager patrons who had bought down-front seats in good faith, which also had been sold to them in good faith. Most of those patrons, for every performance both matinee and evening, understandably became quite angry. Never mind that White had published an explanatory ad in the newspapers, and news stories also had carried the explanation; that simply didn't appease patrons who had rushed down, some two weeks ahead of time, to grab those choice seats. A few demanded refunds, and some vowed never again to darken the Civic Center's doors; but most, albeit grudgingly, accepted the alternative seats, which really afforded an excellent vantage point. It was, as White and Finocchiaro termed it, "the week that was." Showbiz has its problems, but this one not only wasn't anticipated, it also wasn't deserved by a promoter who had been bringing class entertainment to Savannah for years and finally had access to a building large enough to accommodate the crowds he had longed for.

●The very first performance in the Civic Center, which was before the ceremonial grand opening and the ice show, was a Savannah Symphony concert, staged in the theater even while workmen, across the lobby in the arena, were applying finishing touches. Originally the plans did not call for an acoustical band shell for orchestral concerts, but the symphony people insisted on one and the city acceded, which proved the right thing to do. The band shell remains standard equipment. Nor had the city anticipated the purchase of music stands for the symphony, the presumption being that every musician owned his or her own stand. But for uniformity's sake, the city relented, and that, too, proved the right thing to do. The conductor's podium used in the old auditorium was brought over to the new theater. But in the afternoon of the day the symphony was to play at 8:30 P.M., manager Finocchiaro noticed that the recycled podium was battleship gray, and it looked like a sore thumb against the black chairs and music stands. He quickly corrected the inconsistency by ordering—only three hours before the concert—a hasty application of quick-dry black paint for the podium. Since then, a new podium has been acquired; it's black. That first concert, with all the physical nuances in place, went off beautifully, and before a sold-out house.

• The theater's sound system proved the worst bugaboo in the entire Civic Center. It was state-of-the-art, designed by a sound engineer of high repute, with credentials a mile long. Alas, one glitch in the sound system after another turned up, and for months on end; solve one problem, there'd be another. The system sometimes crackled, sometimes echoed, sometimes just plain didn't work. The architects demanded that the sound engineer return to Savannah and straighten matters out; he did, several times, and spent hours upon hours fine-tuning an intricate and sensitive electronic monster. Promoters complained. Performers complained. The first time that Fred Waring brought his Pennsylvanians to the new building, he commended Savannah from the stage on its new performing palace, gushing accolade after accolade. And then, after the audience applauded in response to the compliments, Waring added with a scowl: "Now, if you'll just get this awful sound system fixed . . . " Complaints still arise occasionally, but the sound is much better. Many attractions set up their own sound systems and operate them from portable control panels. But with the early reputation of lousy sound, whenever a show's own sound is foul, patrons and reviewers still hark back to the original problems and blame the Civic Center—proving, of course, that first impressions are lasting.

• On the arena side, across the common lobby from the

theater, an unlikely problem arose early on. The building's equipment included an excellent boxing ring, the very latest kind, although to the uninitiated one boxing ring looks like any other. And for boxing matches, this one was excellent. But whoever would dream that a boxing ring isn't compatible with showoff rasslin' (not to be confused with the legitimate sport of wrestling)? I would learn that the difference was that rasslers need a certain amount of bounce in their rings, considering that bounce is conducive to putting on a good show. Also, boxing rings do not have sufficient resonance to make the sound that those realistic-looking falls reverberate. Aaron Newman, the owner of a small arena across town and a regular promoter of rasslin', came to the city's rescue. He had looked forward to promoting in the new facility to attract more customers than his small arena could hold. So he generously offered the loan of his own ring. He delivered it, supervised its installation, and left it in the city's custody; to my knowledge the late Aaron Newman's ring is still in use. He virtually donated it and never charged a dime for its use; and although it did benefit him, he graciously shared his ring with rival promoters. Aaron Newman was a class act.

●There were other, yet smaller problems, and solvable. Such details as placing signs directing patrons to restrooms, the box office, the theater on one end and the arena on the other, and to the several sections of the arena, weren't completed until the very last minute. So was seat-numbering a late-solved problem, simply because the metal numbers were late arriving. Such things are small in the overall context of a building that ended up costing ten million dollars instead of the anticipated seven million, but they're as important as the orchestra pit, the backstage superstructure, pulleys, curtains, and stage lighting—all of which the public takes for granted.

When opening night arrived—an extravaganza billed simply as "Grand Opening"—few ever guessed that not everything had fallen routinely into place. The special show, put together by native sons Johnny Mercer and Hal Kanter, ran three hours, a full sixty minutes longer than customary stage shows; but the audience packing the house loved it all and would have welcomed even more. Kanter, a Hollywood producer as well as a writer, brought nearly the entire cast from one of his TV sitcoms. Julie Adams and John McGiver were among them, the latter remembered especially for his role as the jeweler in *Breakfast at Tiffany's*, the movie featuring "Moon River" as its theme song, with Academy Award–winning lyrics and music by Mercer and Henry Mancini. Pat Buttrum, a supporting comic in TV's popular "Green Acres," came and wowed the audience with his homespun humor. Other performers were George Kirby, the popular black comedian; Bobby and Cissy, Lawrence Welk's dancing duo; and Freda Payne, the throaty torch singer. Composer Sammy Fain, Mercer's longtime songwriting friend from Hollywood and New York, gave a twenty-minute recitation of songs he had written, including "Love Is a Many-Splendored Thing" and "I'll Be Seeing You." Local musical genius Kenny Palmer provided the band—one hundred percent Savannah musicians.

Yet, with all the talent that night, Mercer and Kanter were the show's stars. Although Kanter was known principally as a writer and producer, he bared still another side—standup comic—his jokes and marvelous satire spoofing everything under the sun and keeping the audience in stitches. Mercer, behind a microphone and lectern holding only bare notes to cue him on sequence, sang a medley of at least thirty of his great songs—"Laura," "That Old Black Magic," "The Atchison, Topeka and the Santa Fe," "In the Cool, Cool, Cool of the Evening," on and on. His finale, of course, was "Moon River," but not until he had sung "The Days of Wine and Roses." The audience was enraptured by "Our Johnny" and "Our Hal," two hometowners who had made it to the big time.

This was their night—the audience's. They had waited years for this magnificent facility, and here it was. The reception in the arena ran another hour or so; and after most people had gone home, Johnny Mercer summoned bandleader Kenny Palmer to the piano, leaned on it, and sang some more, into the wee hours. Those who came for the show got their twenty bucks' worth, which was the price of all seats—orchestra, loge, and balcony—for Grand Opening, and none reserved. The number of tickets printed matched the number of seats in the theater, and every one was sold. A few tickets were set aside for invited out-of-town guests, mostly public officials, but Mayor John Rousakis and the aldermen paid for those "freebies." It was the most democratic opening ceremony of any kind, and all but the set-aside tickets went on a first-come basis.

As for the three million dollar cost-overrun, the city rolled that into the budget, and I cannot recall any citizen or advocacy group raising any objection. Savannah had waited too long for this. The Savannah Civic Center remains one of Savannah's showpieces, capable of accommodating simultaneously shows in the arena and theater, a prom upstairs in the ballroom, and meetings in rooms on all three levels. In 1995 work began on adding more meeting rooms, putting new seats in the theater, new carpeting everywhere, new lobby decorations—all amid a broadened program of solicitation for business. The new appointments are magnificent, reminding those who were present at grand opening of their night to remember.

Worthy of note is the fact that Johnny Mercer and Hal Kanter came to Savannah a week before the grand opening to start planning the show, and they charged the city only bare expenses. Moreover, with the exceptions of George Kirby, Freda Payne, and Bobby and Sissy, whose agencies wouldn't agree to Kanter's pleas for a fee reduction, all the other stars came from Hollywood to Savannah at their own expense, and only reluctantly agreed to accept checks from the City of Savannah for a bare three hundred dollars each. Mercer didn't even charge his transportation costs, and when pressed to reconsider he remarked: "What the hell, Savannah is my home, and if you'll pick up the hotel bill that's good enough." A notation on his bill stated that Mercer had paid for all meals and other incidentals charged to his suite during that week.

Names—Nick and Otherwise

Miss Capulet, a popular character in Shakespearean drama, wondered out loud what was in a name, discoursing at the time over the silliness of the family feud that kept her and Mr. Montague from making their romance overt instead of covert. Heck, Juliet and Romeo would have preferred shouting it from the housetops, as most ordinary boys and girls in love do. Whenever I think of Shakespeare, I usually think also of Savannah names, sur- as well as nick-, for our town does have an interesting assortment of such.

In *Only in Savannah* I dwelt on Savannah's ecumenicity and how various ethnic groups get along reasonably to exceptionally well. One reason for that, I've concluded, is that Savannahians, both natives and longtimers who have stayed more than a half-century, have a knack of knowing how to pronounce names that sound odd to outsiders. They take pride in it, and, invariably, the first "Savannah name" they'll show off pronouncing for newcomers and outsiders is Gignilliat. That name has abounded in Savannah longer than even the eldest of the surviving Gignilliats care to speculate. It is, I am told, of French derivation. I have several favorite Gignilliats, some now deceased, including Arthur, Robert, Thomas, Michael, Heyward, Polly, Peggy, Ravenel, and, by all means, Clifford, who was a woman. Clifford Gignilliat partly eliminated the confusion caused by her masculine given name by marrying, and thus, in proper Southern-lady style, becoming known in social circles as Mrs. Walter Sewell. Still, some of the confusion remained, especially their friends' references to Walter and Clifford Sewell as "a couple." This would cause those who didn't know them to raise eyebrows, suspecting perhaps a same-gender "relationship," as the term goes. Clifford Gignilliat Sewell was a free-lance writer whose byline often appeared in newspapers and on a couple of her books. Letters to the editor responding to her writings always had to be read carefully lest they refer to "Mr. Sewell." Most of the reading public, I'm certain, thought she was a man, whereas in fact she was every inch the genteel Southern lady. One of her cousins, John Gignilliat, became a sub-editor on the local newspaper's staff, but finally abandoned journalism for other pursuits, including commercial exploratory diving with his brother Van in Florida.

All of the Gignilliats I have known have been nice people, and among the nicest was Thomas Heyward Gignilliat, the one I became closest to by virtue of his having served as our newspaper company's attorney. An expert on libel, he mostly kept us out of court and usually won the cases that did go into court. We were not his only clients; he had many substantial ones, and all those fees allowed him to die a wealthy octogenarian. But whenever the newspapers delved into, explored, and exposed the unsavory elements of Savannah life, with the risk of libel running high, Tom Gignilliat seemingly spent as much time on our premises as he did his own. A newspaper lawyer's job is to hold editors and reporters on solid ground, impetuous and gung-ho as they might be. He had three standard answers whenever an editor checked out a story with him, and he would offer only one of the three: (1) "Go ahead, you're safe"; (2) "Well, I can win it on an appeal"; and (3) "Don't touch that sonofabitch [meaning the questionable part of the story] with a ten-foot pole." (Tom Gignilliat could say "sonofabitch" as one word, and with such dignity as to make it sound unprofane.)

In the relating of long tales about life on New York's Great White Way, the famed Damon Runyon often used the phrase "a story goes with it"; and a story goes with this reference to

Tom Gignilliat. It not only is interesting, but it also tells you how to pronounce that name I've already written about a dozen times, and that's something I'm sure you've been wondering about since you began this chapter.

Gignilliat had been involved in litigation (not a libel case) that made the news wires. In fact I was the very one who punched the story into the Associated Press's state wire that day. About an hour later AP messaged a query: RADIO ASKS HOW TO PRO-NOUNCE GIGNILLIAT. You see, radio newscasters got most of their news off the AP wire, courtesy of newspaper enterprise. The query landed on the desk of *Savannah Evening Press* editor John Sutlive, who then walked to the teletype and messaged: GIN-LAT, EQUAL EMPHASIS ON EACH SYLLABLE. The AP came back: HARD "G" OR SOFT "G"? Sutlive, without batting an eye, typed: "GIN" AS IN MARTINI. The AP came back: THANX.

The name Gignilliat trickled into Savannah from South Carolina (Thomas Heyward Gignilliat was a direct descendant of Carolina's Thomas Heyward, a signer of the Declaration of Independence). It came along with such names as Legare and Huger. But don't pronounced those names as they look. It's "Legree," just like author Harriet Beecher Stowe's Simon Legree; and "You-gee," with equal emphasis on both syllables.

Greek names are abundant in Savannah, the reason being that Greek immigrants around the turn of the century found this community to be, indeed, the land of opportunity they had heard about. Also, Savannah was generally friendly to foreign-ers, with so impressive a friendliness that they invited kith and kin in the old country to follow them here. The Greeks them-selves were friendly—with their invitations for kinsmen to follow, they also sent portions of the earnings they had amassed through enterprise, entrepreneurship, and frugality. Savannah youngsters, growing up alongside the children of the Greek immigrants, learned quickly how to pronounce their Hellenic names. First, they were cued by their Greek-American play-mates, but as they matured the Savannahians discerned that if you look hard at a Greek name—and if you know phonics—the pronunciation comes almost naturally. Longtime Savannahians find it difficult to understand why Greek names baffle new Savannahians who have moved in from the hinterlands.

Take, as a starter, the name Rousakis, belonging to John Rousakis, a first-generation Greek-American who became Savannah's mayor and served twenty-one years, longer than anyone else in that office. Break the name into syllables: Rou-sak-is; there can be only one way to say it unless, for some strange reason, you pronounce the first syllable to rhyme with "row" (as in argument, or as in paddle your boat) instead of "roo," which is the right way, rhyming with "rue" (as in regret).

Rousakis has a cousin, George Chiotellis, in whose surname the only perceivable problem might be the first syllable. He rhymes it with "chee," and if you follow golf you logically think of Chi Chi Rodriguez, and instantly say Chi-o-tell-is. Once you get the hang of a few Greek names like that, syllable by syllable, the rest come easy and flow from your lips: De-mos-then-ese, Kar-a-tass-os, Kol-gak-lis, Tass-a-pou-los, De-mop-o-lous, An-est-os, Lia-kak-is, Fess-o-pou-los, to cite a few. Your only problem may be whether to broaden the vowels, but Savannah Greeks couldn't care less whether you do or don't.

Italian names might cause new Savannahians some difficulty, but very little, because syllables are helpful. Much depends upon whether consonants are hardened or softened. Prominent in Savannah's Italian community (which is scattered all over town because Savannah has no such settlement as a "Little Italy") are the brothers Finocchiaro, Mike and Frank, whose surnames Savannahians master well, saying Fin-o-cair-o, giving that penultimate syllable a slight twist. Understandable, though, if someone misses on the first try. It's just about as easy with Cirincione, if you remember soft consonants and that the final syllable isn't like the numeral "1" but rhymes with Tony. Not all Italian names, however, start with soft consonants or apply the "oney" sound to endings; there was, for example (but in Chicago and not Savannah) the late unlamented Al Capone, whose surname everyone can pronounce.

Many Savannah Greek and Italian families shortened and Americanized their names, yet never forswore their old-country heritage, of which they remain proud to this day. The Mateos became the Mathews, some of the Tassapoulos family shortened their name to Tassey, one of the Mamalakis brothers became Manners, and others have changed and shortened to names bearing similarities to the original.

An interesting story (that goes with it) concerns a native Alabaman, John Tidwell, who came to Savannah in the 1970's to become a city official, recruited from Tupelo, Mississippi. Tidwell was born and bred in the briar patch of Fairfax, Alabama, just west of West Point, Georgia. A promising athlete, he won a football scholarship to Auburn, coached high school sports after graduation, played some baseball in the minor leagues, then went into public recreation. But seldom during his pilgrimage to Savannah did Tidwell encounter people with foreign-sounding names; he was more accustomed to Jones, Smith, Brown, Jackson, and the like. So Tidwell was baffled his first day on the job in Savannah after meeting Mayor John Rousakis; Mary Kolgaklis, the mayor's secretary; George Chiotellis, another city official; Eli Karatassos, in the planning department; and Mike Finocchiaro, who managed the Savannah Civic Center. "The United Nations, all in a single day," Tidwell remarked. He was advised that he "ain't seen nuthin' yet," and eventually he met people with such names as Mamalakis, Karacostas, Antonopolo, Eliopolo, Anestos, Cafiero, and—oh, yes—Gignilliat.

It's strange, though, that some Savannahians do not perceive the difference between Greeks and Jews, ignorant of the fact that Greeks are Christians, and about the only similarity between their Orthodox churches and Jewish synagogues is that both use cantors in their liturgies. One noted illustration of this came from the late Tom Gary, a police sergeant in the days when I covered law enforcement, who had to forward to Chief Bill Hall a complaint from a Greek who operated a fruit stand. The complaint was that a foot patrolman of Irish extraction had come into his place of business and started filling a paper bag with apples, oranges, bananas, and assorted other fruits. The complainant said he had no objection to a cop taking an occasional apple or orange, but a whole bag of his goods was simply a case of overkill. Yet he wasn't complaining about the quantity involved, but about the policeman's rudeness when he asked the cop to return the merchandise. The complaint was that the policeman called him a "Jew sonofabitch." Next day, after Chief Hall read the complaint, he went personally to the fruit stand to apologize for his officer's behavior, stressing that his policemen were under strict orders never to direct profanity at citizens. He related that he had given the offending officer a two-day suspension and a reprimand, with instructions that the officer, during the suspension, drop by and make his own apology. Pleased with the chief's visit, the proprietor gave him an apple, and as the chief was leaving, munching the apple, the proprietor reportedly remarked: "Chief, I just want you to know that I'm not Jewish, and if I'm a sonofabitch, I'm a Greek sonofabitch."

Most of the German-origin names in our midst are easy to pronounce. They include Mingledorff, Zittrouer and Zittrauer, Ziegler and Zeagler, Haupt (they say "Hope" around here), Zipperer, and Gnann, to mention just a few. Gnann gives newcomers trouble; they don't pronounce the "G" the same way you don't sound that initial letter in gnat. The Gnanns hereabouts, though, sound the letter; it comes out: Guh-nan.

I have omitted other strange-sounding names from faraway places in order to turn to nicknames, of which Savannah has had its rightful share. Marjorie, whom I married in Florida and brought to Savannah in 1989, is originally from Cleveland, and says that neither in Florida nor Ohio has she encountered so many nicknames. One night, already accustomed to hearing them, she burst into uncontrollable laughter while I was catching up on things with Lester Crapse, my boyhood buddy whom I hadn't seen in some thirty-five years. Lester himself never had a nickname because his surname, Crapse, was sufficient to trigger many fights in defense of the family honor. Well, on this night Lester pulled from his pocket a list of names, friends from boyhood days, and proceeded with the whatever-happened-to questions. The first name on the list was Jughead Knight, whose given name actually is Carlton. Then Marjorie listened to Duck Griffin, Cocky Ellis, Pinky Townsend, and Googie Cody. What broke her up was Poopy Martin. Imagine, someone named Crapse asking about someone named Poopie.

Lester went on with Bunk, Rusty, Goose, Rags, Stinky, and Fag, respectively for William Thomas Browne, both Russell Bridges and Russell Morris, Bill Gaudry, Gene Smith, Hugh

Miller, and Walter Simmons—all of our vintage. Fag needed some explaining, since the word nowadays is a pejorative for homosexual, which Simmons definitely was not. Fag was a flyweight boxer in high school, and friends attributed his slight build to the fact that he smoked cigarettes; in those days fag was another word for cigarette. There is, in fact, a line from the World War I song "Pack Up Your Troubles" that goes, "While you've a lucifer to light your fag/ Smile, boys, that's the style." (Lucifer was another term for match.)

Later, while I was discussing nicknames with retired athletic coach M. A. Spellman, wife Marjorie marveled further as he reminisced on having coached a fellow named Goose Anderson, as well as the lad's brother, Little Goose. Also, Spellman recalled the coaching of Keith "Grasshopper" Hendrix, and having an assistant coach named Chan Highsmith, the nickname inspired by the fact that Highsmith's facial features resembled those of the movie detective Charlie Chan. I threw in some from the local newspapers' typesetters: War News Cler, Wompie Chalmers, and Lula Belle Lewis, so-called because he resembled Lula Belle, a character in the "Wash 'n' Easy" comic strip. I also recalled a former reporter, Henry Hathaway, who had two nicknames—Ace and The Stoker, the latter a pen name under which he wrote fictional stories. Also, the late *Morning News* editor, William J. Robertson, was called Judge; the soul of dignity, he resembled some learned and robed jurist. For the same reason a copy editor, George Lindsey, was called Judge—he looked like one, and was a sagacious soul.

Other Savannah nicknames I can recall include Butthead, Jarhead, Snake, Tiger, Buck, Bubba (many of them), Fatty and Fatso, Skinny and Slim, Blubber, Horse, Horsecollar, Bulgy, Snakehips, Jellybelly, Buzz (several local athletes, all of whom

103

were fast), Chicken and Nookie (the Barnwell brothers), Chicken and Biddie (the Little brothers), Iron Bosom (she looked like Lana Turner in a sweater, and of course the nickname was uttered behind her back), Little Bit (she was petite; no reference to bosom size, which was considerable for a small girl), Shorty, Phantom, Glider (the late Ed Weeks moved effortlessly as he danced), Gump (Chester Warner was nicknamed for comic-strip hero Andy Gump's son Chester), Flapper (Mahany was a good softball player who flapped his hands as he ran the bases), Foureyes (anyone who wore glasses), Baldy, Dick (his name wasn't Richard; he acquired the nickname in the locker room), Brylcreme (after a once-popular hair dressing; the fellow's hair flew in all directions, as in the "before" picture in the ads), Onion (Sibley Durant, who was killed in World War II, was one of the earliest athletes with a crew cut), Turnip, Pike (the story was that he fell into the river and came up with a fish in his pocket), Terp, Twirp, Flip, Skip, Drip (the late Rusty Bridges hung that one on me because of my surname), Mercury (the late reporter Clayton Carter, dubbed that by copy editor Joe Purvis because Clayton moved fast), Bean (another copy editor, the late Harley Cabaniss, called me that; you know, coffee bean), Fingers (jazz pianist Claude Domingue), Scooter, Shooter, Nig (a Caucasian baseball player with Negroid features, called that even by his black friends, and of course in an earlier era), Piggie, Biggie, Poopdeck (Hugh's last name was Pappy, the nickname stemming from Popeye the Sailor's dad, Poopdeck Pappy), Wimpy (Winifred Waters preferred it to his real given name). Also, I must include Fifty-six; he learned that seven times eight equals fifty-six, but when he got to the "eight-times table," he stalled at eight times seven. I kid you not. And there were many others, as you'll find in any town. Plus one more Rusty, for reasons best known to those who hung it on William Frank Fennell, the Associated Press telegrapher assigned to Savannah's newspapers, who went by his middle name but preferred Rusty.

Now, to my knowledge, only two Savannahians bear the nickname Pappyshooter—Eugene Powers and myself. We call each other that, and a story goes with it. After World War II both of us back from military service discovered that we had been in the same Army division, the Thirty-seventh, which before mobilization had been the Ohio National Guard. The term stems from a story, which likely isn't true, that in prewar years, when the Ohio guardsmen were called out to quell strikers at an industrial plant, one of the guardsmen actually shot his own striking father. Thus, after the Thirty-seventh was mobilized for wartime service, the replacements in the outfit referred to the original members as Pappyshooters. I was told by one of the original members that what actually happened was that a guardsman did take his own father, who was becoming rambunctious on the picket line, into custody, mainly for the unionist's own protection. Gene Powers and I, whichever sees the other first, will greet with a "Hi, Pappyshooter."

Back to Cocky Ellis, mentioned earlier. His real name was Wilfred, and he was a swimmer, diver, and football player for Savannah High School. His friends were about evenly divided on the origin of his nickname. Some said it was because he was brash and cocksure. Other said he earned the nickname in the locker room. Cocky as he was, he preferred the latter.

The Tree Guardians

In *Only in Savannah* was a chapter on Savannah's urban forest, Savannah's heavy growth of tree cover, and one of the city's chief assets, which not only enhances Savannah's beauty but also figures importantly in the ecological balance. Savannah has hot summers, temperatures often exceeding a hundred degrees, but without those trees the heat would be unbearable. Visitors marvel as they encounter Savannah's many "tunnels of trees" formed by overhead branches arching from one side of a street to the other, and touching one another. As a newspaper columnist, I often marveled in print over Mother Nature's great gift to our community. That's what led to my involvement in the formation of the Savannah Tree Foundation with several ladies and one other man, our purpose being to save the trees in the face of burgeoning development in which some developers displayed a conviction that the best way to develop was to cut down all the trees and then build upon a clear lot.

A certain two Savannah ladies winced whenever they even thought of a tree being felled to make way for development. Ironically, both ladies depended upon harvested trees for their livelihood. Page Anderson Hungerpiller's husband, Jim, was employed for years as an executive with Union Camp, whose huge Savannah plant turns pine trees into kraft paper. He later changed his place of employment—better job and with no dependency upon trees as raw materials. Lynda Guerry Beam was born into the family that owns Guerry Lumber Company, a business her husband, Kirby Beam, manages. But never mind the irony; Savannah's trees are not the ones that paper companies and lumbermen cut down to grind into pulp and saw into boards. Commercial tree-cutters find their materials elsewhere, in rural forests benefitting from sound tree management, which demands replantings after harvesting. They would never dream of messing with Savannah's live oaks, pines, gums, sugarberries, dogwoods, crepe myrtles, and many other varieties and species. Developers would—and they did.

Equally zealous in their concern for Savannah's trees were two retired gentlemen, Remer Young Lane and Stewart "Scotty" Forbes—the former, a member of a prominent Georgia banking family; and the latter, a horticulturist and arborist who had worked for Savannah's Park & Tree Commission and had cultivated botanical gardens for some of Chatham County's residential showplaces. Lane was an appointed member of the Park & Tree board, but one day he quit in disgust, contending that the city was naming people to the board who, in his words, "wouldn't know an oak tree from their own ass." He and the retired Scotty Forbes decided to become sideline tree activists. They, as well as Mesdames Hungerpiller and Beam, lured me into becoming a tree advocate.

One day in the late-1970's Remer Lane invited me to lunch, and when I arrived at Johnny Harris' Restaurant, Forbes and the aforementioned ladies were already seated. Trees immediately became the discussion topic. Mrs. Beam, seated beside me, asked if I would consider devoting one of my five columns each week to a "tree of the week." No, I replied, because I'd soon run out of trees to write about; besides, mine was an editorial column devoted to a broader range of topics. Lynda pursued: "Well, how about a tree of the month?" I told her I'd think about it, and in a few weeks I came up with "Spotlighting Our Trees" one Sunday a month, shifting its location on the editorial page from the usual lower-left corner, placing a photo-illustration of the selected tree in the spot where an editorial cartoon usually went, with the article on the tree just beneath it.

This feature became an immediate hit with readers, many of whom phoned or mailed in suggestions for future tree columns —a huge live oak in Vernonburg, a minuscule municipality south of Savannah; a gingko at Beaulieu, a waterfront community; a redwood (yes, Savannah has redwoods, though smaller than those in California) off Skidaway Road, and another on the grounds of the old Central of Georgia Railroad Hospital; pistachios beside the lake in Daffin Park; another mammoth oak tree, this one appropriately in Live Oak Park. On and on, the series of Sunday tree columns ran for five years, until I figured I had spotlighted most of the varieties and species.

Besides the call-ins and letters, most of my resource material came from Messrs. Lane and Forbes. They were a delightful duo, the personification of such movie characters as "The Odd Couple" and "Grumpy Old Men." Though fast friends, each attempted to put the other down on how much either knew about Savannah's trees. Perfect gentlemen, they nevertheless shared a propensity for mild profanity. Scotty Forbes was a native of Scotland, thus his profanity bordered on the classic. There's nothing quite like "son of a bitch" with Gaelic shading. Mind you, neither of the two ever called the other bad names; they simply made epithetical references to those who showed no respect for trees, including Park & Tree executive director Don Gardner, fairly new in Savannah at that time and instilling fear in these old-timers that he wanted to replace all live oaks with crepe myrtles. Lane and Forbes would have dueled him any high noon to prevent such a catastrophe, and to ensure their success in the duel they'd have made it two against one. These gents were serious, so much so that they once inventoried Savannah's trees and paid for publication of a small tract, for public distribution, containing their findings.

The Tree Guardians

Once I started writing my monthly tree columns, I could count on fresh material in bountiful supply; and if readers hadn't made suggestions, Lane and Forbes would have kept me supplied with sufficient topics. Now and then, usually on a Tuesday morning, one or the other would telephone me: "Tom, are you aware of Savannah's redwoods?" Baring my ignorance, and thinking that redwoods grew only out west, I'd welcome their offer to pick me up at the newspaper office and drive me to see the redwoods. With them, I always knew it would be a full day out of the office, zipping hither and yon, to view other trees they offered as good examples for size and rarity.

Strangely, although Lane and Forbes lent financial and moral assistance to the founding of the Savannah Tree Foundation, they opted to stay off the organization's board of directors, figuring they could help keep the urban forest's integrity by having no ties to any special-interest group. They remained as valued sideline advisers. Mrs. Hungerpiller headed up the foundation as its charter president. The other founding members were Mrs. Beam; Suzi Williams, a housewife; Mary Helen Ray, who was chairman of Park & Tree and active in lawn and garden projects; Hans Neuhauser, who headed the Georgia Conservancy's Savannah operation; and myself, with little real knowledge of trees but ever willing to learn. I served two years, then resigned in 1988 as I began preparing for retirement the following year from the Savannah newspapers. An early addition to the board was Simone Van Stolk, Paris-born wife of a Dutchman, and reputedly owner of the greenest thumb in Savannah. Her friends contend that she can make *anything* grow, just by looking at it.

Page Hungerpiller, stepdaughter of a wealthy businessman, entrepreneur, and philanthropist, never revealed to board members where she obtained the seed money to set up, incorporate, and start the Savannah Tree Foundation; without saying a word to one another, however, we all guessed the source. The organization's stated purpose was to educate Savannahians on the worth of trees, both economically and aesthetically. The foundation brought in tree experts for evening lectures to which the public and city and county officials were invited, and to meet with developers for the purpose of convincing them that landscaped real estate, containing good stands of trees, could sell for more than land completely denuded of its vegetation. Another aim was to persuade city and county governments to enact ordinances placing certain restrictions on development of tree-covered tracts. Both local governmental bodies were supportive of the foundation's intents and purposes, but they moved cautiously lest accusation of property-rights abridgment should arise. It was a long and hard pull, getting the ordinances enacted, but persistence paid off. Not only that, real estate developers began to cooperate, and finally provided input into the drafting of the tree ordinances.

Not enough can be said of Mrs. Hungerpiller and Mrs. Beam, the ringleaders whose love affair with trees was so strong that it wouldn't have surprised anyone if either or both of the ladies had chained themselves to some live oak in defiance of bulldozers. Movies have featured such scenarios, but no scriptwriter or director ever conveyed on film such zeal as these charming and attractive ladies exuded. Besides getting the tree ordinances enacted, they tamed Park & Tree director Gardner, who really might have gone on a crepe myrtle binge. Gardner instead— while planting a lot of crepe myrtles along public rights-of-way —has planted a lot more oaks beside new roads and in their medians. The foundation these ladies spearheaded has raised sufficient money from private contributors to partly fund salaries of arborists for both the city and the county, and they continue to bring experts to town for lectures and consultations with developers and the public sector.

The Savannah Tree Foundation has grown in mission and scope, its board of directors broadened to include business and professional people as well as tree activists. Its annual *State of the Trees* report has wide dissemination, and the community pays attention to its observations and recommendations. New plantings are much in evidence, ensuring that Savannah's urban forest has a comfortable future. Two presidents, Beth Glass and Cacey Ratterree, have followed Mrs. Hungerpiller, and the group now employs an executive director.

If anyone wonders why it's so important for a community to have abundant tree cover, look at it first from the standpoint of beauty, and compare Savannah with towns in the Old West where pesky mesquites and scattered cottonwoods grow, and shade comes at a premium. Then, from the standpoint of health, recall an early grade-school teaching about the interdependence of humans and vegetation, summed up: "Plants inhale carbon dioxide and exhale oxygen, and animals do just the reverse." Remember that, and if there's an open spot in the yard —plant a tree.

His Own Airfield

Not every soldier holds the distinction of having a military base named for him while he is still alive. Savannahian Frank O'Driscoll Hunter may have been the only one. Actually the late General Hunter was so honored twice with the same airfield. First, the World War I flying ace made his hometowners so proud of his military record and exploits that the city fathers made Savannah's municipal airport his namesake after he came home wearing the Distinguished Service Cross, the nation's second highest decoration for valor (and though he didn't receive it, he also was a nominee for the Medal of Honor, the highest). Came the war clouds in 1940 that soon would burst and wash the United States into the second world conflict, the Army Air Corps commandeered the municipal airport for military purposes, at first called it Savannah Army Air Base, and then later acceded to pleas from the city—which had deeded the airport to the government—that General Hunter's name be retained. The general then, still in the peacetime military service, was stationed elsewhere, and later would become the first officer to command the Eighth Air Force Fighter Command in the European Theater of Operations.

Hunter was a fighter pilot, starting with those flimsy crates in which dashing Americans staged dogfights with dashing German pilots over France and Germany in World War I. As military-aircraft quality, design, and technology advanced, "Monk" Hunter similarly advanced. The First Air Force became his last combat command during World War II.

He was called "Monk" because—as legend holds and his late sister, Jeanne Hunter, often attested—he was a cut-up in his youth: brash, devilish, fun-loving. Another version held that, because he was a lifelong bachelor, his fellow airmen assigned

112

him the nickname. But he lived unlike any monk. He was hand-some, debonair, with an eye for the ladies, and with all the officer-and-gentleman qualities that would cause ladies to have an eye for him. Some said he looked like actor Clark Gable; Jeanne Hunter once told me, with a knowing and twinkling wink that established her as definitely close-kin to him, "and he often tried to act like Clark Gable." I did not ask her to elaborate.

Leaving the service after World War II, Monk Hunter returned to his hometown to savor the accolades heaped upon him so often. The Army had deactivated his namesake base, and it reverted to civilian control—again, as the municipal airport, and called just plain Hunter Field. The newly formed United States Air Force meanwhile had located the Second Bomber Wing, of the Strategic Air Force, on Chatham Field, Savannah's other airport; but later the Air Force worked a swap with the city and shifted operations to Hunter Field because its runways could better accommodate the newer bombers. Hunter is now an Army airfield, an adjunct to the Third Infantry Division based at Fort Stewart, forty miles away. General Hunter turned over his memorabilia from the two world wars to the field bearing his name. His medals, uniforms, diaries (at least, the military ones), portraits, and candid photographs (one picturing him with Edward, the Duke of Windsor, and former King of the British Empire) remain on display there.

Occasionally the Air Force would hold Monk Hunter testimonials, mainly for the benefit of its newer airmen, and the general relished every bit of the adulation. He also relished Savannah, his hometown, and he was a familiar figure down-town daily until sidelined by the illness that preceded his death. He was an imposing presence in what were perhaps the most stylish civilian outfits in Savannah. After lunch he would go home for a rest, change into different garb for his afternoons downtown, and change clothing again for dinner.

In one downtown cocktail lounge a local artist executed a behind-the-bar mural, a collage of Savannah scenes and people. One of those in the painting looked for all the world like General Hunter. Advised of this, the general ventured into the lounge, surveyed the painting, and then disputed any contention that the figure in question was himself. He noted that the brightness of the painting suggested a morning setting, and said, "I'd never dress like that in the morning." In spite of his argument to the contrary, longtime Savannahians stoutly maintained that the fellow in the picture definitely was Monk Hunter.

Was Monk Hunter a fop or a dandy, a throwback to days when gentlemen stood aloof? Absolutely not. While an impeccable dresser, he was one of Savannah's most down-to-earth hail-fellows-well-met. He was delightful to be around, entertaining, witty, outwardly the soul of dignity but inwardly a polished good ol' boy.

Although he was perhaps the only American, or at least one of the very few, to see a military base become his namesake, General Hunter also saw Chatham Field, where the municipal airport is now located, named for another Savannah general, Robert J. Travis, Jr., after the latter was killed in a crash at an Air Force base in California. Travis Field actually was named for two Travises, the late General Robert and his surviving brother, William, both West Pointers; the latter retired from the Air Force as a colonel. Also, the base in California where Robert Travis was killed in a crash was renamed in his honor by the Air Force. Not every city has three airfields named for its sons.

114

More Little Stories

Saving the Squares. Savannah's squares were explained in *Only in Savannah*. Reputedly, the first of the squares was laid out as a rallying point for the colonists of the eighteenth century, just in case the Indians should attack—although Chief Tomochichi and his band of Yamacraws were nice Indians, as it turned out. The squares grew in number, following the plan of General James Edward Oglethorpe, the Colony of Georgia's founder in 1733. There are twenty-two squares remaining of the twenty-six that once dotted the Historic District; only Crawford Square is a neighborhood playground, as several of the squares used to be, and the rest are placid parks, beautified and adorned. The tourists love them.

So do the home folks love our squares; at least, most of them do. Remaining are a few Savannahians who in the past have insisted that the squares be opened to north-south traffic, the better to move cars downtown without having to drive around what they call those "cussed squares." They constitute a quite small minority, those antisquare people, but in earlier days they were a majority. In fact they'd have gotten their way if it had not been for the Park & Tree Commission and the dedicated, farsighted chairman of that body, banker Joseph Huger Harrison. Over his dead body would those squares have been opened to traffic. The mistake had been made earlier on Montgomery Street, the western-most north-south artery, the squares of which were cut through in the mid-1930's, when U.S. 17 was routed through town. No more, said Joe Harrison.

The last of several proposals for driving through the squares came on strong in 1952, previous efforts having been beaten back. But this time it seemed that the proposal would go through. Those were days before shopping centers began to spring up on the southside, to be followed by huge shopping malls, each new such development siphoning business from Broughton Street, which for years was Savannah's principal retail center, with department stores and class-act shops for men and women. Advocates of change insisted that shoppers needed to get downtown faster than they already could by traveling one-way Drayton Street northward and returning southward by one-way Whitaker Street. The city fathers (there were no women on City Council back then) seemed sold on the idea, ignoring Park & Tree's pleas for the status quo. The daily newspapers editorially endorsed the change. The squares seemed doomed, all except the ones on Bull Street, each of which contained a monument dead-center, but Bull Street was exempt from the proposal anyway.

Joe Harrison sprang into action for what surely seemed to him like same-song-next-verse, because he had fought the battle before. He organized public meetings to discuss the travesty that was about to befall Savannah. He went on radio forums (no TV in those days). He issued statements to the newspapers, which they obligingly printed even though they editorially opposed Joe Harrison. Then he went before City Council, whose members seemingly had their minds made up, and appealed to them, one-on-one, from the standpoint of preserving Savannah's historic integrity. No other city, he said, had such an asset as public squares laid out symmetrically. They should be beautified, all of them, the way those on Bull Street already were. Please, he urged, allow Park & Tree to embark on a beautification program. Joe Harrison had a certain power of persuasion into which he interlaced his distinctive smile. He could be angry as hell, yet he never scowled while venting his anger. It was, indeed, a winning smile; and it never worked

better than the day he pleaded with City Council. The mayor
and aldermen suddenly switched and voted not to open the
squares to traffic. And in the years that followed, square beautification became a reality, thanks to such benevolent individuals
as banker Mills B. Lane, Jr., who as head of the Citizens &
Southern National Bank was also Joe Harrison's boss. Mills
Lane donated considerable money to improve squares, and
other Savannahians did likewise.

Ironically, the squares on Abercorn Street and Habersham
Street already had been opened to through traffic for streetcars,
fire and police vehicles, and ambulances, but after the streetcars
stopped running, replaced by transit buses, Park & Tree had
rounded off the corners of the squares to make it easier for
emergency vehicles to drive around them. That, Harrison
insisted, should have been concession enough—if the emergency
vehicles now could travel north and south with little inconvenience or lost time, so should ordinary motorists, he said.
And he won!

After the matter was settled in 1952, John Sutlive, editor of
the *Savannah Evening Press*, who editorially had supported
opening the squares, did some research in retrospect and came
up with a plausible theory that General Oglethorpe had never
intended for the squares to be violated because he never
imagined them as a traffic impediment; indeed, he envisioned
Savannah's growth to develop eastward and westward rather
than southward, paralleling the Savannah River. Thus traffic
could move unimpeded alongside the squares, on the east-west
streets bordering each square on the north and south sides.
Editor Sutlive was satisfied, glad after all that Joe Harrison had
parried his editorial thrust.

Savannah did develop eastward and westward, but more

industrially than residentially. Residential development went southward.

Finding Gwinnett's Grave. Button Gwinnett was one of Georgia's three signers of the Declaration of Independence. The other two were Dr. Lyman Hall, who like Gwinnett was from St. John's Parish (now Liberty County), south of Savannah, and George Walton of Augusta in St. Paul's Parish (now Richmond County). Gwinnett, after the American Revolution, was mortally wounded in a duel with General Lachlan McIntosh of Savannah. He died of gangrene from a pistol ball in his right leg, and as time marched on his burial place in Savannah's Colonial Cemetery disappeared from topside view, the gravestone apparently having been snapped off, either by vandals or careless cemetery workers. Since record-keeping in those days left much to be desired, the exact location of Gwinnett's grave became unknown.

In the 1950's modern history buffs renewed concern over the grave's location; and one of those most concerned was Arthur J. Funk, a retired high-school principal who was (as they say today) into many pursuits, one of them being American history. Funk, on his own, began to walk every inch of the cemetery that lies in the heart of Savannah's Historic District, situated on Oglethorpe Avenue, hard by the police station and just across Abercorn Street from fire headquarters, a location which, when you think about it, is well protected. It took Funk days of moving, row by row, alongside gravestones and above-ground burial vaults, probing, making calculations on a clipboard, and peering intently at every square foot of bare ground. Finally he spotted something he thought to be a jagged piece of marble jutting ever so timidly above the surface. He knelt down, took a trowel, and began to scoop dirt away from the piece of stone.

Sure enough, it was the bottom portion of a tombstone, or Funk would eat his hat.

Next day Funk had summoned others interested in Gwinnett's final resting place, and with great care they removed the slab of marble from underground. Upon inspection, they determined that the slab, about a yard wide and a yard long, was the broken-off remainder of a gravestone that likely jutted out about three or three and a half feet above ground. But how could anyone tell whether this was Button Gwinnett's or someone else's gravestone? All the lettering had been on the above-ground portion of the slab. Funk then took a whisk broom and began to brush the caked dirt from the slab. Lo and behold, on the slab was a large "G," the initial letter of Gwinnett's name. Moreover, it was a fancy, flourishing "G." Funk and the others immediately took heart, reasoning that stonecutters, in making grave markers, likely made their practice carvings on the part of a stone that would go beneath the ground's surface. Surely that had been the case here. They looked at other tombstones of this type and noted that on some of them the initial letters of deceased persons' names were fancily done. This, Funk reasoned, had to be the place.

In a few days archaeologists from the state were in town digging carefully into the spot beneath the slit where the slab had been, just as meticulously as archaeological diggers probe into burial sites in such places as Egypt and Israel. They used small shovels, trowels, and brushes to sweep away loose dirt. In a day or two the diggers had reached a skeleton, and the operation then began to proceed most carefully, only trowels, scoops, and brushes being employed. But, finally, a supine skeleton lay fully in view, and with a splintered right shin bone. In his fatal duel Gwinnett had taken a pistol ball in his right leg. Everyone surrounding the grave was ecstatic, Arthur Funk particularly. "See if you can find the bullet," he shouted to the diggers, who then probed carefully beneath the skeleton and, just below the splintered pan of the bone, found a piece of lead, unmistakably a bullet. This had to be Button Gwinnett.

But not necessarily so. Dr. Antonio Waring, Jr., physician and history buff, observed the skeleton and speculated that it could be that of a woman—thus, surely not Gwinnett. Fiddle-sticks, Funk retorted. Fiddlesticks, hell, Waring shot back. A bitter argument ensued, but archaeologists agreed with Funk that this was the skeleton of a male, someone fitting the physical description of Gwinnett from the standpoint of height (he was not a tall person) and cranial structure. Dr. Waring shrugged and retired from the argument, yet it was obvious he didn't change his opinion. But Arthur Funk was in control of the project, and after the bones were removed and placed into a box, Funk took charge of the box.

The next phase of the project was to raise money and build a monument to Button Gwinnett, to be placed on the site where the bones were exhumed, with a reburial of the remains once the monument was in place. That was done under the auspices of Savannah's Sites and Monuments Commission, the funding coming mainly from local patriotic societies, including the Daughters of the American Revolution and the Sons of the Revolution.

But while the monument project was under way, where do you think the mortal remains of Button Gwinnett reposed? Arthur Funk took box and bones to his bachelor home at the Isle of Hope and kept them on a closet shelf until time for their reburial. And he had a lot of fun as keeper of the bones. A visitor to his home invariably would ask about the bones, and

Funk would reply that they were in the closet. "Go in there and ask Button what he's doing up there on that shelf, and he'll say nothing," Funk would advise, emphasizing *nothing* as if it had quotation marks around it.

Forrest Gump's Bench. Just about everyone who saw the movie *Forrest Gump* remembers the park bench as the place where he sat and related his life story to others sitting on that bench and waiting for a public bus to come along. And most of them know that the bench scenes were filmed in Savannah. Tourists, therefore, will ask to see "Forrest Gump's bench," and they'll be disappointed when a native tells them "there ain't no such animal."

Well, there really "ain't." The bench, fashioned expertly to match the benches in Savannah's downtown squares, actually was a movie prop made by the film company's technical crew. For filming purposes it was placed at the north edge of Chippewa Square, with James Oglethorpe's statue showing in the background over the shoulder of Tom Hanks, who won an Academy Award for playing the title role so well. And although a bus would ride across the foreground occasionally in the movie, it actually was proceeding on the wrong way of a one-way street. In short, the bench wasn't really alongside a bus route. Hollywood has a marvelous way of fabricating, and at the end of filming, the bench was moved and traffic along the square again was opened to the public.

Some in the community have suggested erecting a bench on the edge of Chippewa Square and placing a marker identifying it as the "Forrest Gump bench." That wouldn't be correct, though, because no one knows what happened to the bench the movie crew built. Also, historic preservationists take a dim view of injecting something that's not historic into the Historic

District and making it a landmark. History, dammit, is history; and while it was a good, entertaining movie that won many Oscars, *Forrest Gump* was pure fiction. Sorry about that, say preservationists, but that's the way it is.

With or without a bench or marker, however, the memory of the Forrest Gump bench lingers in the minds of people who saw the movie and then visited Savannah. They want to know where the bench stood as the movie was filmed. And if that's not an opening for Savannah's several tour-guide services, then nothing ever will be. Not a one—horse-drawn, mock trolley, or just plain tour bus—fails to stop at the approach to Chippewa Square and say words to the effect of: "Now right there, ladies and gentlemen, is where Forrest Gump sat and spun his life story." Even though there's no bench actually there. Who needs it?

The Fraternals

I never joined the Masons, although it was not for any particular reason, and certainly not for any dislike of the Free and Accepted Masons. My late mother-in-law once asked me why I wasn't a Mason, as did several other friends when I was younger. Even a Mason asked me, and my reply was, "For one thing, no one ever invited me to join." His response was that the Masons do not invite their members. One must volunteer by making his own application. That suited me as to why I'd never been invited in, but it wasn't too long after that conversation that another Mason invited me to join. That was by telephone, and before the day was over he had dropped by the house with an application blank, and again renewed his invitation.

Perhaps that recruiting Mason never got the word about not going after members. I still have that application form. It's buried somewhere in papers I seldom go through, but whenever I do go through them and come across that form, I regard it as man's triumph over mother-in-law. She, you see, was wrapped up in the Order of the Eastern Star, a Masonic-sponsored group for women, and I mean *wrapped up*. She went to her own chapter's meetings and to every other chapter's. Hardly a night went by that she wasn't, as we called it, Eastern Starring. She was so wrapped up that she thought everyone else should belong to a lodge of some kind—especially her son-in-law. And knowing about the application blank I had, she frequently dogged me to fill it out and apply. Staying out of the Masons, therefore, became a challenge, and I suppose I did, after all, have one particular reason for not joining.

The fact that I never joined in no way dims my respect for the Masonic organizations (nor, for that matter, my late mother-in-law, whom I loved very much; with her, it became a game). Blue lodges, Scottish Rite, York Rite, Knights Templar, Shriners, Jesters, Sojourners—every one of those organizations falling under the aegis of Freemasonry is worthy of respect. They all do work for the uplift of mankind. For example, the Shrine hospitals treat crippled and burned children at absolutely no fee. Lord knows how many youngsters have learned to walk in those free Shrine hospitals. And think how beneficial free treatment of burns has been—kids entering those hospitals parched and seared, and coming out months later with handsome skin-grafted features. I cannot count the number of stories our newspapers have printed on Shriners who have learned of children needing hospitalization, and who have prevailed on community leaders to donate their corporate jets to fly those children to their places of treatment. That's why, whenever someone pokes fun at fun-loving Shriners in street parades, I rise quickly to their defense and enumerate all the good they do. Similarly, the Scottish Rite hospitals for children perform notable service, and like the Shriners, the Scottish Rite provides a wide range of free treatments for youngsters who incur serious ailments.

Though not a member, I likely know as much about the Masonic organizations (with the exception of their "secret work") as many of their members do. As a young reporter, one of the assignments city editor Jack J. Cook handed me was to cover the Masonic beat. I learned much about Freemasonry's structure from those in the know. I learned about lodges, consistories, commanderies, temples, valleys. I learned about degrees at a time when I thought the term applied to the calibrated numbers on a thermometer and to academic achievement. I learned that KCCH is an acronym for Knights Commander of the Court of Honor, and that anyone writing KCCH after his name is just a short step below attaining the Thirty-third Degree, Masonry's highest honor. I learned that those pillbox hats some Masons wear are symbolic of their having attained that honor. I learned that when one Mason bows from the waist to another, he is according an honor to someone of higher, or "grand," rank.

I also learned that there are a lot of Masons of one kind or another in Savannah, many of whom belong to a number of affiliated groups, and that a camaraderie prevails about as strong as the bond in combat between infantry soldiers in the same squad. Masons have a secret handshake, and as they exchange it one can see what seems to be a dissolution of whatever barriers, real or imagined, might have existed before the handshake. Having watched Masons greet, and closely scrutinized their handshakes, I have come to appreciate that bond within the secret order. I know what the challenging handgrasp is because I've received it from Masons who must have thought I was one; alas, I am ignorant of the responding handgrasp, so there may still remain a barrier between me and card-carrying Masons who have shaken my hand. Even so, they've been friendly enough, so there can't be too much of a barrier.

The Masonic-sponsored Eastern Star is something I am more familiar with by virtue of my late mother-in-law's deep involvement. Without divulging any of the secrets, she apprised me of the fact that an Eastern Star chapter cannot open a meeting unless a certain number of Masons are present. The ladies of the Eastern Star even allow Masons to hold certain offices; for example, for every worthy matron (the head officer) there is also a worthy patron; similarly, an associate patron for every associate matron. The "Star sisters," as they refer to themselves, also allow outsiders to attend their installations, and even rise and be introduced. For example, the new matron introduces her family, any or all members of which may say a word of congratulation to the incoming head lady.

The ritualistic installation service is impressive, reminding me very much of what we Episcopalians call "high church" in reference to certain liturgical services in which our bishops, priests, deacons, and acolytes bow and genuflect considerably more so than during a "low" service. The installing officer seemingly walks a mile or two during the proceedings, moving all over the place while accompanying the several new officers to their stations. The geometrical truism about the straight line being the shortest distance between points does not apply to the Eastern Star. Star sisters (and their relatively fewer brothers) also visit around, attending installations and other meetings of the other chapters, and afterwards getting together to compare how "they did it" with the way they do it back in their own chapters. Once I overheard an impassioned discussion over the way one chapter had brought the open Bible into the hall—not at all the way it "should be done."

I have learned, through years of kibitzing and eavesdropping (though never able to learn the "secret work"), that Freemasons and their affiliated organizations take their inspiration from the Holy Bible, which is commendable. A few have told me they "get more out of" Masonry than from church. Indeed, I recall as a boy at St. John's Church the excuses a wife made for her husband's absence on Easter Sunday. He was a pillar of that church, but on that particular Easter he was "so tired" after the vigil at the Masonic temple that he simply couldn't make it to church. Although I paid little attention in those days to holy days of obligation, I thought then, as I do now, that Easter is a "must" lest God and St. Peter add another twenty years or so to one's wait for a welcome through the Pearly Gates.

I do not disparage Masons, however, even if the aforementioned incident still hangs in memory. Their charitable work, especially with children, is a wonderful contribution to God's people and society in general. Nor do I disparage Masons who also are Shriners. A late colleague, reporter Kenneth Palmer, did take a dim view of Shriners, calling them "grown-up Boy Scouts" because they scooted around on midget motorcycles, or donned clown costumes and makeup, or played weird-sounding music (Palmer was also a musician) in their Oriental band, or strutted in their patrol unit while wearing fancy brocaded costumes. Alas, Palmer went to his grave never agreeing with me that "grown" men can in fact band together to do good while having fun at the same time.

Still, professional newsman that he was, Palmer could cover a Shrine event beautifully, describing in detail, for example, the fancy drills of the Alee Temple Patrol. He and another colleague, the late Harley Cabaniss (also not a Mason), knew all the Masonic and Shrine titles of rank because they often had to write about them. They even knew what the acronyms stood for. They explained to me, when I was a cub reporter, that "Alee" (pronounced "eh-lee" and not "alley") was not an acronym, but the name of the local Shrine temple, and that the temple's auxiliary, Eela, was simply Alee spelled backwards. The Shrine acronym is AAONMS, which stands for Ancient Arabic Order, Nobles of the Mystic Shrine.

There is another Shrine temple in Savannah named Omar, more reflective of the Middle East than Alee. Its members are Negroes, who engage in about as many charitable activities and stage as many parades and ceremonials as their white counterparts. Also, the Prince Hall Masons have black-only membership, and the story is told that Masonry once was lily-white, and it became racially mixed because, in slavery days, one of the slaves assigned to keep the hall clean fell asleep behind a partition during a lodge meeting, and he was summarily admitted to the order on the outside chance that he had been playing possum, and actually became privy to the secret work. By enrolling him, and impressing on him the sanctity of the secret work, they made certain he would not divulge it to others. That might have been Prince Hall himself. Whoever it was, he started something big in the black community. It is interesting that our local lodges and temples are still segregated—whites to themselves, blacks to themselves.

I have been exposed, by virtue of newspaper assignments, to other fraternal groups, male and female, including the Independent Order of Odd Fellows, Fraternal Order of Eagles, Royal Arcanum, Benevolent and Protective Order of the Elks, Order of Rebekah, the Dramatic Order of Knights Khorrassan, and the following Masonic affiliates: Order of Amaranth, Daughters of the Nile, Knights Templar, the Jesters, and the Sojourners. Their purposes are lofty, their devotion to their orders admirable, and their works beyond the lodge doors beneficial to mankind. With so many Savannahians belonging to these groups, and some to more than one, the puzzle is that any evil at all has crept into our community. The puzzle intensifies whenever one considers that nearly eight of the telephone book's Yellow Pages list churches, and that there are still other churches content to be listed only in the white pages, and still others without telephones.

Suffice it to say, by way of possible explanation, that Satan stays at work day and night—possibly due to the stifling environment of Hades, which surely inhibits sleep—while the good guys and gals, even those who aren't members of lodges or chapters, take a few hours nightly to slumber. As the King of Siam said to Anna: "Is a puzzlement."

The Tunnels

Savannah's most famed tunnel may not now be a tunnel. At least it no longer runs from the promontory nearest the Savannah River down to the river's right bank; and I'm not sure whether the operators of the Pirates' House Restaurant, where the start of the tunnel is one of the restaurant's showcases for capturing the imagination of visitors and locals alike, know exactly where the tunnel terminates. For that matter there may never have been, after all, a tunnel leading from the Pirates' House to the river. That could be mere myth, and what appears as the leading end of a tunnel actually may be only a passageway into what once was the basement of the place.

This is not, however, to dispel the romance and glamour of the Pirates' House tunnel. I eat there sometimes, and still enjoy stealing a look into that shaft where, legend holds, seamen enjoying a night ashore, and having overimbibed, were rendered unconscious by a club or blackjack, then dumped down the shaft to waiting accomplices, and subsequently taken to a ship ready to sail on the morning tide. That process was called shanghaiing. America once fought a war over, among other things, the impressment of seamen. This procedure was impressment by the direct and manly way; those clubbed into unconsciousness would wake up, walk to the rail, look over the side at miles of ocean, and then shrug in concession that they would work as crew members of that ship for the duration of the voyage. After all, it was a long swim back to Savannah, and sharks plied the waters. Seamen, and likely some inebriates who had never been aboard a ship, were shanghaied in those days because help was hard to get and the pay was paltry.

Conceding, though, for the sake of moving along, that the Pirates' House tunnel once actually served as a conduit for shanghaied sailors, it may well be the only tunnel that Savannah denizens can discuss with any degree of knowledgeability. That's because Herb Traub, who for years owned and operated the restaurant that he converted from a museum that the late Marmaduke Floyd had converted from a closed-down saloon, had a flair for public relations. Traub accepted Floyd's conclusion of why the tunnel's end was there, and he exploited the tale, the better to draw and entertain diners, especially those visiting from hither and yon. That's why locals and tourists know about the tunnel. If ever an imaginative entrepreneur graced our scene, it was Herb Traub, along with his one-time partner, Jim Cayce. He also exploited the legend of Captain Flint, a fictional pirate; and in an upstairs room that Traub would allow tourists to peek into, he displayed a pirate-costumed mannequin in bed, and seemingly dead. That, Traub said, was Captain Flint. Anyone who has read Robert Louis Stevenson's *Treasure Island* will recall that the story's plot is a quest for treasure buried on an island by Captain Flint, who, Stevenson wrote, "died in Savannah." Why not, for the sake of flair and exploitation, lay claim to the Pirates' House having been the place of Captain Flint's demise? Traub not only laid such a claim, he also furnished that upstairs room, complete with the mannequin.

Savannah has had at least two other tunnels of note, and there is no myth, or suspected myth, surrounding them. Not everyone, however, knows about them; those who do, agree that the tunnel from a hospital, under Drayton Street to Forsyth Park, played a significant role in Savannah's history. The yellow fever epidemic of 1820 was a devastating blow to Savannah. The mosquito-transmitted disease claimed many lives. A hospital at the corner of Huntingdon and Drayton streets was where stricken patients were taken for treatment, but far more died than survived. Their bodies, according to legend unchallenged, were moved from the hospital through a tunnel that led to the park across Drayton Street, and in the park the bodies were loaded aboard carts and wagons to be transported during the night to a burial ground.

The hospital's building survives to this day, now used for certain medical-related purposes in the wake of Candler Hospital's relocation to larger quarters elsewhere. Before the Methodists acquired the hospital and named it for Bishop Warren A. Candler, it was publicly owned and called Savannah Hospital. Long before the Candler operation was relocated, the tunnel reportedly was filled in, but longtime associates of the hospital would point to a bricked-up doorway as the spot where the tunnel began.

Another tunnel, also running under Drayton Street, was called "the bishop's tunnel" for obvious reasons—the Roman Catholic bishop used it to go from his abode to the cathedral church, located diagonally across Drayton at Perry Street. That was in days before the present Cathedral of St. John the Baptist was built at the northeast corner of Abercorn and Harris streets.

The bishop's house, later occupied by the Fuchs and Hoy families, was a two-stories-over-basement mansion closely resembling Savannah's famed Juliette Gordon Low Birthplace, a national Girl Scout shrine commemorating the Savannah woman who founded the Girl Scout movement in her hometown. The cathedral was situated on Perry between Drayton and Abercorn streets, and some Savannahians will remember the property as the location of Stephen Harris' automobile agency on the Drayton corner, the Eagles' hall just east of it, and Abercorn Street School on the corner of Abercorn and Perry.

Long after the new cathedral was built, the school was razed and the Catholic Chancery building was erected in its place. The chancery has since moved to another location. The Savannah Symphony offices now occupy the former chancery building.

Little else is known about the tunnel, except that it was later filled in. Peggy Hoy Sterling, who grew up in the former bishop's house, recalls seeing evidences of the tunnel when she was a child. The bishop's house has long been razed.

There may have been other tunnels, but it's doubtful because the community long has harbored a fear of digging too deep on account of the city's high water table. Even the tunnel that ought to be built probably won't be, and because of that fear. Still, the suggestion arises now and then for a tunnel beneath Bay Street, from East Broad to Martin Luther King, Jr., Boulevard, for the purpose of alleviating the heavy traffic on Bay. But each time the water-table factor comes up as well as fear that the vibrations from drilling equipment might seriously damage some of the historic buildings downtown.

Perhaps the fear of damaging landmarks in Savannah's famed Historic District is valid. But the water table? Wouldn't one say that such tunnels as New York's Lincoln and Holland, the one beneath Mobile Bay, and certainly the Chesapeake Bay tunnel in Virginia, have been constructed, maintained, and traveled through in spite of water tables considerably higher than Savannah's? Still, don't count on a tunnel under Bay Street within the foreseeable future of the very youngest Savannahians.

Lady Astor—Words in Her Mouth

The adversarial relationship between politicians and journalists is legend. Sometimes politicians can be so pleased at what they see in print about themselves that you'd never know the relationship was so fraught. Other times it's patently obvious just how difficult it can become. All of that depends, of course, upon how the politician looks, not only to himself or herself in print, but also to the public upon whom a politician relies for survival in office. Anything flattering makes the journalist the politician's friend, if only for a little while.

Lady Nancy Astor was a politician, a member of Parliament in Great Britain, this American-born woman who married a nobleman, and she was one of the most outspoken peers of the realm. She rivaled Winston Churchill in candor, and the story goes that once, in a dispute with Churchill, she remarked that if she were married to him she'd put poison in his drink. To which Churchill rejoined: "Nancy, if I were married to you, I'd drink it."

In the Year of Our Lord Nineteen Hundred Forty-five, Providence, or at least Fate, deemed that Lady Astor would visit Savannah in December while on one of her revisits to her native land. Just why she came to our town, I cannot recall, but there was some advance notice that she was coming, and *Morning News* city editor Bill Harris tapped his best reporters to cover Her Ladyship. Bill Fielder, only recently back from World War II and a sub-editor at the time (he later would become managing editor), got the assignment. Lee Banks, also back from the war and destined later to become city editor, would accompany Fielder as the photographer. In those days reporters snapped their own pictures; Banks was basically a reporter, and a thorough one, but he also was a crackerjack photographer. A good team, those two.

They met Lady Astor at the appointed time. She wanted to see Savannah, so they accompanied the renowned tourist, interviewing her as they rolled along. Much of the downtown area, later to become known as Savannah's Historic District, reminded Lady Astor of her adopted England. She was complimentary of the places and things she saw. But alas, an inordinate amount of litter, strewn seemingly everywhere and terrible on such a windy day, disturbed Savannah's visitor. The parks and squares were a mess. Savannah overall was not a pretty sight, and, outspoken as she was, she voiced her dismay. Savannah was beautiful, she said, but . . .

So from that interview came the quote that citizens still repeat, more than fifty years later, whenever our town begins to look shabby and neglected: "Savannah is a beautiful lady with a dirty face."

This many years later, the record needs setting straight. That's not precisely what Lady Astor said, although she did say it *in effect*. It was Bill Fielder's creativity, his imagination, his flair for getting the story, which was responsible for the quote becoming fixed in Savannah's annals. Bill, and maybe Lee, whispered something to round out the phrase, put the words in her mouth. "Would you say," he asked Lady Astor, "that Savannah is a beautiful lady with a dirty face?" Yes, she replied, that was precisely how the city impressed her.

Back in the newsroom, Fielder related to city editor Harris what had transpired, and how he had suggested the dirty-face analogy to the famed visitor. "That's it!" Harris exclaimed. "Lead your story with that quote." But, Fielder injected, she had only agreed with an assessment of Savannah that Fielder actually had concocted; she didn't, in so many words, state it like that. Never mind, Harris countered, she had, after all, agreed, and Harris was sure Lady Astor wouldn't claim she was misquoted. "Hell, she'll be glad you thought it up," he told Fielder.

Bill Harris was an innovative newsman himself, always alert to the sensational, the "good lead," something to catch the imagination of the reader at the very beginning of a story. Most good newsmen are like that, and Harris was no exception. His flair for creativity was a trait that propelled Harris in prewar days out of the newsgathering business into newsmaking. He latched on to a politician from nearby Ailey, Hugh Peterson by name, and became his public relations man as Peterson sought Georgia's First District congressional seat. Elected, Peterson took Harris to Washington with him as his secretary, a title now known on Capitol Hill as chief administrative aide. Later Harris would leave the city desk to run for sheriff of Chatham County, an office he would hold for more than a decade. His campaign for sheriff exemplified his creativity, because he convinced voters that he was qualified to become the county's chief law-enforcement officer when, actually, he had never served a day in law enforcement, his only experience with firearms having been a three-year stint in the Marine Corps, most of it in combat.

The story in the next morning's local edition impressed readers, in Savannah and elsewhere, because the story made the newswires. Indeed, Harris fed it to the news services. The story also impressed the authorities. Mayor Peter Roe Nugent immediately ordered a beef-up of street-cleaning and litter control. It impressed garden societies, which launched beautification projects. It impressed residents, who spruced up their premises. Savannah's facewashing occurred virtually overnight.

The old town never looked prettier. The cry went up: "Bring Lady Astor back and let her see Savannah now."

The story also impressed Lady Astor, who relished the quote. The following March, she did return, by invitation of the Rotary Club. She was treated to another grand tour on a Monday morning, the tour ending at the DeSoto Hotel, where she would be Rotary's guest speaker. The main ballroom of that grand hotel was packed with Rotarians and guests. It was a grand occasion. *Morning News* editor William J. Robertson introduced Lady Astor to his fellow Rotarians as "her incomparable ladyship." She rose to speak and remarked that the Savannah she had just toured was "like a beautiful lady without a curl out of place."

So Bill Harris was right when he insisted on using the quote that wasn't originally hers. It also proved that Bill Fielder knew how to make a good story better. And mainly, it proved that politicians, when misquoted, don't mind it if the misquote not only makes them look good, but also inspires beneficial results.

"Ball Game Tonight"

What was "Seaboard's" name? Why was he called that? Why, for that matter, didn't some of us who saw him almost daily think to ask him? If anyone in the community should have known, it was Westley W. Law. One of Savannah's earliest civil-rights activists, W. W. Law also is a fountain of knowledge on black culture and history. For example, he can tell you off the top of his head who was the pastor of this church or that church in whatever era you choose to ask him. He can tell you just about anything you want to know on anything that concerns Afro-Savannahians, past or present.

Oh, he remembers Seaboard all right. But Seaboard's name and his background remain as much a mystery to Law as they do to me. So this story will use only the man's nickname.

I first encountered Seaboard when I was a kid on a newspaper route down the east side of West Broad Street, in recent years changed to Martin Luther King, Jr., Boulevard, in honor of the martyred civil-rights leader. Seaboard was shuffling along the sidewalk and saying, repeatedly, words I could not understand. He shuffled because his legs were deformed. He seemed both knock-kneed and bowlegged, his thighs rubbing each other and his calves never touching. I assumed it was a condition from birth. As for his manner of speaking, I would guess it to be a blend of the Gullah-Geechee dialect with the speech impediment Southerners call tie-tongue, referred to by Yankees as tongue-tied. Seaboard directed his gibberish to nobody in particular and to all in general. I would learn later that he was plugging some kind of patent medicine. The Knight family, owner of several drugstores, marketed its own N-R, which stood for Nature's Remedy, and I think he might have been mumbo-jumbo-ing N-R, or perhaps its slogan: "N-R tonight, tomorrow all right." I surmise that because there was a Knight drugstore on West Broad, close by the spot where Seaboard and I always crossed paths. If that was the product he plugged, he was performing a service because a lot of Savannahians swore by N-R.

I often crossed paths with Seaboard on my *Evening Press* route, and we'd always exchange waves of greeting as we passed. A time or two, whenever I had an extra paper, I'd give it to him. One day I turned and looked back and saw him selling the paper I had just given him, which was all right because I never believed, even at an early age, in tying strings to gifts.

One day as I was passing the old Savannah Hotel (now the AmeriBank) at Bull and Congress streets, I saw Seaboard shuffling along and proclaiming words I could understand: "Ball game tonight!" He said "ball game tonight" over and over to passersby, and I realized he was informing the downtown crowd that the baseball team was back in town. He was plugging baseball as an ambulatory public relations man. I belonged to the Knothole Club at the time, an organization of boys and girls who, for a quarter, could buy a button that was their admission ticket to any and all of the Savannah Indians' home games, the only stipulation being that club members sit in the left-field bleachers, as a group. The Knothole Club was an arrangement several adults, including lawyer Victor B. Jenkins and Baptist pastor John S. Wilder, had made with the Indians' owners to allow virtually free admission to youngsters struggling to grow up in the Great Depression.

So at Municipal Stadium, each time I rode my bike out to watch a game, I'd always see Seaboard shuffling around outside, touting "ball game tonight" right up until game time. Anyone that close to the ticket window knew about the game anyway, but this was a way for Seaboard to wrap up his daylong project. He knew, of course, that he soon would feel the arm of the ball club's general manager, escorting him past the turnstile into the park and to the left-hand section of the grandstand, which was reserved for Negroes during those Jim Crow days. Also, the general manager each time would hand Seaboard a dollar bill, small payment for a whole day of being a walking advertisement for the team.

That was in the mid-1930's, five or six years before I finished Savannah High and went to work in the local news room as a copyboy who, by virtue of the $50-a-month salary he drew, also was an apprentice reporter. The editors would allow me, when I wasn't otherwise busy, to write a few brief items, and what seemed some days like a hundred obituaries. Eventually sports editor Walt Campbell would ask me to cover some sports events, and sometimes the baseball game. Outside the stadium it was as if nothing had changed where Seaboard was concerned. He was there on game nights, shuffling outside the park, saying "ball game tonight"; and in the spring of 1946, after I had returned from military service and resumed reporting, Seaboard was shuffling around town, touting the evening's sports fare at the stadium.

The next year, 1947, Walt Campbell resigned his sport editorship to become general manager of the professional baseball team. Club owners Wallace Brown and Dr. Eddie Whelan made him an offer he couldn't refuse, a job right down the alley of someone who, besides writing sports, had been an athlete and coach in his youth and had three sons who played sports. I stopped by Walt's stadium office one afternoon and Seaboard was with him, just leaving and pocketing a dollar bill Walt had handed him. I asked Walt to clue me on Seaboard.

"Well, he doesn't talk plain, and he's kinda crippled, but he does a good word-of-mouth job for us. I let him in free and slip him a few bucks now and then," Walt said. No, Walt didn't know why he was called Seaboard because it was obvious that someone in his physical shape would not have worked for the railroad of the same name. Maybe it was because he lived on the coast, but that was only a guess. One thing he did say, very plainly, was "ball game tonight," which is why the baseball moguls utilized his talents. And it's why Savannahians from that era who are still around remember him fondly as someone who, though limited, made an impression on his community. My gripe about Seaboard—he was grossly underpaid.

The Bleacher Fans

Behind first base at Grayson Stadium have sat some of Savannah's most ardent, and loyal, baseball fans. Many still sit there. Gone, however, are the bleachers behind third base. They've been torn down, their surviving former occupants now scattered through the grandstand, but most of them clustered just behind the visitors' dugout and all the way up to the grandstand's highest tier. That's close to third base, but it lacks the intimacy that the former bleachers provided to both the fans and to the third basemen who have played for and against Savannah teams.

The loss of the third-base bleachers was offset by a gain of equal rights and privileges for the Negro fans; they moved out of the dewy night air (and the blistering sun when day games were played) into the covered grandstand, although many of them harbored mixed feelings over giving up their place in order to keep pace with the social changes accruing to their benefit. It was a rather bittersweet development for the beneficiaries as the final vestige of Jim Crow days headed toward eternal rest.

While in pre–Jim Crow days the racial makeup of the bleachers facing first and third bases differed, there was little difference in the amount of noise and cheering emanating from the two sections. On the first base side, where the makeup of fans was all white, Irving McKinney and a Mr. Drake, both now privileged to cheer on the haloed and hallowed baseball players in the Great Beyond, led the cheering. In the "colored" section directly across the field from them, Mrs. Bertha Jackson and Mrs. Ella Maxwell and their cowbells led the noisemaking. As the games intensified in excitement, with lusty-yet-mild coaxing and urging from the grandstand fans in box seats as well as the upper tiers, the two sections of bleacher fans would be uninhibited in their outward and audible expressions of root-root-root for the home team. And from either of the bleachers, no umpire ever endured an entire game without their razzing. It was a classic example of baseball fandom at its ultimate.

Some of those first-base bleacher fans from those halcyon days of pre-television baseball, when the crowds were huge because there was no competing entertainment in Savannah's living rooms and dens to keep them away from the ballpark, still come and sit where they've always sat. They have gained new "members" of their coterie, many of them much younger than they were in a time when they claimed squatters' rights on the general-admission seats in that bleacher section. And many of these johnny-come-lately bleacherites bring their children who, immediately upon settling in with their parents, scoot off to the far seats of those bleachers that extend almost to the right-field corner of the field. The kids position themselves strategically in anticipation of shagging baseballs fouled in their direction. The old order continues, but it has changed; not nearly as lusty noises now emanate as in days of yore.

As for the former bleachers behind third base, where the black fans sat, they never were as solid seats as those behind first base. Actually they were fashioned atop an unfinished portion of Grayson Stadium. Reconstruction of the stadium began as a government-funded project in 1941, to replace the former Municipal Stadium devastated by a hurricane in the fall of 1940. The stadium would have been completed, as a symmetrical park with equidistant foul lines, had not World War II diverted the priority of steel from recreational projects to defense needs. The reinforced concrete grandstand, which had been completed as far eastward as a point about forty feet beyond the visiting team's dugout, was all that would be built for the war's duration. However, the basic structural steel for a continuation of the grandstand was already in place, so a section of wooden-board bleachers more temporary than permanent was built atop the steel beams. That was where the segregated black fans were relegated, except for one section of the grandstand's extreme left, which was roped off from the rest of the seating. Blacks willing to pay more for tickets were permitted to occupy that section, but they could not venture beyond the ropes. And underneath that section of the grandstand, separate concessions and toilet facilities accommodated the blacks. (Post-war, those bleachers were never completed, and finally the steel was removed to convert that section of the stadium into a picnic area.)

Since segregation was the norm until the late-1950's, the black fans accepted second-class seating and loyally supported the home teams each season. The cowbells of Mrs. Jackson and Mrs. Maxwell rallied the black fans to yell and cheer, and there was a certain black man whose voice could be heard anywhere inside the stadium, and likely in the homes and places of business near the stadium. He delighted in jeering the visiting players, and sometimes his jeers would run long and involved. Once, as best I can reconstruct from memory, this is how it went as a visiting player, who tried to steal second base, was walking toward his dugout after being thrown out by the Savannah catcher: "Yeh, man, ya tho't you was gonna steal that base, didncha? Dontcha know stealin's wrong? Ya ain't count on Astroth (Savannah's catcher) havin' no throwin' arm. Ya ain't know he da best in da league. Ya think he jes gonna stan' dere and watch ya run on down, but he wise to ya, an' ya ain't get nowhere but out. Go sit down a spell, and doncha ever try dat again, y'heah?"

That was just typical. He'd spiel on and on, lecturing one player after another. He and a buddy, whenever a visiting manager would make a trip to the mound to settle down a pitcher, would alternate giving the manager advice. "Take him out," one would yell. "Leave him in," the other would counter. And then after a few repetitions, the one who started out saying "Take him out" would switch to "Leave him in." The other then would switch to "Take him out." Once, after a manager had left his pitcher in the game and was walking back to the dugout, he looked toward the bleachers, and with a laugh shouted, "I wish you guys would get together."

The black fans left their perches behind third base about 1953, after several of the clubs in the South Atlantic had signed black players. Savannah was the first team to do so, signing Al Isreal to play third base and Fleming "Junior" Reedy to play second, about a month before spring training started. A few days later the Jacksonville club acquired Henry Aaron and Felix Mantilla as their first blacks, the former destined to break Babe Ruth's home-run record and become enshrined in the Hall of Fame at Cooperstown, New York. With blacks in the league, a few Savannah black citizens, led by Dr. Henry Collier, approached management with the observation that it was now time to end segregated seating. Management balked at first, and one of the city's first racial demonstrations formed outside Grayson Stadium one night, and re-formed the second night, but before week's end management had relented. The fans who had endeared themselves to teams and white spectators alike over the years moved into the grandstand—and the rope came down. It was a moment as significant in baseball annals as the toppling decades later of the Berlin Wall.

Some of the "freed" blacks assimilated themselves into seats amid the white spectators, but most of them sat together, as they always had, in the previously segregated part of the grandstand—as near to third base as they could get. And to this day, most of the black fans sit together, including the two ladies who still bring and ring their cowbells.

Whenever excitement begins to mount in a baseball game, those black fans usually are the first to grow audible. The long-spieling fan who once heckled the opposition (and occasionally an umpire) no longer comes, probably enjoying, along with Messrs. McKinney and Drake, and all the other bleacherites who have departed this life, those baseball games in the Great Beyond. And they probably sit side by side in the unsegregated Promised Land.

As for the picnic area where the Jim Crow bleachers once stood, it is a component of modern-day baseball in the minor leagues, which more and more has become attuned to families. Civic groups come to the park early and bring their kids. Little League teams come early to eat hot dogs and hamburgers before the games start. They file into the grandstand, and some go to the first-base bleachers, after the National Anthem is played and the umpire cries "Play ball." Perhaps some should walk to the chain-link fence behind third base and watch for an inning or two from that vantage point, and then listen closely. Perhaps they'd hear ghostly cheering from years gone by. An era fondly remembered by the dwindling few of us who experienced it firsthand.

Half-rubber, Savannah-born

It is debatable (in other climes and places) whether the sport of half-rubber originated in Savannah. Home folks are convinced that Savannah was its birthplace, and at least two other authors have written researched tomes that I wouldn't dare dispute. So call it Savannah's original game, and it's unfortunate that its local inventor, whoever he was, didn't patent it before a toymaker came on the market with a packaged game called "Half Ball." Perhaps the inventor was too busy having fun.

And a fun game it is. Half-rubber is a derivation of baseball, and its required equipment is simple—a sponge-rubber ball cut in half, and a broomstick. That's it. The game can be played with as few as three participants, and as many as opposing teams agree to place in the field. Fielders can vary from one upward in number. The rules vary, as agreed upon by the players, but they cannot be changed in the middle of the game. No umpires are required, but it's best, for the sake of holding down argument, to have at least one.

It works this way. The pitcher sails the half-ball toward the batter holding the broomstick. The batter swings at the half-rubber. If he (girls, too, can play, but let's stick with the male pronoun and call it generic; also, grammatical) hits the pitch, and no one in the field catches the half-rubber, he is credited with a single, double, triple, or home run, depending upon how far the missile travels. Distances for base hits are predetermined by the participants. Say, the batter gets a single; he has one runner on base. Say again, he then hits a triple; the imaginary runner scores and there's a man on third. Say, he misses; strike one. Misses twice again; strike three, he's out, and next batter is up. A fly ball caught by a fielder is an out. Also, a foul tip is a strike, and a third-strike foul tip must be caught by the catcher to make it a strikeout. Just like baseball, but with imagination added as a dimension of the game.

Half-rubber usually is played in a sandlot or on the beach, but there's an annual tournament in Savannah, sometimes drawing competitors from out of town, played in Grayson Stadium, the local baseball park. It's a popular game in which veteran pitchers actually develop a kind of control in sailing the ball.

The story goes that half-rubber, invented in Savannah (and don't dispute that), became an international game during World War II, Savannah soldiers, sailors, Marines, and airmen having introduced it to their comrades in arms wherever they served. Yankees (who invented stickball, a similar but different game) took it home. So did mid-Westerners, Westerners, and far-Westerners, and other Southerners. One of those who took it home likely is the fellow who marketed "Half Ball." Probably some enterprising New Yorker. Alas, Savannah's loss economically, but chances are that half-rubber is played best in Savannah.

The Head Irishman?

Savannah comprises several "communities," as do most cities, especially those along the Atlantic seaboard where immigrants settled. The Irish community, the German (some say Dutch) community, the Black community, Jewish community, the Italian community, the Greek community, the Chinese community, and so on, including in recent years the Indian community (from India and Pakistan, not the American Indian, which ironically was Savannah's very first community and greeted the white man). There's also a small Arab community, dating back generations, and enhanced in recent years by newer immigrants.

Well, who, if anyone, heads those several communities? Who is the one to whom other members turn for counsel and wisdom? Good questions, but the answers don't come readily because in a free society "community" members learn quickly to fend for themselves and to assimilate themselves into the warp and woof of Savannah. The Irish community, though, has seemed to this observer to have had, now and then, a head Irishman. There was the late John J. Bouhan, for years the political boss of Savannah and Chatham County, who without question was the head Irishman. Mamas trying to help sons and daughters would "call Mr. Bouhan," usually with success. He could direct job-seeking youths to jobs either in local government (police, fire, public works, City Hall, or Courthouse bureaucracy) or in the private sector, calling on business owners who owed him for political favors ranging from curb cuts to free topsoil delivered by public servants who had stripped it from public property, usually the crust of new garbage landfills. Bouhan, a lawyer, ran his own personal employment agency, knowing that everyone he found a job for would be a voter for his side.

The Head Irishman?

Bossism, however, started to wane in the mid-1950's as political reform set in, and when Bouhan died he had lost most of his clout. So, from recent observations I have deduced that Savannah has had several head Irishmen, all at the same time, people of position and influence to whom Irish families turn more for advice and counsel rather than favor-seeking. One of those was Walter Corish, a natural leader from the days of his youth, possessing the wit and blarney one associates with the Irish across the sea, who at age eighty died in January 1995. Walter, who became my close friend, was seven years my senior, so I did not know him personally until I was well into adulthood, a rookie sports editor of the *Evening Press,* and was his around-the-corner neighbor. He owned an insurance agency and, as diversion, was much a part of the sports crowd. He had been an athlete while a cadet in Benedictine Military School, a Roman Catholic–run high school. He continued, particularly after his World War II service, as one of the most visible sports boosters in town, always raising money for and providing leadership to the Benedictine Athletic Association, and lending moral and material support to other sports organizations. He also was active in the elite Irish-heritage Hibernian Society, the Roman Catholic Church, the Knights of Columbus, and such.

Successful in the insurance business that he had inherited from his father, Nicholas Corish, and that he passed along to his namesake son, Walter Corish found himself in a position to offer a helping hand to Savannah Irish who couldn't have cared less about sports—sometimes with money, sometimes as liaison between job-seekers and businesses, much the same way the late John Bouhan had done, yet in a nonpolitical way. Politically, in fact, he never ran for office, yet he supported candidates, not all of them Irish. Unquestionably he was one of the head Irishmen, and he held the respect of non-Irish (defined in Savannah as Crackers, Jews, and Blacks). Corish was an Irishman whom his fellow-Irishmen and lassies would believe without question if he "said it was so."

I am told (and I believe it) that he established himself as a leader in the Irish community not too many years after he had graduated from Benedictine, when he became head of the school's athletic association. The association numbered (and still does) just about every Benedictine alumnus in town. Its mission is to provide uniforms and other sports equipment for the school, and otherwise to see that the athletes in such a small-enrollment (seldom more than 350 or 400) all-male institution compete with distinction in a classification against public schools of much higher enrollment.

When Corish became head of the athletic association, the athletes traveled to the practice field and out-of-town games aboard a bus nicknamed "The Tea Ball" because, worn and grimy, it much resembled a tea ball that bore the stains of many submersions in the teapot but seldom if ever in the dishpan. The Tea Ball's engine and interior closely matched its outward appearance. Often the engine suddenly would conk out, necessitating repairs paid for from the association's coffers.

The situation was becoming ridiculous, so Corish decided that the Tea Ball might be all right for taking kids to practice fields, but for road trips it was downright impractical; besides, the team always traveled with the lingering fear that the bus would break down and the boys would arrive either late for the game or not at all. So Corish approached the Reverend Father Boniface Bauer, who by virtue of his pastorate of Sacred Heart Church was also headmaster of Benedictine School. The football team was scheduled that weekend to play Sidney Lanier High School in Macon, one of its fiercest rivals.

"Father Boniface, that's a long trip to Macon, and it's hilly country up there," Corish said to the priest, who held veto power over expenditures of the athletic association, the reason being that control over athletic teams (as decreed by the Georgia High School Association) rested with the institutions and not booster clubs. It's a good rule, lest win-happy boosters exploit, pamper, and spoil youngsters who are in school primarily to get an education.

Corish raised the issue of hilly country because he reasoned that the Tea Ball would have difficulty negotiating elevations much higher than near-sea level Savannah. Father Boniface balked at first, seeing no reason why the Tea Ball, with careful piloting by the driver, couldn't make the trip to Macon and back. Corish pleaded further and finally won his point, gaining permission to charter a better bus for the trip. Father Boniface relented, albeit reluctantly.

The kids enjoyed riding on a "real" bus, with stuffed seat cushions and good ventilation, not to mention more room. The bus was particularly comfortable for tired athletes on their nocturnal ride home, most of them nursing bruises and aches incurred on the football field. They won that game, incidentally, and Corish accorded much credit to traveling conditions.

The next week Benedictine had another out-of-town game against Glynn Academy of Brunswick, some eighty miles down the coastal plain from Savannah. Feeling a precedent had been established by the Macon trip, and on a roll, Athletic Chairman Corish chartered the same bus for the Brunswick trip. The day before the game he felt it prudent to advise Father Boniface of his decision, convinced that the good but tough headmaster would simply nod approval. But Father Boniface didn't. "Walter," he said in a sort of sing-songy tone priests sometimes use outside the sanctuary when they aren't chanting the liturgy, "there aren't any hills between Savannah and Brunswick." The kids made the trip down the Coastal Highway aboard the Tea Ball.

That may have been the only time head-Irishman Corish failed in his usually successful power of persuasion. But look at it this way—Father Boniface Bauer wasn't Irish, but of German extraction.

Even More Little Stories

The Crystal. A visitor downtown will ask where's a good place for an inexpensive lunch, and a Savannahian will answer, "The Crystal." The visitor then will say he had something a little better than "instant" in mind, and the Savannahian, who intentionally was leading him on with that reply, will laugh and say, "I don't mean 'with a K, but with a C.'" Then the Savannahian will explain that our city has restaurants with names that sound alike but are spelled differently. In fact, the ones that begin with "K" enjoy six locations in Chatham County, but there is just one Crystal, and its full name is Crystal Beer Parlor. It's located at Jones and Jefferson streets, where it was established, circa 1930, by the late William B. "Blocko" Manning and his wife, Connie, who, age ninety-eight, died in the spring of 1997. Grandson Conrad Thomson and his wife, Carol, now operate the business, as well as a new midtown Crystal.

The Thomsons serve, of course, beer, because it's the Crystal Beer Parlor, but it's their hamburgers for which the Crystal is better known. They buy choice beef and grind it themselves, daily. Then they grill it in a special and secret way—the kitchen is off limits to outsiders—and such adornments as onions and certain condiments are customer's choice. Their own potato chips are also special, sliced in the kitchen and fried "just right." The Crystal also serves a special luncheon steak, delicious salads, and cole slaw that tastes different from most, and the menu offers several other choices in meat dishes. Most diners, though, order either hamburgers or steaks. And the term "most diners" embraces an eclectic clientele of tourists, local lawyers, bankers, educators, newspaperpeople (of course), stockbrokers. The whole "downtown crowd" has counted itself among the Crystal's customers at one time or another. It's a neat place, indeed.

What makes the Crystal so neat is its adornments. The walls are spotted with pictures from days of yore, ranging from former President Truman's visit to Savannah for a St. Patrick's Day address to the Hibernian Society to former Potentate Robert Sieg's presentation of a plaque from Alee Temple to Hollywood Shriner Charles Coburn, the famed late movie character actor who grew up in Savannah and started his theatrical career distributing programs in the old Savannah Theatre. The presentation was made on one of Coburn's many sentimental visits to his old hometown.

All of the pictures are priceless from a reminiscing standpoint—the 1939 football team of Benedictine Military School, for instance, several of whose players became citizens of note. The prone figure of Leo Center, knocked out in the finals of the 1941 Golden Gloves tournament in New York's Madison Square Garden, appeared on the back page of the late and still-missed *New York Mirror* the morning after the tournament. (Center, who became a successful businessman and served seventeen years as a Savannah alderman, made the finals again in 1942—and won. Leo later ran up a respectable record as a professional fighter. He is one of the enshrinees in the Greater Savannah Athletic Hall of Fame.) The framed adornments include front pages from Pearl Harbor Day and other noteworthy events in history. There's a photo of Jack Dempsey, plus others of sundry sports luminaries. For Savannahians, every picture recalls "something" that they can relate to. The Crystal really is an art gallery of contemporary history, and one of the photos, showing John Rousakis kicking a football for the Savannah High School team in the 1940's, has the fellow who served twenty-one years as Savannah's mayor looking not at the football but at the camera—a portent of a future politician who, his friends kiddingly remind him, never met a photographer he didn't like.

Leo Center's Picture. Scott Center, youngest son of businessman and former city alderman Leo Center, enjoys telling the story of how the photograph of his dad made it to enshrinement on the wall of the Crystal Beer Parlor. The photo is not very complimentary. The boxer's eyes are glazed. The caption in the *New York Mirror* read "Leo Center of Savannah, Ga., hears the birdies go tweet-tweet-tweet."

Scott's story is that advertising man Chuck Tallman, who collected many of the pictures for the Crystal's walls, contacted Scott's mother, Miriam, and asked whether she had a photo of Alderman Center from his days as a boxer. Miriam obliged by giving Tallman the unflattering picture of the fighter lying prone on the canvas. Now, the reason Miriam Center chose that certain picture, according to son Scott, is that when Tallman came by, she and Leo were near the point of divorce, of which Tallman was unaware. It was purely a case of Miriam Center being "ticked off" at Leo. Her way, son Scott said with lingering amusement, of getting back at his father.

Scott Carter, incidentally, has an older brother, Tony, who lives in the Atlanta area and is an active Democrat like his parents and brother. He was one who dared to challenge Newt Gingrich in one of the congressman's bids for reelection—before Gingrich became Speaker of the United States House of Representatives.

Coburn and Mercer. Two of Savannah's show-biz luminaries were Charles Coburn and Johnny Mercer, the former a character actor of esteem and the latter a lyricist whose songs

America still sings. Coburn, who was born in Macon and reared in Savannah, often made sentimental visits home. Mercer, a native son, returned to Savannah more often than Coburn—to see his mother and siblings as well as his boyhood friends, with whom he'd get together for a party or two.

Both happened to be in Savannah in December 1945, three months after the end of World II. Coburn was visiting his sister and brother-in-law, the Stephen Harrises, and lodged in the penthouse of the old DeSoto Hotel; and Mercer stayed at his mother's home. I had just returned as a reporter on the staff of the *Savannah Evening Press*, and city editor Jack Cook assigned me to get the two Hollywood gentlemen together for an interview and photograph. It was a choice assignment—imagine, interviewing two such famed former Savannahians.

I first telephoned the Mercer house, and Johnny answered. He was more than willing to meet with Coburn for an interview. When would be a convenient time? I asked. "Whatever time is convenient with him," Mercer replied. "He is older, and I'll let him decide." This was indicative of the kind nature of Johnny Mercer, ever willing to accommodate someone else. Mr. Coburn, telephoned at his suite, set the time for 2 o'clock that afternoon, saying, "I'll be more than glad to meet Johnny," a remark I thought strange at the time, but soon would fathom.

At 2 P.M. photographer Helen Jones Wheeler, her camera in hand, reporter Kenneth Palmer, and I walked through the hotel's lobby to the elevator, and there was Johnny Mercer, already having pressed the elevator button. The four of us rode the lift to the penthouse suite, and were warmly greeted by Charles Coburn. "Come on in," he said cheerily, and directed us promptly to the table on which bottles of Scotch, bourbon, gin, and appropriate mixers were displayed. "Fix yourselves whatever you like," Coburn said, the genial host. Helen, Kenneth, and I made our drinks after Mercer, and then we settled into chairs, and the two gentlemen from Hollywood began to chat as if they hadn't seen each other for years. Just before we sat down, Helen snapped a priceless picture (which I still have) of Coburn and Mercer raising glasses in a toast to Christmas, just a few days away.

As the afternoon progressed, Coburn and Mercer told us that this was the first time the two had ever met, and that explained Coburn's "I'll be more than glad to meet Johnny." Imagine, two Hollywood figures (who didn't live too far apart in the movie capital), from the same hometown, so busy in their work that neither had ever met the other. It was a memorable afternoon, and when Helen, Kenneth, and I took our leave, the two former Savannahians were into at least their third drink, chatting merrily about memories of Savannah and mutual friends in Hollywood.

I've always wondered, if that interview hadn't been arranged, whether Coburn and Mercer ever would have made acquaintance. Years later, after Mercer's death in 1976, I had the photograph copied and sent a print to Ginger Mercer, Johnny's widow, in California. She had not been with Mercer on that 1945 visit, and apparently he never mentioned the interview to her. Ginger's thank-you note said that she was unaware their paths ever crossed. A copy of the Coburn-Mercer picture taken that day now hangs in the Johnny Mercer niche in the Savannah Visitors Center.

Quickest Resignation. Reporter-photographer Helen Jones Wheeler was one of the *Evening Press*'s wartime staff members, she and several other women writers outnumbering male staffers who were too old for military service. World War II marked the first time in the afternoon paper's history that more than two women served on the staff at the same time. It was a man's world in prewar days, but like the legendary Rosie the Riveter, they became pioneers in sex-mixed journalism in Savannah. After the war both the morning and afternoon papers hired numerous women reporters, and at one point, when the *Evening Press*'s staff had more women than men reporting, the rival staffers of the *Morning News* sneeringly referred to the afternoon sheet as the "Panty Press," the jealous bastards. In the 1970's one of those "Panty Press" reporters, Kathy Beatson Haeberle, became the first female city editor of the combined news staffs of the morning and afternoon papers. That sure-Lord showed the scoffers.

While serving as a wartime reporter, Helen Jones Wheeler combined talents with another staffer, Barbara Sutlive (editor John Sutlive's oldest daughter), to write true accounts of notorious criminals for crime magazines, under the joint *nom de plume* Wheeler Sutlive, picking up some extra money on the side. Two enterprising young ladies.

Helen came to the Savannah paper unmarried, but soon wed an Army officer stationed near Savannah; and her married surname Wheeler then became a part of her byline. Captain Wheeler in due course went over seas to fight the war, and she promised to wait for him in Savannah. Well, it was only a few days after the aforementioned interview with Charles Coburn and Johnny Mercer that Helen, after a long telephone conversation during which her eyes welled with tears of happiness, cradled the phone, and walked into editor John Sutlive's office and resigned. That phone call had been from her just-returned husband, who was back from overseas and in Savannah. He would be by the office in just a few minutes. Helen began to clean out her desk, and by the time hubby arrived she was ready to go.

Just like that, she was out of there. Editor Sutlive, visibly shaken over losing so suddenly one of his best writers who also knew how to take pictures, sat at his desk shaking his head after Helen's goodbye embrace and peck on the cheek. "Most expedited resignation I ever had," he lamented, adding: "Ah, Love!" Helen and the captain headed toward the door, waving to the rest of us, and happy as larks, not to mention doves.

Pinky Masters. Although he became a legend in his own time, I never really warmed up to the late Pinky Masters, who ran a bar at the corner of Drayton and Harris streets (it's still there), because as a city editor and then a managing editor I regarded his bar as a pain in the ass for the plain reason that so many of my reporters hung out there. In days of yore, drinking reporters were the norm; in fact, peers regarded nondrinkers as odd balls. Drinking during working hours, however, has become sort of an unwritten no-no for the working press. I am not a teetotaler by any means, and in younger days I frequented barrooms, but usually after hours. And I chose places where my reporters did not come because, frankly, I saw enough of them during the workday, and regarded my social life as separate and distinct. Only twice in my life did I ever enter Pinky s establishment, each time on the way home from boxing matches at the old Municipal Auditorium. Pinky would call me now and then and ask why I didn't drop in more frequently.

But his place represented the source of the visible hangovers some of my reporters came to work nursing. It's one thing when you're a reporter, but something entirely different when you're an editor trying to manage a staff and expecting staffers to be alert at all times. Not every reporter was a Pinky person, but enough of them were to make me just plain dislike the Pinky Masters establishment.

Nevertheless, I was in a small minority because Pinky's place became famed not only as a watering hole but also as a hotbed of politics. Politicians, especially those running statewide, would hobnob with the Pinky's crowd, thinking they'd spread the word in their behalf. Also, Pinky became known as an endorser of candidates. Those he favored, statewide and local, would have their posters placed in the south window of his establishment, visible to thousands of motorists who daily drove to downtown on one-way Drayton Street. And the most famous of those politicians was Jimmy Carter, ironically a Baptist teetotaler who never drank anything stronger from Pinky's bar than a Coke with ice in it. Carter was a nondrinker, but he knew that many voters drank; hence, another source of a growing constituency.

Carter's first visit was at the behest of Michael Joseph "Toby" Buttimer, a beer distributor and a loyal Democrat who took a liking to Carter when the politician from Plains was a state senator running for governor. Carter lost that bid, but four years later came back to win Georgia's highest office. Toby Buttimer was one of Savannah's dearest Irishmen, who one year was chosen grand marshal of the St. Patrick's Day parade, considered the very highest honor for a Savannahian of Irish heritage. He liked Carter the first time they met, assessed him as a politician with much potential, so he squired him around whenever the candidate visited Savannah. And he told Carter he simply had to get acquainted with Pinky and his bar's customers because they could help him politically—which turned out to be true, because in both of Carter's gubernatorial races Pinky placed Carter signs in his window and gave him the red-carpet treatment during the candidate's Savannah visits. Needless to say, when Carter was making his successful run for President of the United States, Pinky went all out to tout his candidacy, both in the window and across the bar, and when President Carter visited to be the speaker at the Hibernian Society's annual St. Patrick's Day banquet (at Buttimer's invitation), he made a special stop at Pinky's for the dedication of a plaque Pinky had mounted on the barstool where Carter had sat. Upon Pinky's death President Carter issued a glowing tribute to the Savannahian, and sent a personal representative to the funeral in St. Paul's Greek Orthodox Church.

Still, while I accorded Pinky Masters all the credit he deserved for becoming a living legend respected by even the leader of the Free World, he and I never could hit it off, which I'm sure never bothered him. Once, after an itinerant reporter had worked for me about six months and moved on to another clime, place, and newspaper, Pinky telephoned me demanding that the *Morning News* pay a bar tab the reporter had run up and skipped town on. It was a considerable sum owed to Pinky. That's just tough, I told him, but there was nothing in my budget to cover debts owed by long-gone employees. "Then I'll just sue you," Pinky threatened, which was music to my ears. "Go ahead and sue," I encouraged, "and then try to explain to the state revenue people how you violated the law by selling booze on credit." Then and there, I believe, Pinky and I buried the hatchet. He laughed, admitted that he had illegally accorded credit to a customer, then said, "Well, Tom, you can't blame a guy for trying." I laughed with him, and we chatted frequently afterward over the telephone. But I never bought another drink from him, try as he might to seduce. I shed a tear when the news came of his passing, and so did thousands of other Savannahians who had known him pleasantly.

The Put-down. This is a tale of old-school pride, male chauvinism, female wit, and good-natured kidding. Its elements are Sister Mary Faith, R.S.M., a Roman Catholic nun; Donald "Rosie" Rosenblum, a retired three-star general; the Rotary Club of Savannah; and The Citadel, which is the military college of South Carolina. Sister Faith is one of the top administrators in the office of the Diocese of Savannah. She came to Savannah to be president and CEO of St. Joseph's Hospital, but after more than a decade in that post she stepped down to assume her diocesan job. She holds a Ph.D. General Rosenblum is a career officer who became smitten with Savannah when he commanded the Twenty-fourth Division at nearby Fort Stewart. He retired here and opened a consulting business after commanding the First Army, headquartered at Fort Meade, Maryland. He also is a graduate of The Citadel and demonstratively proud of his alma mater.

The Rotary Club of Savannah comprises most of the community's top executives and professionals, and until the early 1990's was all male in membership, as were Rotary Clubs across the United States. After Rotary International voted to give local clubs the option of admitting female members, the issue came before the local civic organization. There was debate, Rosie Rosenblum taking the negative side, maintaining that Rotary always had been male and it always should be. His side lost, so Rotary set about selecting its first female member and decided upon Sister Faith, who accepted the invitation. She had gotten wind of the debate, so she knew it had been the general who spoke against allowing women in. Rotary moguls knew that she knew that, and thus decided that a nice gesture would be to assign the general the role of introducing Sister Faith to the club, which he did with all his officer-and-a-gentleman manner, surprising his peers and endearing himself to the good sister. And soon it would be that Rosie Rosenblum, admittedly a male chauvinist, would find himself, as many alumni were and still are, anguished over the attempts by a young lady in South Carolina to become the first female to enroll in The Citadel's cadet corps.

From the time of her induction, Sister Faith and Rosie sat near each other at the Rotary meetings, and engaged in kidding banter, especially women's rights and his alma mater's problem with trying to keep a female out of the cadet corps. I shall not relate all the points for and against that were advanced because I'm not a Rotarian and wasn't privy to the friendly exchanges. But I am told by several Rotarians of acquaintance that it was entertaining, and club members reveled in listening to the two. Sister Faith, I should add, is not a feminist in the sense that members of the National Organization for Women are. Lord only knows, as a holy woman in the Roman Catholic Church, she does not espouse abortion on demand. Her personal thrust on behalf of women's rights has been her own demonstration that women are capable of doing jobs that men do. Physicians, staff, patients, and the Church hailed her as one of the best administrators ever to head St. Joseph's, and her involvement in many community activities endeared her to Savannah.

Then one day I was the luncheon guest of Rotarian George Fawcett, a longtime friend. Sister Faith sat at our table and Rosie, at the table beside ours. The previous week the news media had reported Sister Faith's resignation as president of the hospital and her statement that she would go into other work. As Rosie sat down and saw Sister Faith, he said he was sorry she was leaving St. Joseph's and then asked what, specifically, would her new job be.

Without hesitation, not the first pause to ponder a reply, Sister Faith said, in sufficient voice volume to be heard at the nearest tables, "Why, I'm going to become dean of women at The Citadel." Now I have seen some put-downs, and been the object of some, many of them quite clever. That one, in my book, was champion of them all. And, I would guess, for the first time ever Lieutenant General Donald Rosenblum did not have a barb to shoot back. He laughed, by the way, the heartiest of all present.

Atlanta Noses. There exists a natural resentment between any state's capital city and the cities, towns, and hamlets out in the hinterlands. The resentment is based on a suspicion that capital city folks want to control everything in the state. That's because capital citizens exude what outsiders perceive as an elitist posture, a superior attitude, as if saying to the rest of the state, "We know what's best for you, and you don't deserve anyway what you've already got." New Yorkers speak sneeringly of Albany, for example, and South Carolinians are often disrespectful of Columbia. Such is especially the case in Georgia, whose capital city of Atlanta also is the economic hub of the South. To us on the coast, Atlanta, as well as being the seat of state government, seems to have everything already in the way of roads, central headquarters, industries, all kinds of other amenities, yet Atlanta always seems to want even more of the same. Let new road work begin in Atlanta, and a Savannahian who goes up there and sees the work in progress will come home and say to neighbors, "That's where the money for *our* roads goes." A Savannahian, whose name isn't as remembered as well as his saying, once put it this way: "If Atlantans could suck as hard as they blow, they'd have the Atlantic Ocean up there."

With that background, picture now the Atlanta regional headquarters of the American Civil Liberties Union (ACLU) and an independent-minded Chatham County Commission chairman named Joe Mahany. Former chairman Mahany is, among other things, a born-and-bred Savannah Irishman, and like many of our own who trace ancestry to the Auld Sod, he has a quick temper. Moreover, he is a Savannah chauvinist, proud of his community and the county whose government he headed, and not very receptive to damnations emanating from outside Chatham's borders, especially Atlanta.

Also picture such a one's reaction when a letter arrives one day conveying the ACLU's concern over the custom of opening county commission meetings with prayer—a custom Mahany and his governing board inherited, but against which they held no reservations, political or personal. Every member of the county's governing board was a God-fearing person, and no two were of the same religious persuasion. So, for that matter, is Savannah a God-fearing community; it's hard to find any neighborhood without a church.

When Mahany received the ACLU's letter, which it said was prompted by an objection from a citizen it deemed prudent not to identify, his Irish temper came zooming to the fore. The very idea, trying to pull that church-and-state business on him and his commission. Wherinell does the ACLU get off with that kind of stuff? He was angry, make no mistake, and if it had been a few years earlier, when politics wasn't as genteel (by comparison) as it is today, Mahany would've invited an ACLUer to come down and settle the matter with fisticuffs in downtown Johnson Square—any high noon of the ACLU's choosing.

Instead, Mahany shot off a reply, bluntly telling the ACLU person to keep his "Atlanta nose" out of Chatham County. There was a further exchange of correspondence, but the flap ceased and, to my knowledge, that ACLUer kept his Atlanta nose in Atlanta. Thus, the latest manifestation of the contention that "if Atlantans could suck as hard as they blow, they'd have the Atlantic Ocean up there."

Entrepreneur and Chauffeur. When the late Herschel V. Jenkins was publisher of the *Morning News–Evening Press*, during the years of the Great Depression and through late 1957, he preached to his employees the doctrine of hard work and frugality. "If you earn a dollar, put a dime in the bank" was his advice, and I first heard that admonition as a kid delivering the afternoon paper, when Mr. Jenkins frequently would attend the every-other-Friday mandatory meetings of the carriers. He was a good father-figure for all of us, and it may well be that we made it far into adulthood before appreciating Mr. Jenkins' interest in his boys.

Alonzo Ninons was one of us, a black carrier boy, obviously a little older than most of us because when we were in high school he was enrolled in Georgia State Industrial College, now known as Savannah State University. From a poor family, Alonzo was working his way through college. Not only did he earn money from his paper route, he also filled little jobs hither and yon, one of which was "doing" lawns, and publisher Jenkins' lawn happened to be one of them. Mr. Jenkins was impressed with a "colored boy" so early-on into the free-enterprise system. Alonzo was majoring in agriculture and was particularly interested in horticulture. No one knows for sure, but it's a good guess that when Alonzo opened Ninons' Florist business after graduation he got a financial boost from publisher Jenkins. And his business became a success. Alonzo was one of the very few black entrepreneurs in the florist business, and his clientele in the black community grew. (I should add that a few times I ordered flowers from Alonzo, out of pure friendship and for auld lang syne.)

After going into business, however, Alonzo Ninons never wavered in his allegiance to Herschel Jenkins, the white boss who had been his longtime booster. As Mr. Jenkins grew older, and his eyesight made driving difficult, Alonzo would leave his business and chauffeur the newspaper tycoon to places he wanted to go. Alonzo also mowed the small lawn on the Jenkins premises at Thirty-seventh and Lincoln streets. He always could find time to help Mr. Jenkins and his daughter, Victoria, in many ways. After the death of Mr. Jenkins, Alonzo was Miss Jenkins' stalwart support. He ran errands for her, drove her places, oversaw contractors she engaged to repair her home. He was, always, at the beck and call of "Miss Victoria," and he would have gone to China, if necessary, if she had asked him.

One day, long after her father had passed away, Miss Jenkins telephoned me, and in a tearful voice said, "Tom, I just wanted to tell you that Alonzo died yesterday. I've lost one of the best friends I've ever known, and I know he was your friend, too. Just wanted you to know." Alonzo Ninons was, indeed, my friend also. I never got a promotion at the newspaper that Alonzo didn't drop by to extend congratulations. He'd always say that he knew "Mister Jenkins would be proud of you, because you were one of his boys." Alonzo was one in a million, an exemplar of success in business, but mainly, an exemplar of loyalty.

The Girl on the Ledge. Harben Daniel, who came to Savannah in 1939 to open the city's second radio station, WSAV, liked for things to go just right. He forbade his announcers to bring outsiders into the control room, and for good reason—someone unfamiliar with the setup could accidentally hit a switch and throw the station off the air. He was suspicious of a certain announcer who worked the late shift, almost certain that the fellow was bringing his girlfriend into the studio after hours. So one night, after attending a movie with Meredith "Tommy" Thompson, his chief engineer, and their wives, he suggested they drop by the station and check. The studio was on the top floor of the ten-story Liberty Bank building at Bull and Broughton streets.

Upon exiting the elevator, Daniel and friends immediately sensed a strong odor of perfume. Aha, Daniel reasoned, we've caught him. Daniel and Thompson went straight to the control booth, only to find the announcer there alone. Apparently he had heard them approaching. Inside the booth, the perfume smell was even stronger, but no one else was present. Daniel noticed the window onto the precarious tenth-story ledge was partly raised, but he said nothing and promptly motioned Thompson that it was time to leave. Back in the elevator, Daniel and Thompson began to laugh. The curious ladies, who had stopped by the restroom, asked that they share their source of amusement. Still laughing, Daniel informed them that their hasty exit was necessary, lest "that poor girl on the ledge" either freeze or fall to the street below. If the announcer needed female company that desperately, who were they to interfere? A further touch of wit was added by one of the other announcers, as he would tell that story in later years: "The boss and Tommy left suddenly because they didn't want to get arrested, and charged with disturbing the piece."

How Old Was Everett? Commercial High School, which was closed down years ago after the other public high schools became comprehensive by absorbing commercial subjects into their curricula, fielded several good athletic teams. One of the stars in the 1950's was Everett Todd, a three-sport athlete and one of the hardest, steadiest, and most dedicated players ever coached by Murtagh Aloysius Spellman, who ultimately would become athletic director of the Savannah-Chatham County School System. Todd was a thorn in the side of all Commercial's rivals, and he became the most "investigated" player ever to don a uniform.

The Georgia High School Association, which governs and sets rules for competitive athletics in the state, stipulates that no athlete can be certified as eligible to compete for a school if he has reached the age of eighteen before a term begins. Todd was eighteen when he graduated, but he was seventeen as he began his senior year. Yet, when he was only fifteen, this gifted young athlete became the object of suspicion by coaches of all the teams Commercial High played. They simply suspected that he was too old to play for his school, and for good reason—Everett Todd matured early, and from the day he enrolled in Commercial he could have passed for twenty-one. He had broad shoulders, seasoned features, and a voice that sounded even more gruff than it does now because he was going through the changing-voice stage of life.

The coaches of rival teams, therefore, would challenge Todd's eligibility before they would play Commercial—not every coach every year, but every coach who hadn't previously challenged Todd's status, with the exception of one coach, who having challenged Todd the first year he played, came back each succeeding year for reassurance. Somehow, he couldn't believe that someone who looked as old as Todd did could be as young as Todd actually was. "It's like a game unto itself," Principal Arthur J. Funk said. "They come into my office and ask to look at Todd's record in our files. I pull his card and show it to them; moreover, I have stapled a copy of his birth certificate to the card to save them the trouble of checking with the health department."

That process of continuous checking and double-checking, Funk said, had caused Todd's file card to become worn and dirty from such frequent handling. "You know how I locate Todd's card?" Funk asked. "I just pull out the file drawer and look for the card with the dirtiest top edge. It stands out like a sore thumb. And of course, the stapled-on birth certificate makes Todd's location slightly thicker than the other cards'."

Everett Todd, who, off the playing field, was more a shy kid than an outgoing one, was unaffected by all the furor over his eligibility status. He never seemed to mind being called such things as "the old man" by kids on the opposing teams. He merely played, and won several trophies and other forms of recognition by scoring touchdowns, shooting baskets, and getting base hits. But one die-hard local coach, years later, remained unconvinced, saying, "I still believe Todd was too old to play."

Mallowmars. Nearly everyone has tasted and savored Mallowmars, those delicious chocolate-covered marshmallow cookies produced and marketed by Nabisco. They are a delectable treat. But because they are covered with chocolate, and chocolate melts easily in warm weather, Mallowmars are not sold in balmy Savannah the year around. Stores stock them during the cooler months. So Savannah has its own Mallowmars season.

For years, whenever the Mallowmars arrived, *News-Press* columnist Archie Whitfield became the first to know. Whitfield wrote the popular "City Beat" column, conveying to readers interesting tidbits of goings-on in Savannah, little items that otherwise wouldn't make print. Whitfield would get the tip-off on Mallowmars from George Thomas, first manager and later the owner of Smith Bros., a grocery store on Habersham Street catering mostly to Savannah's carriage trade. By some arrangement with the food brokers, Smith Bros. was always the first to receive a shipment. Thomas would call, and if Whitfield wasn't in the office, he would leave a message with me to pass along: "Tell Archie the Mallowmars are in." Archie dutifully would inform the readers, and a day or two later Thomas would drop off a case of Mallowmars, which Archie would share with fellow staff writers.

This story becomes more interesting when one realizes that readers often confused Archie Whitfield with me. Both of us wrote a column, with our pictures. Both of us were veterans of the newspaper staff. Both of us had gray hair (mine more so, but who can tell the difference from black-and-white mug shots, a half-column wide?). And we were close friends, often seen together in public (which we still are, in retirement, at least every Wednesday when the 1-2-3 Club meets for lunch). The story becomes more interesting still when one realizes that after I retired, and then Whitfield retired a couple of years later, George Thomas also retired from Smith Bros. and sold the business.

Now, with that background, picture a next-time-around married man—myself—some two years after Marjorie and I, two widowed souls who fell very much in love, took our vows. Whitfield was no longer on the paper's staff, thus he no longer wrote "City Beat," and Smith Bros. was under new management. The phone at our house rang, and Marjorie answered. I was in the living room with a neighbor who had stopped by. I could hear Marjorie say, "What!" and then, "OK, I'll tell him." Marjorie came back into the living room, a funny look on her face, and stood silent for a few seconds. Then she said, "That was some woman who said to tell you Mallowmars are back." Then, after another period of silence, Marjorie ventured: "Is that something I'm supposed to know to become a Savannahian?" There was also a slight implication that the message may have been some kind of signal—perhaps "the coast is clear."

Marjorie had been in Savannah only two years, having come home with me after our courtship and marriage in Florida. She didn't know anything about Savannah's Mallowmars season, although I'm certain sunny Florida also has one. I burst out laughing, and then explained the Mallowmars routine to my bride. I then called Archie Whitfield to relay that prime bit of intelligence on the chocolate-covered marshmallow cookies and told him the circumstances under which the information came to me. I don't believe he has stopped laughing yet.

Wings for Everyone. Not because it would embarrass him, but because it might embarrass three long-married ladies whose husbands may still harbor a tinge of jealousy, I shall call the principal of this story "Joe," and with assurance to anyone whose wife might have once dated some fellow named Joe that this Joe has an entirely different name. But this Joe, I want you to know, was one of Savannah's Casanovas of yesteryear.

Joe was a member of a socially prominent family, and he dated debutantes by the dozen, and maybe by the score. He was tall, handsome, witty, kind, considerate, and gallant—all a girl could ask for in a male companion. Thus, he charmed many. Also, he fell in love with most of them, and particularly the three mentioned earlier. It is significant that the three mentioned earlier were close friends and also roommates in college.

Joe was drafted into the Army during World War II, but didn't serve very long because the war ended shortly after he finished basic training. He returned to Savannah, got a job, and resumed his custom of dating pretty young ladies. About a year after returning to civilian life, Joe decided to reenlist in the military service, qualified for flight training, and became a fighter pilot in the Air Force, by then a separate branch of the armed forces. He was proud of winning his wings, and would remain a proud member of the Air Force for many years, finally retiring with the rank of colonel and with considerable air combat time in the two wars following the big one.

As a new pilot Joe would come home on short leaves, each time dating one of those certain three girls—one at a time, and on different leaves. Joe took off his wings and pinned them on each of those young ladies—one at a time, of course. Such a gift of wings, the insignia of a bona fide pilot, was in World War II days tantamount to an engagement ring. It is not known whether, at the time Joe unpinned wings from his breast pocket and pinned them on his date, he proposed marriage. After one of them told me this story, my impression is that it was a tacit sort of understanding.

It is strange that none of the three young ladies ever

mentioned to the others having Joe's wings, at least not for a few months. Not until one day, when the three were unpacking in their college dormitory room, one of them placed a picture of Joe on her dresser. The remaining two looked at each other, surprised, as their roommate also placed flyer's wings at the base of Joe's framed photograph. They then informed their room-mate that they too had Joe's picture—and Joe's wings. All three then compared notes and recounted how each had been pinned by Joe on one of his visits home. If ever there was a scenario of "aha, gotcha," it occurred then and there.

My understanding is that when Joe came home next time the girls' college had a spring break, he was spurned by all three when he telephoned to ask for a date. Each said she had another engagement. At another time one of them finally told him that all three now were wise to him, and he might as well find someone else to pin his wings on. Thus ended not a triangle, but a quadrangle that had been unbeknownst to three of the four sides. Joe later married a nice lady elsewhere, sired a family, completed his career as a flyer, and settled into a nice civilian job several states removed from Savannah, the hometown to which he has returned for visits only a few times. The three ladies, now well into their sixties, are still buddies, and at least one of them relishes telling her tale about Joe's wings, even in the presence of her husband and their two sons.

The 1-2-3 Club. The 1-2-3 Club is perhaps the loosest organization of males ever formed, and regarded by its members as Savannah's "most exclusive club." The title of the club is patterned after a much larger organization in St. Louis to which many prominent business and sports figures belong. Former players, managers, and executives of the professional sports teams in St. Louis are members, and the main topic of weekly discussions is, of course, sports. The title comes from the 1–3 P.M. hours the club meets for lunch—one to three.

Jim Bayens, a longtime member of the St. Louis Cardinals' baseball organization who served in many roles, from farm director to road secretary to scout, migrated to Savannah when the Cardinals bought the Savannah minor league franchise in 1987. With his experience in the organization, he was assigned to be the general manager of the local farm club. Jim one day invited four of his newfound friends in Savannah to lunch and broached the idea of getting a few guys together for lunch each Wednesday. The four were John Tidwell, Savannah's director of leisure services; Jerry Rogers, a radio station's general manager; retired Army Lieutenant General Donald "Rosie" Rosenblum; and myself, a soon-to-retire newspaper editor. We agreed, and the next week a fifth "member" came aboard, Andy Calhoun, a soon-to-retire banker. We settled on copying the St. Louis group's title, but because we would be lunching at 12:30 P.M. instead of one o'clock, we justified our title by using the first three digits of the half-past-twelve numbers.

Others came aboard: Archie Whitfield, a soon-to-retire newspaper columnist; Al Jennings, a just-retired radio executive; Charlie Brooks, a lawyer. That made eight members. Joining later were Kevin Rawls, a distributor of packaged peanuts, crackers, chips, and other snacks; Bucky Johnson, a newspaper advertising director; and Joe Shearouse, who succeeded Tidwell as head of leisure services after the latter left Savannah to manage the Cotton Bowl in Dallas. Tidwell is still welcome if he should happen to visit Savannah on a Wednesday. Kevin Rawls, our youngest associate, died at age thirty-six in 1995, succumbing to cancer of the pancreas, which came upon him suddenly. Rawls was an inspiration to us and to his many other friends, always the last one to sit down because nearly everyone in our restaurant would hail him as he approached the table. Our group sat together at his funeral, and Rosie Rosenblum delivered a moving eulogy in tribute to a popular young Savannahian.

The 1-2-3 Club has no officers, no dues, no by-laws, and only one rule: "No broads." Chauvinistic as that may seem, our wives approve, so long as we hold an annual Yuletide party and invite them. It's an irreverent group, each of its meetings taking the form of a roast as the participants hurl barbs at one another. The three main topics of discussion are sports, politics, and women, not necessarily in that order. We discuss women not in disrespect, but in admiration—particularly of some who may be dining in our restaurant. On sports, discussions settle on such questions as whether Thomson's pennant-winning home run, or Mazeroski's, to win the World Series, was the more spectacular in the annals of baseball. Calhoun is a Clemson fan, perhaps the South Carolina university's most ardent. Rosenblum touts The Citadel, his alma mater that he left to rise to three-star rank. Shearouse was one of the great track stars of Georgia. Brooks boosts Georgia Tech, his school. Jennings is as rabid a Florida fan as Calhoun is Clemson. Johnson, a South Carolina grad, sings the praises of the Gamecocks. Rogers is our resident expert on all sports; he's originally a New Yorker, reads several sports publications, memorizes statistics, and even knows horse-racing. Whitfield and I claim no alma mater, each of us having only passed through institutions of higher learning; he's for Georgia Tech and I like Georgia. Tidwell was an Auburn athlete, and the late Kevin brought the "War Eagle" cry back to the 1-2-3 after Tidwell left town. Sadly, the two, with such a mutual interest, never met.

On politics, the range is equally as broad. Brooks is our resident moderate-liberal, Rogers our flaming liberal, and the rest of us are conservative-to-moderate in varying degrees. Brooks is our only politician per se, having served as chairman of the Chatham County Commission and still a loyal Democrat, but with a few reservations.

But sports, politics, and women aside, the main thrust of the 1-2-3 Club is fun. Even differences over candidates and issues, players and teams, blondes and brunettes are aired jovially, and too often loudly. Others at lunch time, especially those regulars who sit near our reserved table, kibitz our debates and sometimes throw in a sideline remark. Those who don't know us gawk, and some shake their heads in disbelief—that adult males can seem so happy when they're together. Once a couple at a nearby table kept eyeing the 1-2-3 table, and as they left the lady stopped and remarked: "Just who are you? I have never seen gentlemen enjoying themselves so much as you." The couple hailed from Michigan, tourists who stopped to have lunch in the Historic District. We introduced ourselves, offered a one-minute capsule history of the 1-2-3 Club, and thanked them for noticing. Before leaving, the lady kissed each of us, and walked away laughing.

We call the club exclusive because our table, when all attend, cannot accommodate anyone else; even so, because not all attend every week, membership has been broadened to include Skip Jennings, a lawyer, and Bernie Cleary, a retired public-relations executive. But once, when in a fit of levity we decided to propose others for membership, every one was voted down—the governor, our two senators, the mayor, the Pope, and even Mother Teresa. The famed and good nun's name was advanced only in jest in the first place, but she too was voted down when one of the group reminded the rest: "No broads." All in fun, Mother Teresa. Indeed, two of our number are Roman Catholics, and to a man we love you and admire your good deeds.

I cannot apply *Only in Savannah*, the First Book's title, to Savannah's 1-2-3 Club, because there's another in St. Louis. But I seriously doubt if they have as much fun.

Ol' Man River ... and His Front

It would be only a matter of time, Savannahians reasoned, before Savannah would extend its river walk to the Radisson Hotel, on the eastern end of the downtown river front. The Radisson was a Johnny-come-lately to the banks of the Savannah River, built just east of Savannah Electric's office building. But there was no direct route for the hotel's guests to walk to the Rousakis Riverfront Plaza, with its restaurants, bars, boutiques, candy shops, and many other kinds of places appealing to tourists. The hotel was separated from the grand esplanade by a busy street as well as private property used by one of the two towboat companies serving the port. That, of course, didn't stop a flow of guests from the Radisson, but there was the inconvenience.

After only a couple of years of becoming established as the Radisson, the hotel's name changed to the Marriott. For reasons best known to the owners, a franchise arrangement with the latter worldwide hotel chain seemed preferable, so Marriott it now is, and forget Radisson. Not many months after the hotel's name changed, the city fathers and mothers (women serve on the council too) approved a riverwalk extension to the Marriott. The connection to the rest of the restored waterfront runs westward from the hotel, parallels the power company's parking lot, goes past the statue of the legendary Waving Girl to a sidewalk running behind the towboat company's offices and docks, and ultimately makes the hook-up with Rousakis Plaza. The distance from the Marriott is a quarter of a mile or so.

The construction entailed, of course, a temporary removal, and placement into storage, of the Waving Girl's statue, which has become a must-stop-and-snap-some-pictures for tour buses while the tour narrators explain that the late Florence Martus, spinster sister of the lighthouse keeper some eighteen miles downstream toward the Atlantic Ocean, lived with her brother, and on the widow's walk of the home they shared near the lighthouse she would wave at every ship entering the Savannah River channel. Every ship, understand, and not just a ship here and there, or now and then; and each ship's captain, aware of why she was waving, would blow his ship's whistle in salute to Miss Martus. The legend holds that Miss Martus kept hoping that her sailor boyfriend, who had promised to return and marry her, would be aboard one of those ships. Alas, the bounder never returned. It is said that the cause of the demise of Miss Martus was something other than a broken heart, but that she took a broken heart to her grave nevertheless.

Now, the Waving Girl's statue, sculpted by the famed Felix deWeldon, whose works include the well-known statue of the Marines in World War II raising the American flag atop Mount Surabachi on Iwo Jima, was bought and paid for by Savannah's Altrusa Club, a women's civic organization. The Altrusans raised the necessary $60,000 by soliciting donations from the public, the largest single gift being $5,000, and the smallest, $5. The Altrusans donated the statue to the city, to be placed on River Street, just east of the towboat company's property. Ships nowadays accord their whistle salute to the Waving Girl when they pass that point, the old lighthouse keeper's residence downstream having been razed. The Altrusans are understandably proud of their contribution of this visible memorial to their city. They bask in the glow of satisfaction that they truly have done something worthwhile. It is easy to understand, therefore, the Altrusans' chagrin when the city requested that they share in the expense of moving, storing, and then replacing the Waving Girl's statue, necessitated by the extension of the riverwalk to the Marriott. Once they gave the statue to the city, they felt, it became the city's responsibility, a contention I'm sure most Savannahians support.

So the Altrusa Club, whose membership is only about forty women strong, sent a formal rejection of the city's request to the city manager in a letter dated August 16, 1995. The letter reviewed how the statue came to be, and concluded with this firm, but cordial, turn-down: "We feel that we have done our part in providing this wonderful asset to our City, and we hope that you and our elected leaders will be able to provide for 'her' continual maintenance from the general fund, as 'she' has certainly been there for all of us to enjoy."

While some rightly will accuse the city of looking a gift-statue in the mouth, no one can say that the city hasn't kept beautiful and utilitarian the popular Rousakis Riverfront Plaza (named for John Rousakis, who was mayor when the plaza was completed to climax an urban renewal project that spanned his and two previous city administrations). The red brick esplanade is popular for promenaders. The first Saturday of each month, the owners of the River Street businesses cosponsor, through the Savannah Waterfront Association, a festival featuring band music and displays of wares along the plaza—one grand and glorious outdoor flea market, once a month. The Savannah Symphony Orchestra performs, under the city's auspices, several times a year, and listeners bring their folding chairs and picnic baskets, and fill every square foot of space in front of and behind the musicians. Every St. Patrick's Day (Savannah's major festival) activities along the waterfront begin a few days ahead of March 17th, and some revelers stay a day or two beyond. Paddle-wheeled excursion boats use the plaza as their base of operations. Small cruise-line boats come and go, tying up alongside the plaza. Ships from our Navy as well as foreign countries make occasional visits. The esplanade attracts skateboarders and roller-blade skaters, sort of a hazard to promenaders, but how can you stop the kids from enjoying themselves? And, of course, every night on River Street is a festival unto itself. It's popular with revelers, and some have likened it to Bourbon Street in New Orleans. It's not quite that, but somewhat similar.

The coming of the Marriott, née Radisson, complemented River Street immensely. The older large hotel is the Hyatt Regency, locally owned and built by entrepreneurs Merritt Dixon and Mitchell Dunn. It has been host to many conventions and is popular among locals for banquets, cotillions, and meetings. The Hyatt bridges River Street, so its main restaurant, the Windows, affords diners a magnificent view of the Savannah River and the oceangoing ships moving upstream and downstream. Besides the two large hotels, several smaller intimate inns now overlook River Street, utilizing the upper floors of the old cotton-warehouse buildings, the lower levels of which accommodate the many shops and eating and drinking places for which Savannah's riverfront has become noted.

And one of cobblestone-paved River Street's fascinations, especially to visitors, is the railroad track running down its center. Visitors at first think the track is obsolete, a remnant from older times. They register surprise upon learning that it's an active track for freight trains hauling cars from docks on the upper end of the seaport to docks on the lower end. Now and then the train must pause until the owner of a double-parked car blocking the track returns to move his vehicle. Providentially the owner usually is somewhere nearby and makes a beeline to his car upon spotting the approaching train. But, out of custom and habit, the engineers are a patient lot. They'll wait for a reasonable time before summoning a tow truck. One of the railroad engines, incidentally, is equipped with a sound system upon which tapes of Dixieland music are played as the train moves along River Street. The music not only is enjoyable, adding a touch of the old South, but it also sounds a loud warning that the train is coming, and if your car's blocking the track, you'd better hustle. You see, there's more to River Street than the Waving Girl.

Greening the River

Picot Floyd was one of Savannah's most interesting public figures, and in retrospect he had to be interesting because of his parents, Marmaduke and Julia Floyd, who were interesting people. Mr. Floyd was a civil engineer with a flair for history and preservation; Mrs. Floyd was a writer with a flair for history, preservation, and detailed research. The Floyds started a museum in a historic tavern site on East Broad Street, just south of Bay Street, and it became a meeting place for various groups interested in history and culture. They called it the Pirates' House, and ultimately it became a restaurant under the same name, of world renown, perhaps the best known of Savannah's many eating places, even more so than Mrs. Wilkes' Boarding House.

The Floyds's son, Picot, was their only offspring, although each had children by previous marriages. Together the Floyds instilled into Picot a deep sense of history, so it was no surprise that he, after a stint as a Coast Guard officer during the Korean War, would become the first executive director of the Historic Savannah Foundation, the privately funded organization that has been the group most responsible for the restoration of Savannah's famed Historic District. But Picot gravitated into public administration, and from 1966 to 1972 was the city manager of his native Savannah.

Picot's first job in public administration, in the early 1960's, was that of Savannah's assistant city manager; and one of his early assignments from City Manager John Hall was to go through the long-stored documents, artifacts, and memorabilia in the basement of City Hall and to sort out those holding any historical significance. He found many past references to St. Patrick's Day, and he also noted that most of the documents—

canceled bonds, proclamations, resolutions, etc.—were adorned with green-colored illustrations and fancy borders—Irish green, of course. Then one day, as another St. Patrick's celebration was approaching, a citizen contacted City Hall with a suggestion that the Savannah River be dyed Irish-green for the occasion.

That intrigued Picot Floyd. He had been seeing all that green on the old documents, and now here was a suggestion for a river of green. In the city manager's office, which overlooked the Savannah River from the fourth floor, Floyd asked his boss to take a look at the river, and then passed along the suggestion of dyeing it green. Hall may or may not have thought much of the idea, but he thought very little of spending taxpayers' money to try such an experiment—only, he said, if the river dyeing was funded privately. Also, Hall, an engineer, cautioned, it would be a difficult task to achieve because the river's currents were so strong they'd probably obliterate any infusion of green dye. Floyd was persistent, so Hall finally relented and told him to work up a proposal for him to review. (City managers never act without first having a proposal; they call that procedure "completed staff work.")

Floyd took the project on and obtained calculated opinions from some local engineers and other experts. His proposal was to use an oily green dye that would float on the river's surface, rather than a soluble dye the swift water would absorb and dissipate quickly. Hall took the proposal to City Council, which approved it with the proviso that the project not entail any city funds. Floyd then recruited some outside help to raise money from private sources. He also recruited many boat owners, who were intrigued with the idea and happy to be of service in spreading the dye. The plan was to dye the river on March 16, the Eve of St. Patrick.

Greening the River

Came the day, and came the volunteer flotilla equipped now with barrels of the green dye. The number of boats on the river rivaled in size the motley fleet that evacuated the British soldiers from the beaches of Dunkirk in the early days of World War II. Yachts, skiffs, bateaux, shrimp boats, nearly every kind of craft except canoes, which would have been too light in such a swift stream. At about 4 P.M. the flotilla boats poised about a half-mile upstream from City Hall, Floyd gave the signal, and the dyeing began as the boats drifted downstream, volunteers aboard pouring the dye from barrels onto the water's surface. Unfortunately the wind began to blow harder than it usually does. A few whitecaps formed, the breadth of the river. The dye, instead of spreading evenly, formed into streaks of green. It wasn't entirely, not by a long shot, as Floyd had envisioned.

So, did the Savannah River really get dyed green that windy day in mid-March? Yes and no. It was green, all right, but not the same as, say, the Danube, which in reality is more green than its Strauss-waltz-fabled blue; I've seen it. There was not what you might call a patina, yet the streaks of dye made it green enough to satisfy some onlookers. And the onlookers were many—thousands lining the right (south) bank of the river, many cheering lustily as the green sheen began to materialize. Many of the spectators, in true St. Patrick's Day fashion (Savannah style), and to counter the chilling effect from the wind, had brought along bottles of alcoholic refreshment. They toasted the grand experiment, several times. Some began to sing a parody of the novelty song of the 1930's, "A-tisket, A-tasket." They chimed in: "Was it green? Yes, yes, yes-yes." Some had come to the riverbank earlier than others and had begun to toast the experiment with a head start; so frankly, Miss Scarlett, they didn't seem to give a damn whether the river was green or sky-blue-purple. They simply enjoyed the afternoon.

This may have been the key event—ah, the *coup de grâce*—to put Savannah "on the map" with its St. Patrick's festival, which had been getting more and more nationwide publicity by the year. The news services came down to cover the greening project, which also made national television. Those who may not have known about Savannah finally did, thanks to the perseverance and creativity of Picot Floyd.

And to answer the question whether, scout's honor, the Savannah River turned green, *Morning News* reporter Archie Whitfield went straight to Mayor Malcolm Maclean, who had watched the operation from a second-floor window of City Hall. Maclean, with Whitfield at his elbow, said, in his most official voice, the way the Pope might deliver an encyclical: "I hereby declare and proclaim, as mayor of Savannah, that the Savannah River is green."

The Mayor of Yamacraw

My transformation from managing editor of the *Savannah Morning News* to assistant city manager of the City of Savannah (a post I would hold for five years before returning to newspapering) was so abrupt that it made my head swim. The year was 1969, and I should have been on cloud nine, running the morning paper's newsroom after having been managing editor of the *Evening Press,* the smaller of the jointly owned dailies. It was a career high in journalism, becoming M.E. of the big paper. But alas, the Augusta-based corporation that owned our papers and others fell into an ownership dispute that landed in court, and the local papers fell into somewhat of a holding pattern, with executives not knowing whether to straddle the fence or jump to one side or the other. For the first time in my life I felt disenchantment with the newspaper business, in which I had started as a route carrier in 1935.

Curtis Lewis, who was then mayor and one of Savannah's wealthiest entrepreneurs, was branching out from his Ford automobile dealership, planning to open the city's third television and radio operation, which became WJCL. I had spent eighteen months in TV as WSAV's first news director (1956–1957) and discussed with Curtis Lewis the possibility of joining his new venture. A day or two after our conversation, a call came from City Manager Picot Floyd: "Curtis tells me you're unhappy where you are. I have an opening. How'd you like to be my assistant city manager?" It was that abrupt, and while I knew little of the inner workings of municipal government, longtime friend Picot (one of our reporters a few years earlier) ventured that managerial skills were transferable, and except for the larger scope of city government, that there wasn't much difference between running a newsroom and running a city. A day or two later we discussed terms. I resigned my editorship and headed toward a working environment in which I would encounter all kinds of people and situations, some even more interesting than news writers encounter. Especially, people!

One of these people was Mrs. Susie Gardner, a black lady in her sixties (give or take), whom my newfound colleagues in City Hall knew as "the Mayor of Yamacraw." Yamacraw was the name of the Indian tribe General Oglethorpe found here when he established the Colony of Georgia hard by the Savannah River in 1733. Yamacraw Village is the name of a public housing project on Savannah's westside, situated generally on the site where the Yamacraw Indians lived. "Miss Susie," as people affectionately called her, was a charter resident of the project built in the 1940's—Savannah's first venture into slum clearance. Miss Susie not only lived in the project, she also was born and reared in the Yamacraw section before anyone ever thought of slum clearance. Since about the 1920's, Yamacraw had been a neighborhood of black families; earlier its population had been a mix of many poor-white Irish, many poor blacks, and a few Jewish families. My father was born to an Irish family in 1897, in Yamacraw, in a house where the Greyhound bus station now stands.

Susie Gardner, as a charter resident, gradually assumed the role of Yamacraw Village's elder stateswoman and citizen-advocate. The other residents, except for those much younger and those who had come actively to the fore during the racial revolution, looked up to Mrs. Gardner. They came to her seeking mediation whenever they had grievances with the Savannah Housing Authority. She helped those who earned enough to fill out their income tax returns. She sat all night with sick neighbors and contacted social agencies for those needing assistance. She was everything from counselor to midwife. They (save for the younger ones) loved her dearly.

Mrs. Gardner was large of stature. She had broad shoulders, a large bosom, and a bellowing voice of only two volumes, loud and silent. Had she been a sailor, she could have stood on the deck of a destroyer, in a gale, and been heard on the bridge of an aircraft carrier a mile away, without any amplification. She also was a lay-preacher in her church, and her living room bore testimony to her religious devotion—several Bibles, a picture of Jesus, a crucifix (she wasn't Catholic or Anglican), copies of *Guideposts*, and religious tracts. She believed in God, no question.

But in her assumed role as citizen-advocate for Yamacraw, Mrs. Gardner could be so positive, and so piercingly vociferous, that someone who didn't know her would conclude that she was Lucifer-incarnate. She never spoke softly, and figuratively carried a big stick. I came to know her, in line of duty, when I would have preferred she swing a real stick, something I could dodge, rather than fire those verbal slings and arrows, which I couldn't dodge. Trucks speeding through Yamacraw, headed toward an industrial area just west of the housing project and across a canal, had become the big issue over which Mrs. Gardner took her neighborhood's grievance to City Hall.

I was assigned by Mayor Lewis and City Manager Floyd to "work something out" after she appeared before City Council to air her grievance. At that council meeting she stepped to the microphone, which of course she didn't need. For about fifteen minutes Mrs. Gardner berated the elected mayor and aldermen for allowing big trucks to speed through Yamacraw Village, endangering children at play, especially those children who attended kindergarten in the community house and who had to cross the trucks' route in going to the playground. Those trucks, she admonished, had to be stopped immediately. Mayor Lewis was aghast at his first encounter with Mrs. Gardner and was surprised that the problem she had outlined existed. "We'll work something out," he assured her, and thanked her for coming.

"I can't leave here until we pray over this matter," Mrs. Gardner shouted, and then commanded (it was a command, believe me) everyone to "bow your heads." As they did, she opened a prayer that ran about five minutes with a boisterous "Our Heavenly Father."

"Working something out" proved to be not so simple a task as I envisioned. Next day, and very early, I was in Mrs. Gardner's living room, asking her to walk the area with me and to point out, on site, the nature of the problem. At first she wouldn't hear of it. "I already told you what the problem is. Fix it!" she roared within the confines of her little apartment. At that moment, looking through her apartment's window toward the bus station, I said to her, "My father was born right there where the bus station is."

That sentence worked magic. "Do you mean that nice lady who sold goat's milk, *that* Mrs. Coffey, was your grandmother?" she asked. It was my first knowledge that Dad's mother ever sold goat's milk (and he later said he didn't remember that), but I replied "yes" in a hurry. "Child, come over here and let me give you a big hug," she commanded, still at full volume. I did, and hugged her back, after which she donned a wrap, and away we went to walk the problem area.

Mrs. Gardner and I became fast friends. She didn't exactly remember my grandmother, but she had heard her mother talk about "Mrs. Coffey's goat's milk." And from then on, whenever she called City Hall with any kind of grievance, she would ask for me; and her first words to me on the telephone were "Is this my Yamacraw boy?" I was forty-eight years of age then, and my only intimate knowledge of Yamacraw had come from tales my father spun about the old days, but no one ever became a Yamacraw boy any faster than I did.

Ultimately, after Malcolm Smith, the city's traffic engineer, devised an alternate route for the trucks, the first problem I encountered with Mrs. Gardner became solved. From then until I left city government to return to the *Morning News* in 1974, she and I worked out many problems, including curing the residents of strewing soiled disposable baby diapers along the curbs and gutters rather than depositing them in the trash Dumpsters.

Now, if you're wondering why the younger Yamacraw residents didn't accept Susie Gardner as their "mayor," she provided the answer: "These young people ain't got no manners. All they think about is devilment and theirselfs. They the ones bringing dope into this project. They the ones who shoot each other, and steal from the old folks. They just plain don't listen to me, or nobody else. I can control their mamas and daddies, but they beyond hope." A classic exemplification of "the old order changeth"—and this time, for the worse. Indeed, a sad reflection on the times.

When Susie Gardner died in the 1980's, just a couple of years younger than my father, who would live beyond the age of ninety-five, I asked the city editor to allow me to write her obituary. A wonderful woman, and a dear friend to this Johnny-come-lately Yamacraw boy. I wrote the obit. Tearfully.

The Black and White of It

In early May 1996 an invitation came to attend the opening exhibition of the Ralph Mark Gilbert Memorial Center on Martin Luther King, Jr., Boulevard. I was intrigued by the illustration on the cover of the invitation—a reproduction of a vintage photograph I had used to illustrate an earlier column reminiscing about West Broad Street. West Broad is the street Savannah renamed in honor of Dr. King, the martyred civil rights leader. The picture was snapped many years ago by the late Frank Littlefield; his daughter, Martha Littlefield Summerell, had shared it with me as a curiosity item. Later Westley W. Law, Savannah's best-known black historian, obtained Mrs. Summerell's permission to include the photo among the West Broad memorabilia that he was collecting for future display.

Quite a picture. It was taken in the 1920's with a Brownie camera when Littlefield was in his twenties. It shows the aftermath of a collision between two open-air taxicabs, hard by the old Central of Georgia Railroad station, a gawking crowd of the curious, a number of West Broad landmarks in the background, and several means of transportation—cars, bicycles, streetcars, horse-drawn wagons. All this in one snapshot. And somehow it depicted so graphically the bustling West Broad of a bygone era. This photo became the theme of the exhibit inside the old Guaranty Life Insurance building, where the Gilbert Memorial, honoring an esteemed black clergyman and civic and cultural leader, was taking shape as a project of the black community.

I responded, of course, to the invitation, and for two reasons. First, I hold good memories of the old West Broad because my first paper route was along that street. Second, I was part of the show, one of several reminiscing Savannahians recorded on a

194

continuous-play videotape made in the Savannah College of Art and Design's television studio several weeks before the Gilbert Center opened. Retired Georgia appellate Judge H. Sol Clark and I are the only white persons on that tape; and, of course, Judge Clark also attended the opening.

What impressed me about that opening on a Sunday afternoon was that Judge Clark and I were not the only white people present. The attendees included an impressive mix of the races—I'd guess about fifty-fifty. For the better part of two hours blacks and white strolled through the displays of pictures from a bygone era, when West Broad was recognized as the Negro population's street, yet the white population never hesitated out of fear to go there. It was, make no mistake, Savannah's Jim Crow era, when blacks without question were second-class citizens who voted only if they could afford to pay poll taxes and whose children attended inferior schools deemed by the powers-that-be, who knew better, to be "separate but equal." But in those days little animus between the races prevailed. They lived in a peaceful coexistence, a condition that lasted until the racial revolution of the 1960's came in the wake of the *Brown v. Board of Education* decision by the Supreme Court. Halcyon days, those; a part of the hundred-year hiatus between emancipation and desegregation.

I learned much about black people in those days, mainly because most of my subscribers on that paper route were Negroes, all of whom treated me kindly. I was under strict parental direction never to use the word "nigger," and in retrospect I believe I was among the very few whites to address blacks by the courtesy titles of Mr., Mrs., or Miss (there was no Ms. in those days, although Mrs. came out "Mizz"), adhering to an admonition laid down by my grandmother in Walthourville,

Georgia, one day after she had heard me call one of her black adult friends by her first name.

So it was pleasing to see so many whites at that grand opening, and to realize that they too held fond memories of West Broad Street, now renamed for Dr. King, and its people. It fortified the answer I have given whenever asked by visitors how blacks and whites "get along" in Savannah—"better than in most places." Savannah survived the racial revolution much better than many cities in both the North and the South, the civil-rights demonstrations seldom got out of hand, and then-Mayor Malcolm Maclean sacrificed his political future in order to begin according a fair shake to citizens of color.

In recent years blacks have cracked the racial barrier on all fronts. They serve on all the public bodies and on judicial benches, and some have won election citywide as well as in political districts where blacks form a majority. They serve as principals of schools in white neighborhoods. They hold high rank on the police and fire departments. They live in neighborhoods that for years were lily white. Even so, Savannah still has some all-white and all-black sections. For example, I doubt that white folks will ever move into the Ticklegizzard section on Savannah's westside, and you can count on your fingers the blacks who live in Ardsley Park or other sections where mostly whites live. Also, at many mixed gatherings blacks will walk in and sit together rather than intersperse themselves. Savannah State University, one of Georgia's traditionally black institutions of higher learning, admits white students, but campus dominance remains in black hands.

The election of Floyd Adams as Savannah's mayor attests better than anything else to the lowering of the barriers. Adams won his election citywide, just as he won an alderman-at-large post citywide four years before deciding to run for the top municipal office. As recounted elsewhere in this book, Adams declared at his inauguration that he intended to be the mayor of all Savannahians as he condemned constant references from the outside to his becoming "Savannah's first black mayor." Early on in his administration, just days after he had proclaimed Black Heritage Month in Savannah, Adams attended by invitation the annual Confederate Memorial Day observance in Laurel Grove Cemetery, and made a stirring speech according recognition to anyone and everyone's heritage. "By invitation" is the key phrase here—the invitation came from the Sons of the Confederate Veterans and the United Daughters of the Confederacy. Also, he was accorded a standing ovation when he delivered his State of the City address to the mostly white Rotary Club of Savannah, which for years has invited the city's political leader to speak annually on that subject.

Adams, by a vote of the people, has emerged as Savannah's top black leader, joining a roll of leaders who have included, among many others, Judge and Mrs. Eugene Gadsden (he, now retired from the Superior Court bench; and she, a past chairman of the Savannah Airport Commission); Mrs. Esther Garrison, an educator and school board member; Sol Johnson, a newspaper publisher whose daughter Willa succeeded him as head of the black-oriented *Savannah Tribune*; Robert Gadsden, the judge's late father and an educator; the aforementioned Dr. Ralph Mark Gilbert, for years pastor of First African Baptist Church, Savannah's oldest black Baptist congregation; lawyer Roy Allen, a former legislator who switched from the Democratic to the Republican party, and was one of the few blacks in the United States to speak up for former Savannahian Clarence Thomas during those hectic hearings before the confirmation of

Thomas as only the second black to ascend to the Supreme Court bench; Bowles C. Ford, Savannah's first black alderman since Reconstruction; Lester B. Johnson III, a member of the city's legal staff, who also went to bat for Justice Thomas; a number of physicians, including Dr. Wesley Ball, who became Candler Hospital's chief of staff; and, of course, the aforementioned W. W. Law, who stood up for civil rights before many knew what "civil rights" meant.

Savannah still has racial problems, but they pale by comparison with what they once were. The daily press now heavily focuses more attention on the black community than it ever did in the past. The *Morning News* explores poverty—still a pressing problem—and black-on-black crime, which remains a blight on a race deserving much better. Race-wise, Savannah is by no means out of the woods, and "nigger" has not disappeared from the lexicon of many Savannah whites. As a matter of fact, many blacks accord that term to one another—sadly, in utter contempt, and with seemingly deeper acrimony than emanates from whites, except of course such diehards as the few remaining Ku Klux Klansmen, the skinheads, and assorted other rednecks. But show me any other city, North or South, Midwest or West Coast, where such problems have disappeared. Indeed, I'll show you many that are much worse.

Couldn't Be Bribed

It's risky business, trying to bribe a judge. But then, my friend didn't really regard what he tried as a bribe attempt. That, I suppose, was because gamblers look at things differently. To them gambling isn't a sin or just plain wrong in the first place. They view gambling as an exercise in American freedom—you pays yer money and you takes yer chances, as the saying goes. No one, they insist, ever is forced to gamble; professional gamblers draw enough suckers without having to resort to proselytizing. And never mind that gambling (save for the now-legalized state lottery) is against the law. To them, it's a lousy law, encroaching upon individual rights, same as the Prohibition amendment (No. XVIII, repealed by No. XXI).

My friend shall remain unnamed here, and so will the judge he approached in the spirit of what he (my friend) never intended as a bribe attempt. The story is just as interesting without the names. I have never gambled with this friend; our relationship began and continues through other mutual interests. I should add that he has never attempted even to lure me into a bet, either on such sports events as the Kentucky Derby or in the numbers game, which once flourished in Savannah under the name of bolita, a version of the Cuban lottery.

In the days of political bossism bolita ran rampant. Some of the political and police officials (the ones who held the most sway over how things went) tolerated it, although from time to time, just for appearances' sake, the cops would crack down on bolita runners and on the places where the winning numbers were drawn daily, and the crackdowns would last about a week or so. The heat always cooled quickly, usually when the newspapers began to regard gambling raids as inside-pages news.

Illegal gambling, a state offense, was punishable by stiff fines and/or jail terms up to a year. The tribunal in which stiff sentences were imposed was State Court, which has jurisdiction over misdemeanors, felony-case jurisdiction being reserved for Superior Court. But for a case to reach State Court, it first had to be heard in Recorder's Court, sometimes called Police Court. By any name, that court hears most cases soon after arrest, and determines whether arrest was made properly, and whether police actually have sufficient evidence to remand the case to a higher tribunal. In some cases, felonies excepted, the judge of Recorder's Court may assume jurisdiction and impose a penalty himself—examples: cases of public drunkenness, simple assault, or traffic violations. A wise judge in that court is a modern-day Solomon, tempering justice with mercy in each individual case, often taking jurisdiction to hold down the clutter of cases on the dockets of higher courts. A Recorder's Court judge may, if he chooses, assume jurisdiction in gambling cases, imposing fines up to $200, or thirty-day jail terms. A gambling conviction in State Court results in a fine up to $1,000 and/or a year in jail.

Consider, then, the economics of gambling bosses paying fines of $100 or $200 for their bolita runners rather than $1,000 fines in a higher court, and also risking the loss from the street of a runner, who has regular bettor-customers, during a year's stay behind bars. Over time that's a great saving of money. And when my friend approached the judge, it was because that particular judge had been assigning all bolita cases to State Court. The judge was conscientiously opposed to gambling and felt that accused violators, if guilty, should draw the maximum penalty.

It was a friendly session my friend had with the judge— friendly because the two had grown up together, and in their youth engaged in competitive athletics. They were on a first-name basis, and sometimes would find themselves and their wives in the same social setting. My friend, incidentally, had never been hauled up on a gambling charge; if there's one thing he never was, it was careless.

He walked that day into the judge's chambers, they exchanged howdydos, and settled into small talk. The judge, observant as he was, complimented his caller on the alligator shoes he was wearing. "Must be expensive," he mused. His caller affirmed that they were expensive, then told the judge that he too could afford alligator shoes, or other such luxuries. Indeed, he continued, the judge could pick up an extra two hundred or three hundred dollars a week, and with no extra effort on his part.

The judge became curious as to how such a windfall could bless him, and his caller simply shrugged and said that all the judge would have to do would be to perform his job as usual, though alter his course a tad by assuming jurisdiction in run-of-the-mill bolita cases coming before him. Just fine 'em on the spot instead of sending them to a higher court. Nothing illegal, the caller assured him; after all, the law granted the judge the authority to assume jurisdiction in certain misdemeanor cases. But the caller continued, "I don't suppose you'd be interested. Or would you?" Words to that effect.

The judge, looking across his desk at his caller, without hesitation said no, he really wouldn't be interested. The caller said that, really, it meant nothing to him personally, that he merely had overheard some of the goodfellas say they wished the judge would do that, and he just knew that if the judge were interested the goodfellas surely would be grateful in a material way. The caller left after a handshake with the judge, and the latter continued as before—sending all gambling cases higher.

Couldn't Be Bribed

Telling me about that encounter, years later, my friend said he was still scratching his head and wondering why the judge had turned down such a good opportunity, especially when all he had suggested was that the judge "do his job." "Hell," he said, "I wasn't asking him to turn anyone loose, or show any kind of favoritism to a gambler who was stupid enough to get caught."

As stated earlier, real gamblers conscientiously see nothing wrong in gambling, yet they know that the law views it differently, so they simply take their risks, which in itself is a gamble. As for approaching the judge, my friend didn't consider what he proposed to be a bribe attempt, but merely a business proposition in which he was a disinterested party anyway, having only overheard the lamentations of the goodfellas.

A year or so after my friend related this story, I asked the judge, who by then was retired, if he recalled the dialogue with my friend. He did indeed, he said. Well, I pressed, why didn't he make a charge against his caller? The judge replied that he knew his caller so well (from boyhood, remember?), and knew his philosophy on gambling, that he also knew his caller never considered his proposition to be a bribe attempt, but merely a business matter. Besides, since only the two of them had been present, it would have been difficult to prove. Also, the judge reasoned, his turning down the offer sent a clear message that he would not deviate from his policy in the hearing of bolita cases. No one ever came back, he said, to increase the amount contained in the original offer. Clearly they got the message.

All Under One Roof

Only a surface parking lot now occupies the property where Bo Peep's stood. Bo Peep's was basically a pool hall, opening onto Congress Street about midway down the block between Bull and Drayton streets. Leaving Bo Peep's, one would face directly toward the south outer wall of Christ Church, an imposing and beautiful structure standing on the very site where the first Anglican congregation put down roots as the Colony of Georgia began to take shape in the winter of 1733. Once pastored by the famed John Wesley, it is the mother church of the Episcopal Diocese of Georgia.

The proximity of the church to Bo Peep's always struck me as providentially convenient. Someone emerging from Bo Peep's might have succumbed to several opportunities to sin while inside the place, therefore any such soul harboring penitential feelings had only to step a few feet across the street, enter Christ Church, kneel in one of the pews, and beg the Good Lord's forgiveness. I sadly report, however, that not once during my acquaintanceship with Bo Peep's did I ever see anyone emerge from there and go into Christ Church. Still, there may have been some.

I was never a gambler in my youth, save for a friendly poker game now and then, and wouldn't be one now had not the voters of Georgia approved the institution of a state lottery. Now I spend a dollar a week playing Lotto, always betting the same number, figuring that one of these days it is bound to come up. Had I been a gambler in my youth, I'd have spent even more time than I did in Bo Peep's, which was the ideal place to yield to the temptation. Not only did friend Wolf Silver (may his kind soul rest in peace) own and operate Bo Peep's, he also maintained a counter where one could bet on anything, ranging from the outcome of sports events to, I would imagine, whether the sun would shine tomorrow.

In order to understand how the amiable Mr. Silver could maintain openly a center of gambling, one must also understand Savannah of the period preceding the institution of political reform in the mid-1950's. Although gambling was illegal in Georgia (still is, unless you play the state lottery; and how's that for a double standard), Savannah's officialdom and its populace tolerated it. Who really cared whether someone in Savannah wanted to bet on the Kentucky Derby? After all, people at Churchill Downs were betting on it, so why be so picky over locale? Also, gambling was a debatable moral issue; some said it was sinful and others held differently. Mr. Silver accommodated those who held differently, and it is interesting that the good Christian communicants of Christ Church never complained of gambling going on in a place not more than forty feet from their house of worship.

Bo Peep's, however, was more than just a place to gamble. It was a self-contained place of interlocking subplaces offering all kinds of personal pleasures, and Mr. Silver reigned as lord and master over them all. Let me describe the layout that covered the eastern end of the block on whose western corner stood the Hotel Savannah, later the Manger Hotel, and, still standing, now the AmeriBank.

Walking east on Congress, just past the hotel, you would first come to a magazine stand that Mr. Silver owned but leased out. On sale were any and all kinds of magazines, newspapers, paperback books, and, of course, *The Sporting News*. Girly books were among the magazines sold, but not as explicit as this era's *Playboy*, *Penthouse*, and *Hustler*. From under the counter, though, one could buy books and magazines that would make many of today's Sunday-school by comparison. This was the first stop along Bo Peep's road to personal pleasures.

The very next front door was the main entrance to Bo Peep's, and the food served across the long lunch counter running perpendicular to Congress Street was magnificent. The hot roast beef sandwich was one of the specialties, the absolute best in town. One also could get a quick lunch with three or four entrée choices daily, a succulent beef stew, or a hamburger nearly rivaling in taste the ones served up by the Crystal Beer Parlor, not many blocks away.

Just beyond the lunch counter were the pool tables, and seldom was a table idle. Pool playing was at its peak during lunch hour, with standby players lined up waiting their turn. A lot of gambling took place around the pool tables—private side bets and betting between players. The three or four Negroes who racked the pool balls did well on tips, and at least two of them sold tickets on the daily bolita games—bolita being a version of the Cuban lottery, daily winning payoffs based upon the middle three digits in the total sales on the New York Stock Exchange. I do not know whether Wolf Silver took a percentage of what his black employees received for selling numbers, but Silver had his own gambling section. It was located along a wall just beyond the pool tables, and operated by Johnny Ware, and no nicer fellow would anyone ever meet. Mr. Ware (may his soul rest in eternal peace) "looked like a lawyer," customers would say, and he would jokingly tell bettors that his son, a Roman Catholic priest, prayed daily for his customers to be winners. On the wall behind Mr. Ware was a huge board on which the pairings in sports events were posted, and inning-by-inning scores were chalked in as they came in on the Western Union ticker.

At the end of the lunch counter a door opened into a bar, where beer and mixed drinks were available, and never mind that mixed drinks were illegal in Georgia. The bar had another enticement besides spirits and malt beverages—prostitutes who sat on some of the bar stools awaiting business opportunities, which materialized many times over the course of a day. But then, where would prostitutes, once they had obtained a pickup, go to complete their assignations? Ah, that was another feature of Bo Peep's, because on the far wall of the bar was another door leading into the Victory Hotel, which fronted onto Drayton Street at the corner of Congress. The hotel's registration desk was situated just inside that doorway from the bar. Usually, I am told, a prostitute's customer didn't have to register because the lady he had just paired up with already had a room upstairs.

So you can see that Bo Peep's, from the entrance of that magazine stand to the hotel's exit onto Drayton Street, had the complete answer for any traveling salesman, any seaman in port, any casual visitor who harbored a yen for a grand night on the town, not to mention locals who preferred not to wait until nightfall. And while I was rather familiar with Bo Peep's, and particularly enjoyed his quick lunches, it took a visiting scribe, in days when I was writing sports, to point out to me what a self-contained palace of pleasure Savannah really had. That sportswriter, now gone to his reward, was in town to cover the South Atlantic League's all-star baseball game that day in the 1950's, when he arrived in the pressbox an inning late and asked me to brief him on the game's progress so far. I asked him why he was late, and he replied, "Bo Peep's," with a smile on his face.

"You know, Tom, you've got in Savannah a great place, the

best of its kind in the whole league. In Bo Peep's you can buy a girly magazine, eat a delicious sandwich, play a few games of pool, lay a bet, buy a couple of drinks, pick up a broad, go upstairs, get laid . . . and without getting your feet wet. Wow!"

That was Bo Peep's, and some years later, after Mr. Silver had departed this life and the whole property—magazine stand, pool parlor, hotel, and all—was being razed to make way for a parking lot, the building collapsed midway through the razing process. The building's collapse created a great story for one of my reporters and a photographer to cover just before the deadline of the *Savannah Evening Press*, when I was city editor. Next day I pulled a tear sheet—story and graphic pictures of the flattened debris—and mailed it to that sportswriter. A few days later came his terse acknowledgment of my advisory: "Savannah will never be the same. Hope they got the girls out safely."

Some Slips in Type

The reading public, as well as professional newspersons, delight in spotting typographical errors and other kinds of slips in the written word sold for public consumption. The public likely finds more enjoyment than the professionals, the latter of whom are selective in their enjoyment—they laugh at slips in other writers' work rather than their own. Some writers take it downright personally whenever it happens to them. For example, a former columnist for the *Savannah Evening Press*, back in the 1960's, actually accused a Linotype operator of sabotaging him with an innocent typographical error that brought mirth to everyone else who read it. Beryl Sellers, the columnist, finally calmed down when the typesetter convinced him that it was just an accident. Sellers, in fact, laughed at it himself after consulting with the typesetter. But before then, Sellers was fit to be tied when the error came to his attention. Sellers wrote a local-page column titled "Savannah Vignette," one of those around-town pieces that many newspapers run—strictly a this-and-that column relating everything from anecdotes Sellers picked up on his governmental beat to brief mentions of civic projects, town meetings, and other news. He frequently quoted Lieutenant Robert Funk, the safety officer of the Savannah Police Department, passing along to readers safety tips for motorists and bicyclists.

On the day in question, Funk's safety tip was for drivers to avoid following other drivers too closely, lest a sudden application of the lead car's brakes result in a rear-end collision. The offense is called tail-gating. Mayor Malcolm Maclean, in his City Hall office a block away from the newspaper, was the first to spot the mistake. The mayor telephoned Sellers, laughing and saying something like, "Beryl, I think (ha-ha) there's a mistake (ha-ha) in your column, third item." Maclean hung up, still laughing. A red-faced Sellers, who never liked being laughed at, picked up the first edition of the paper and turned to his column. Sure enough, there in the third item was Lieutenant Funk's quote to the effect that "some of the worst accidents occur while tail-getting." Of course Funk had said "tail-gating," and Sellers had written it (he checked his carbon copy) just as Funk had said it. That's what made Sellers angry—indeed, absolutely livid for a few minutes, until the typesetter, whom Sellers knew quite well, convinced him that it was all a mistake and that he wouldn't have miss-set the type deliberately.

The Wayward Slugline. Then there was Walt Campbell, sports editor of the *Morning News*, whose columns always ran long. Walt believed in unloading all he had in his notebook each time he wrote a column, seldom holding anything for the next column. The amazing thing was that Walt would amass so much material in his column notes, enough to sustain three columns a week. In those days Linotype operators would set a slug line at the beginning of each piece of composition in order to identify the piece. "Campbell's column" was the slug line always placed at the beginning of Walt's by A. B. ("Foxy") Fox, who operated a machine adjusted to set type two columns in width, which was Campbell's format. Well, Foxy, feeling devilish one day, set the slug line "Campbell's longwinded krappe," intending no disrespect for a writer who was a good friend; indeed, Foxy often kidded Campbell about writing long pieces, calling it "a book within a column."

The practice in the composing room was for the printer who was placing type in the page forms to pull the slug lines off the galleys, after proofs had been read and corrected and sent over ready to go. But this time, alas, the slug line didn't get pulled.

Instead, "Campbell's longwinded krappe" became the first line Walt's sports-page readers saw. There were laughs aplenty, and telephone calls (people who spot mistakes delight in telephoning newspapers), yet nice-guy Walt Campbell never let that mistake bother him. He shrugged and took it in stride. The one it really bothered was Foxy, who had initiated the mistake while trying to be cute. He apologized to Walt, to Walt's boss, seemingly to everyone else in the plant because he had embarrassed both the *Morning News* and a good friend.

Not the River Styx. There was a tragic news story on which photographer Jim Bisson spotted a poor headline in the afternoon paper's first edition, yet hesitated for a few minutes before mustering the courage to call it to editor John Sutlive's attention. Jim had not been too long with the paper, and Sutlive was the most respected person in the newsroom, the soul of gentlemanly conduct. Jim would later learn that Sutlive himself had written the headline. If he had known that earlier, he'd have been even more reluctant to step forward. The headline was on a story about the end of a search for the body of a prominent Savannahian who had drowned in a boating accident. The search had gone on for several days. The headline read: DROWNED BOATER'S BODY FOUND AT HELL'S GATE. Actually the headline was factual, Hell's Gate happening to be the name of a point where two rivers in the local saltwater estuary came together at the mouth of a coastal sound. But how would the family feel, reading in bold print that their loved one, after his demise, had made it to the threshold of Hades? Bisson's caution about pointing out the headline to Sutlive proved to be without any basis. Sutlive, who was a personal friend of the drowned man and his family, immediately wrote a substitute headline for the final edition, and several times thanked photographer Bisson for spotting the first one.

One of the funniest typos occurred in earlier days, when the jointly owned local dailies had separate staffs who competed with each other for news breaks and delighted in finding mistakes on competitive pages. Invariably someone would clip out a boo-boo, paste it on a piece of paper, and mount it on the bulletin board the two staffs shared. And usually with some snide comment affixed. So the morning paper's people found much delight in posting an afternoon paper's story about the arrest of a fellow caught on a ladder peering into a lady's bathroom. Not only the headline, but also the story itself, omitted the second "p" from "peeping tom." The note penned beside the clipping read: "She probably had the water running," understood by anyone who ever experienced bladder weakness.

Churches' Victims. It is probably coincidence, but it seems strange that items about church activities seem vulnerable to embarrassing typos. More than once I've seen stories about the Forty Hours Devotion of Roman Catholic churches—some out with an "a" replacing the "o" in the word "forty." References to Sacred Heart Church often appear as "Scared Heart." And for some reason new reporters in town, especially non-Catholics, have had difficulty with the nomenclature of the cathedral. Its name is the Cathedral of St. John the Baptist, but it often has appeared in print as St. John's Baptist Church (there is indeed a St. John Baptist Church in town, without the possessive). A reverse corollary occurred one day when Chris Brady, a cub reporter who later would become managing editor of the *Augusta Chronicle*, suggested that the city editor change the correct reference to the cathedral in a news story. Chris, a native Savannahian who grew up in the cathedral parish, apparently never knew the correct name of his own church. He adamantly maintained that "it's a Catholic church, not a Baptist."

The granddaddy of all church-related typos appeared in an ad for the weekly religion page. Well, it didn't really appear because I happened to catch it while in the composing room reading a final proof of a news story previewing Easter activities in Savannah's churches. At the bottom of the page proof was an ad, two columns wide and about three inches deep, advertising the sermon topic for a certain church's Easter sunrise service. It read: "Have You Washed Any Wombs Lately?" I read it a second time and simply couldn't believe that a pastor would choose such a topic for Resurrection Day, so I telephoned the pastor to verify that something definitely was wrong. "Good Lord!" the clergyman shouted. "No, I telephoned the young lady and told her my sermon topic. What I really said was 'Have You Washed Any Wounds Lately?'—wounds, not wombs. Please change it for me." He repeated his plea, and I assured him we'd make the correction. The sermon was inspired by the New Testament account of the faithful women who went to the tomb to wash the wounds of Jesus and to prepare His body properly for eternal rest. The error occurred through phonetic miscommunication. Actually, editors reading page proofs seldom pay any attention to the advertisements when checking the new items. I suspect Providence took a hand the day I spotted the error.

Missed Headline. I also can recall the missed headline, although in retrospect we wouldn't have allowed it anyway. It was one of those running stories, which began on a foggy night when an incoming ship struck a railroad trestle spanning the Savannah River and knocked the bridge slap-dab off its supporting piers and into the water, thus creating what for several months would bar oceangoing cargo ships from all terminals upriver from the point of accident. Removal of the steel was an ongoing story within the big story. One cannot imagine the time, effort, and difficulty involved in retrieving a steel bridge from the bottom of a channel. Of course there was the Coast Guard investigation, paralleled by the Army Corps of Engineers' separate investigation, into the whys and wherefores of the mishap. The corps, incidentally, made a separate finding, decreeing that the Seaboard Coastline Railroad (now the CSX) would not be permitted to replace the trestle, but instead would have to route cross-river traffic the long way around, using a trestle several miles upriver and beyond the shipping channel. Finally, after several days of hearings, the Coast Guard determined that there had been no negligence on the pilot's part, and what caused the ship to veer suddenly and strike the trestle was shoal beneath the water's surface that had materialized quickly and was not indicated on the chart of the channel.

The afternoon paper's front-page headline read: C. G. FINDS SHOAL CAUSED TRESTLE ACCIDENT. Jim West, a talented news editor who ran the copy desk, wrote the headline. As his managing editor, I sat with Jim and other staff members for the afternoon critique of the paper we had just printed, and I complimented Jim on the way he displayed both the main story and the sidebar explaining what a shoal was, and how a shoal could develop almost overnight due to changing currents and shifting sands on a channel's bottom. "But, Jim," I added, with a wink to the others which Jim did not see, "you really flubbed a great opportunity for a classic headline." Jim looked up, puzzled, that "huh?" look on his face. Then he laughed with the rest of us when I said the headline should have read: THE SHIP HIT THE SAND.

Homophones. A lot of mistakes in print stem from homophones, words that sound alike but have different meanings. Such errors cause many readers—and from the experience of receiving their criticisms I say, v-e-r-y many—to contend that newspaper writers and editors are just plain ignorant. In local and other papers you'll see the misuse of such words as "effect" and "affect," "rein" and "reign" (strange, I've never seen "rain" used any way but properly), "karat" and "carat" (but never "carrot"). Also, a reader's perception of newspaper ignorance becomes enhanced with the misuse of foreign words. Best advice from experts is to avoid foreign words and phrases unless you're writing for a foreign audience, but such advice often goes ignored. For example, the French phrase *coup de grâce* creeps often into print, but not always is it spelled correctly. It means the final stroke, or the blow of mercy that ends one's misery (and life), but it sometimes comes out *coup de gras*, which means a stroke of fat. Typesetters could never be blamed for that one; it's the writers who are guilty, apparently unheeding the admonitions against baffling readers. (Whenever I see foreign words and phrases, I again think of one of the classic foreign-phrase boners—a teenager on an exam paper translating *hors de combat* as "camp followers.")

The Name She Gave. For my money the best slip in type of recent years was recorded in the *Athens Banner-Herald*, a sister paper to the Savannah dailies by virtue of being owned by Augusta-based Morris Communications Corporation. To the best of my knowledge, Wally Davis, executive editor of the Savannah papers, was the first to spot it. Wally is a speedy reader who can spot a mistake faster than most editors, and with that gift he assumed the daily task of scanning all the papers in the Morris chain. On a particular day Wally began reading a story of a mass arrest of prostitutes in Athens, the home of the University of Georgia. Campus and off-campus prostitution is a problem in any college town, and Athens is no exception. Wally, an alumnus of Georgia, perhaps felt nostalgia in reading that the problem lingered many years after his graduation, so he read the entire story.

At the end of the story was a listing of all the young ladies of the evening who had been booked for prostitution. The girls had given their names to the cops, and the desk sergeant had dutifully recorded them on the police blotter as the arresting officers rattled them off. The second from last name in the listing is what caused Wally to burst into laughter and, still laughing, he dialed Bob Chambers, his longtime friend and publisher of the Athens paper. "Don't you guys ever question the names on the blotter?" Wally asked Bob. "Look at the bottom of yesterday's story on the whores." There was a pause as Chambers found a paper, and then you could have heard his "Oh my God!" from Athens, Georgia, all the way to Athens, Greece. The name the young lady had given to the police, and which was passed on to Athens readers of that family news-paper—Fonda Peters!

Enough said about slips that pass in type.

Death of a Newspaper

On November 19, 1891, the *Savannah Press* was born as an independent afternoon paper in competition with the *Savannah Morning News*, established January 15, 1850. An upstart, the *Savannah Press* flew in the face of a daily that had not missed an issue except during a couple of Civil War years, when it went into hibernation. In 1930 Pleasant A. Stovall, who had founded the afternoon paper, sold to Herschel V. Jenkins, publisher of the morning paper, who changed the name of his acquisition to the *Savannah Evening Press*. Although the independent after-noon paper was profitable, Jenkins and his stockholders made Stovall an offer he couldn't refuse.

Jenkins moved the equipment, office furnishings, and staff of his new acquisition two blocks north, from the corner of Congress and Whitaker streets, to the premises of the morning paper at Bay and Whitaker. It was a friendly assimilation insofar as the new kids in the building got along with their new brothers and sisters—except that the news staff of the *Evening Press*, quartered on the west side of the large second-story newsroom, never ceased for a moment trying their best to scoop the morning paper on news breaks. And for years that spirit of friendly but fierce competition prevailed, with the *Press* running up a much higher batting average in the quest for exclusive stories. The beneficiaries of such competition were, of course, the readers of both papers, who could always count on fresh news, twice a day.

But on October 31, 1996, the *Savannah Evening Press* died, going the way of most afternoon papers in America, and leaving Atlanta, with its jointly owned morning *Constitution* and afternoon *Journal*, the only two-dailies city in Georgia. Chang-ing reader habits and the competition of television news are what contributed to the demise of afternoon newspapers. The mounting cost of newspaper production, which poses a daily economic problem, had become simply too much to sustain a market for two Savannah dailies.

Still, it's a sad day whenever a newspaper dies. It was a sad October 31 when Publisher Frank Anderson, his editors, and other officials, as well as a few retirees including this author, stood in the pressroom and watched the final edition of the *Press* roll. The banner headline read: "See you in the morning," meaning that readers henceforth would have to rely on the *Morning News* to bring them their daily news in print. The front-page story by veteran writer Marcus Holland related that the final edition marked the 37,969th day of publication for the afternoon paper over its nearly 105 years of existence. This author, who retired in 1989 as editor of both papers, wrote by request a special farewell column for that front page, recalling the spirit of competition between the two dailies. The age-old newspaper term —30—, which means "end of story," came up in both Holland's piece and this author's column.

The circulation of the *Press* had dropped to just above 10,000. In halcyon days subscribers had numbered nearly 25,000. Circulation figures do not convey actual readership. There's a multiple factor in calculating the number of readers—three-point-something—taking into consideration the average number of people in a household. Which means that on its final day the afternoon paper was being read by more than 30,000 souls—not bad, even considering changed reader habits. But then, there were the economics of daily production to be reckoned with.

It was certainly an emotional day for this author, who began his newspaper career in 1935 delivering the afternoon paper. My farewell column in the morning paper, for which I still write a commentary two days a week, was a tribute to newspaper carriers on bygone days, and the final edition of the *Press* contained a feature story on Mrs. Beatrice Faircloth, dean of all carriers, who delivered to subscribers for fifty-three years. What an emotional day it surely was for that grand lady.

In its last days the *Evening Press* was hardly any competition, news-wise, for the morning paper. Indeed, its pages contained many stories picked up verbatim from the *News*, not a word changed and with no second-day leads at all. In newspaper parlance that's called "boiler plate." About the only differences between the two papers were fresh front-page stories, a few columns and features, editorials (albeit written by the same people but with different slants and subjects), and the comics.

So Savannah, a city noted for slow acceptance of change (or hard resistance to, take your pick), definitely underwent an abrupt change that thirty-first day of October, which coincidentally was also Halloween, when witches rode and hobgoblins said "Boo!" The *Morning News* has become larger in content, with more complete sports coverage, in-depth news stories, and an op-ed page offering more liberal columnists to offset the mostly conservative editorial policy of long standing. Thus, the community wasn't entirely spooked.

No School Today

Childish pranks are as old as history itself. They form the training ground for the strategies of life by embracing the elements of subtlety, intrigue, trickery, and all that. Who can read of Deborah, one of the smartest women in the Bible who sat in judgment of God's people, without concluding that she must have been a prankish child? Recall that she devised a scheme to lure Sisera, the enemy, into her tent, and after wining and dining him into a deep slumber, dispatched him by driving a tent peg through his heart. My observation has been that the most prankish of my school contemporaries grew up to be the most successful.

Do not, however, confuse prankishness with meanness. There's a difference, and if Deborah must impress some readers of Holy Writ as mean-spirited, remember that Sisera was a mean cuss himself, lived by the sword, and finally got what he deserved. Also, do not confuse childish subtlety, intrigue, and trickery with crookedness. There's a difference there, too. It's all in the spirit of how it's done.

Peg Hoy Sterling, one of my contemporaries now, but who finished high school a few years before I did, tells the story of her grandfather, Victor Fuchs, who was a prankish child and grew up to become successful in the cotton business after starting in a lower echelon as a grader. That's a skill, grading cotton. When cotton was king in Savannah, before the Great Depression and before the boll weevil decimated the South's principal cash crops, the sales of that commodity were keyed directly to a cotton grader's assessment of whether the cotton in question was, say, "strict low" or "middling," or whatever. The better the grade, the better the price, and graders had better be right. Mr. Fuchs parlayed his expertise as a grader into much higher advancement in the cotton business.

Victor Fuchs attended Savannah High School in the early 1900's and was a prankster. He lived just a couple of blocks from the school, so getting there on time was never a problem—just a hop and a skip. Mrs. Sterling's story is that Victor arose early one morning and was informed by his mother that snow was falling. It's worth mentioning something like that to an awakening teenager because snow rarely falls in Savannah. Old and young are fascinated whenever it snows. Victor Fuchs bounded from bed, dressed hurriedly, wolfed down his breakfast, then sloshed through the light covering of snow to Savannah High. The school was situated on Bull Street, occupying the entire block bounded on the other three sides by Oglethorpe Avenue and Hull and Drayton streets. The custom in those days was for the girls to enter the building from Bull Street and the boys through a side door facing Hull. It was a segregation by sexes, but for a practical reason because the boys enjoyed heckling their feminine schoolmates.

On that snowy day Victor decided it would be better to play outside in the snow than to attend classes. Once at the Hull Street gate, he decided to return home and obtain a large piece of cardboard. Back at the schoolhouse, he used a large crayon and wrote "No School Today" on the card. He affixed the card to the Hull Street gate, and with a few other boys who had shown up early he went off to throw snowballs and engage in some makeshift sledding the rest of the day. The girls, however, came to the Bull Street entrance, entered the building, and went to their homerooms, and spent the rest of the day attending classes—without any boys. It was an hour or two after classes began that the school officials discovered the bogus sign on the Hull Street gate, and the story Grandpa Fuchs told to Peg Hoy, when confessing his prank years later, was that school officials never figured out who the culprit was.

Victor Fuchs confessed other pranks to his granddaughter, since he was in a confessing mood. The one she remembers best was how he raided his parents' chicken nests every other day, took some of the eggs, and sold them to the family of Dr. Craig Barrow, who lived in a mansion house facing Chippewa Square, two blocks from the Fuchs house. The elder Fuchses didn't learn of their son's enterprise until one day, when the Barrows were out of eggs, their maid came over and asked to see Victor, who for months had been their supplier. Victor's parents had indeed noticed that their hens hadn't been producing as many eggs, but they had attached no significance to the drop in production. Victor, when confronted, couldn't understand the ado over a few eggs. Since the eggs were "theirs," he reasoned, what was so awful about a son's running a small business?

It's a reasonable assumption that Victor Fuchs and his childhood entrepreneurship contributed to his later success in life.

Some Impressive Personalities

I have kicked myself a thousand times for not keeping better notes. In the news business, man and boy, for more than a half-century, I would have had a treasure trove of memos-to-self from which to draw recollections of Savannahians who made an impression. Alas, most of my notes were mental, but they are sufficiently indelible to allow me to pass along to posterity some insights into a few of our city's personalities who made impressions, not only on me but mainly on Savannah:

Alexander A. Lawrence. This work, and its forerunner, *Only in Savannah*, mention frequently the late John J. Bouhan, Savannah's most noted political boss. Alex Lawrence was one of Bouhan's law partners and often was involved with him in political matters, but one never viewed him in an "associate-in-bossism" light. He was independent enough in both his thinking and in his actions. Thus Savannahians viewed him as an excellent lawyer, a civic leader, a historian, and a *bon vivant*. He had still another side—he was a blend of humorist and serious author. Oh, yes, he was a federal judge, one of the best who ever donned a robe and graced a bench, and his written opinions, spiced with humorous asides that must have made other learned jurists wince at times, especially entertained the press, reporters and editors usually regarding as drudgery the task of taking a legal opinion and making sense enough of it to pass it along to readers in some kind of comprehensible fashion.

His books on history dealt with the Revolution and the Civil War. *A Present for Mr. Lincoln: The Story of Savannah from Secession to Sherman* (1961) is a classic, its title deriving from the fact that after General William Tecumseh Sherman ended his infamous March to the Sea at Savannah, he telegraphed President Lincoln, offering the city of Savannah as a Christmas present.

Some Impressive Personalities

Attendance at meetings of civic clubs usually is in direct relationship to the announced speaker. If it's a lawyer or a judge, attendance will not be as high as for, say, such a colorful politician as, say, the late Governor Marvin Griffin and his homespun philosophy. But clubs fortunate enough to land Alex Lawrence as a speaker would draw nearly a hundred percent to hear him. He was that good, and that entertaining, even with a dead-serious topic. And dead serious he was, as well as entertaining, the day in a Chatham County courtroom while defending a bottling company a woman had sued after finding a piece of a cockroach in her soft drink. In summation, he stood before the jury and argued that, even though a cockroach might have intruded into the bottled drink, and while the thought of such an intrusion was not pleasant, ingesting a roach really would cause no harm. In order to prove his point, he extracted from his pocket a matchbox, and from the box he extracted a cockroach, which he proceeded to eat. The jury returned a verdict in favor of the bottling company, and it didn't take too long in reaching its verdict.

His last book, *Tongue in Cheek* (1979), was exactly what its title implied, but it didn't make publication until after the good judge's death, so he unfortunately missed the book's critical acclaim. I'd like to quote forever from it, but just a single footnote from one of his own legal opinions that he included in the book is sufficient to illustrate the real and true Alex Lawrence—jurist, historian, and writer of considerable erudition. The footnoted opinion was in the case of a federal prisoner who had petitioned for release from his sentence in order that he might go to South America and join a group of Chilean freedom fighters. Judge Lawrence noted that the prisoner did not contend that his constitutional rights had been violated, so he had no recourse but to deny the petition. This was his footnote: "I am aware that in November, 1864, convicts were released from the Penitentiary at Milledgeville who volunteered to serve in the State militia in opposing Sherman's March to the Sea. However, the Governor of Georgia authorized the release, not the Confederate District Court. Besides, it was a better cause."

I felt honored to be a part of Judge Lawrence's legacy. I received in October 1979 a copy of *Tongue in Cheek* from its publisher, W. B. Williford, along with a personal note relating that "Judge Lawrence told me repeatedly, both orally and in writing, that I was not to be concerned with getting a review copy of the book to the Savannah newspaper as he would personally take a copy to 'my good friend Tom Coffey.' At the time I thought his repeated reiteration of this plan was a bit unnecessary, but I was at the disadvantage of not knowing either the true state of his health or that he was fully conscious of his impending demise."

Frank Rossiter. My first awareness of Francis Patrick Rossiter, one of Savannah's consummate Irishmen, came when I was a carrier boy for the *Savannah Evening Press* and "employee's rate" appeared beside his name on my list of subscribers. My district manager, Theron W. Griner, told me Rossiter was a reporter on the morning paper's staff, and then I realized that I had seen his bylines in the *Morning News*, which I also read. Frank would become a friend after I joined the afternoon paper's staff as a copy boy in 1940, since I'd see him daily in the newsroom the two staffs shared. As I began to write and advanced to reporter the older Frank often would comment on my stories, variously offering praise or constructive criticism. And we later would work together on the morning sheet's staff.

Frank founded the column "City Beat," which until recently

spiced the local page. Just by happenstance did the popular column come to be. He was the star reporter, working in a dual role as assistant city editor, the latter post requiring him to sit on the city desk on weekends. It was a dull news day that Sunday he wrote the first "City Beat," a potpourri of little items gleaned from notes he had accumulated over the past week. He telephoned off-duty city editor Bill Harris to get permission to print the column, and Harris was so elated that he promptly suggested the title and told Frank to plan on making it a regular Monday morning feature.

As the years wore on, Frank became known as both Mr. City Beat and Mr. Morning News, and he shared with John Sutlive, the afternoon paper's editor, the honor of being the most respected newsmen in town. It was unfortunate that Frank and the newspaper company came to the parting of the ways in the 1960's over what in retrospect was a misunderstanding so trivial in nature, but so serious at the time. His departure was a loss to Savannah journalism.

I know that Frank Rossiter found his new environment, outside newspaperdom, strange and perhaps frightening, but he soon landed a job in the shipping business. Shipping seemed a natural for him, since he had covered the waterfront (along with several other beats) his entire newspaper career, and he knew practically every soul along the Savannah River. He traveled the length and breadth of Georgia soliciting business for our seaport, and was successful at it. But then he ventured into politics and became successful at that too.

In 1960, when John Rousakis resigned from the Chatham County Commission to run for mayor, he assembled an eclectic ticket to run with him—a black businessman, a longtime civic leader, a labor official, a Protestant businessman, a Jewish businessman, and an Irish-Catholic in the person of Frank Rossiter. Rousakis and his entire ticket were popular Savannahians, but none was more so than Rossiter. The vote totals proved it: Rousakis & Team won all seats, with Rossiter garnering more votes than anyone else on the ticket. Consequently, as the new council took office Rossiter was named mayor pro tem. In three subsequent bids for reelection Rossiter would reap more votes than anyone else, and it was only because of the cancer that would take his life that he decided to bow out of politics before the time came to seek a fifth term.

As an alderman, Rossiter was the most independent of all on the Rousakis team. Not always did he vote with the majority; sometimes he could sway the majority his way. But his loyalty to Rousakis, even if voting against him on a certain issue, never flagged. It would be, he explained, simply a difference of opinion. His loyalty was inbred. Rossiter grew up in a political family, his father having been a part of Boss John Bouhan's organization, and while stubborn-Irishman Joe Rossiter sometimes harbored differences with Bouhan, he was always on tap and ready to pitch in come election time. Frank definitely was his late dad's clone in the loyalty department. But becoming an alderman, as well as a success in his second career after leaving the newspaper, was not Rossiter's crowning achievement. That came the year he was chosen grand marshal of the St. Patrick's Day parade. For an Irish-Catholic in Savannah, nothing can be finer, not even the presidency of the Hibernian Society—with which Frank Rossiter also was honored.

I always felt flattered when Savannahians would get Rossiter and me confused, thinking he was I and I was he. The confusion was easy to understand (although he was my senior by some six years)—we both were well identified with the local newspapers, both of us wrote columns in which our half-column pictures were inset, and both of us had white hair. After each election I'd kid Frank, telling him that the reason he always garnered the most votes was "Hell, man, they think you're me." I dearly wish I could have made as many contributions to Savannah's warp, woof, and weal as Frank Rossiter did.

Edward Caughran. That's another Irish name—Caughran; it's pronounced "Corran," rhyming with "foreign." Ed Caughran, though, has never made much over his Irish heritage, but took it for granted and in stride. What he has made a lot of is music. For nearly forty years he was Savannah's foremost music activist, and since his retirement from gainful employment his activism hasn't dimmed very much, if at all. He definitely is "The Music Man" of Savannah, but not at all like Professor Harold Hill, the con man in the popular Meredith Willson musical play of the same name. Ed Caughran really has taught kids to play musical instruments, thousands of them, either one-on-one personally or by extension of his talent and leadership through other music instructors over whom he had supervision.

He came to Savannah in the 1950's, a protégé of James Fillmore, who ranks just a notch or so below John Philip Sousa as a bandmaster and composer of march music. Fillmore taught Caughran, to play trumpet and to be a music teacher, at the University of Miami, after which Ed came to direct the Savannah High School band. He also had a second job as first-chair trumpet in the fledgling Savannah Symphony Orchestra, most of whose musicians made ends meet by teaching either in the public schools or by tutoring private pupils. The SHS band, under years of the late Henry J. Applewhite's direction, had gained the reputation as one of Georgia's best. Caughran made the band even snappier, and made the bold move of adding more strutting majorettes than his predecessor had to what had been an ROTC marching and concert band. His first head majorette in front of eight other high steppers and twirlers was Susan Ford, a statuesque blonde, whom Joan Howard, a petite brunette, followed; and the tradition those young ladies started continues to this day. The band's reputation spread, prompting the great James Fillmore to drive up from Miami to check for himself. Caughran took advantage of his mentor's visit and persuaded him to stay a few days, rehearse the band, and be guest conductor at an evening concert. Needless to say, the Savannah High auditorium overflowed that night for a concert nominally priced and featuring so noted a conductor. Fillmore, incidentally, is one of the great music-makers (along with W. C. Handy, Sousa, and Liberace) whose names *The Music Man*'s composer Willson wove into the lyrics of "Seventy-six Trombones."

It was logical that Ed Caughran should move up in the school system, and he ultimately became head of the music department, in charge of all bands, choral groups, orchestras, and everything else musical—kindergarten through high school. He wasn't content, however, to musically educate Savannah's children; indeed, he spread music through the whole community. To downtown Johnson Square, every spring and over a two-week period, he would bring bands and singers to give public concerts at the noon hour, prompting office workers to bring brown-bag lunches to the park benches, where they could eat, listen, savor, and enjoy. Caughran also persuaded the Georgia Music Educators' Association to make Savannah its permanent convention site, bringing annually the all-star bands, orchestras, and choral singers to rehearse for two days under noted guest conductors, and then to perform Saturday concerts to which Savannahians have been responding for years. He also strengthened a liaison with the Savannah Symphony, arranging field trips to the Civic Center for special morning concerts—the kind Leonard Bernstein made popular on television. He also persuaded the daily newspapers to become cosponsors with the public schools, the Civic Center, and Armstrong Atlantic State University, of free concerts by the Defense Department's several touring military bands—Army, Navy, Marine, and Air Force. For good measure he also engineered performances by Coast Guard bands, although that service, for reasons best known to the federal bureaucracy, isn't a part of the Defense Department except during wartime.

Not content to sit around and listen to recorded music after his retirement, Caughran has in recent years associated himself with the music program of Armstrong Atlantic State University. He invited any and all to join a community band. The band, called "Ed and Friends," gives two concerts a year, featuring patriotic music at midyear and Yuletide music in December. Edward A. Caughran, more than anyone else I know, personifies the popular Coca-Cola commercial ditty, "I'd Like to Teach the World to Sing."

Emma Kelly. Emma Kelly's presence at the piano keyboard in nightspots all around Savannah—for several years now a fixture at Ben Tucker's "Hannah" upstairs at the Pirates' House restaurant—has brightened many an evening for visitors and locals alike. Savannah-born composer Johnny Mercer called her "The Lady of Six Thousand Songs," but actually it's more like ten thousand.

Mrs. Kelly, who commutes daily between her home in Statesboro, fifty miles away, and Savannah, also plays every Sunday in

Statesboro's First Baptist Church. She knows as many people on a first-name basis as she does the music and lyrics to all those songs in her repertoire. She has performed with symphonies as well as combos, and on network television. Name a tune, and she'll play and sing it for you. She'll even invite nightclubbers to come forward and sing with her—self included, a few times, on "I'll Be Seeing You."

Emma tells a story on herself—the same story the late Johnny Mercer would tell when he wanted to kid her. It concerns a time when Mercer was in town with his fellow composer-friend, Sammy Fain (among Fain's many: "I'll Be Seeing You" and "Love Is a Many-splendored Thing"), and they visited a nightclub where Emma was playing. Mercer introduced the two. Later, as the two Hollywood composers sat drinking at a table, Mercer was summoned to the telephone. He walked up and asked Emma to play, while he was away from the table, "some of Sammy's pieces." Emma nodded, but then, suddenly, she drew a blank. "I couldn't think of a single Sammy Fain tune," she admitted. She'll blush as well as laugh each time she tells that story.

Samuel L. Varnedoe. They called him "Big Sam" because he had a namesake son, and he also was large of stature. He was a stockbroker by occupation, whose Varnedoe and Chisholm partnership with Frank Chisholm began in the Great Depression, after the market started to recover, and blossomed from a shoestring beginning on borrowed money to a large business, which in recent years was sold to Robinson Humphrey.

Varnedoe made many contributions to Savannah's progress, but his crowning achievement was successfully prodding from the sideline for an alternate route to Tybee Island, twenty miles from Savannah on the Atlantic Ocean. He envisioned a lengthening of President Street to link up with the existing U.S. 80, and convinced the county government of the feasibility of floating bonds to finance a toll bridge across the Wilmington River in order to make the project doable. Thus, Sam's persistence solved the problem of a traffic bottleneck along the only route to the beach. And the President Street bridge across the Wilmington River is another of his namesakes, the county having so honored him.

Another of his contributions was charting a solution to the problem of getting the City of Savannah out of the pit it had dug itself into by borrowing from the sinking fund in order to make ends meet. Because it hadn't learned a lesson from earlier folly, the city later reached another brink of bankruptcy, and that was resolved in another way; but there's no telling what shape local government would have been in had it not been for Sam Varnedoe's earlier, and voluntary, intercession.

Friends, however, remember the late Sam Varnedoe as a *bon vivant*, a hail-fellow-well-met, and the joke-a-day man. Those friends marveled that he found time to make a living because, no sooner than he'd hear a new joke, he'd telephone friends to pass it along. The phone would ring, and Sam's unmistakable voice would begin, "Did you hear the one about the fellow who . . . ?" The way Sam made a living was dealing, for clients, with stockbrokers in New York and elsewhere—and it was from them, he once told me, that he picked up most of those jokes.

Lee Mingledorff. Born to a wealthy family in the foundry and shipbuilding business, Walter Lee Mingledorff, Jr., became a political malcontent early in life. At Georgia Tech he had earned a commission in the Army Reserve, and was called up at the beginning of World War II. Military service was not to be, however, because the government deemed the Mingledorff contract to build minesweepers for the Navy more critical in the overall defense scheme, and he was discharged against his will to run the shipyard. He fulfilled that mission admirably, and the shipyard won many "E" awards for excellence in boosting the war effort.

On the home front Mingledorff made mental notes of the way Savannah's politics, in an interlocking alliance with established business and industry, was, as he put it, "holding Savannah back." When the war ended and he became president of the Chamber of Commerce, Mingledorff became highly vocal in his criticism of a lethargic Savannah basking in its own contentment with the status quo. That was his theme in speech after speech to the civic clubs. Thus, when a reform movement began to take shape in the mid-1950's, the leaders of the movement deemed Mingledorff the logical person to run for mayor against the established machine.

Mingledorff won the mayorship, ostensibly a part-time job under the just-installed council-manager system, which the reformers had worked for and won in a special referendum. He soon found that being mayor required most of his time, and for good reasons. The new (and first) city manager, Frank Jacocks, needed an omnipresent mayor to bounce things off as he went about professionalizing a city government long entrenched in the political spoils system. Mingledorff was most effective in warding off pressure from the outside to maintain as much of the status quo as possible. Many citizens, some of them the top business executives and professionals, were slow realizing that the changeover in how the city operated would be virtually an upheaval and not merely a slight tremor. Mingledorff and his council had to stand firm and endure many slings and arrows, particularly from the diehard remnants of the old political machine, some of whom were still working for the city and inured to the old ways. For example, diehards regarded setting up a traffic engineering department as something about as necessary as mammaries on a boar hog—gee, hadn't the cops always handled the traffic?

One of Mingledorff's early concerns (speaking of traffic) was the lack of expressways. His efforts and explorations up state and federal avenues paved the way for the coming of the Interstate system to Chatham County. His efforts were expanded upon by future city and county officials, chief among whom was William F. Lynes, who would win the county commission's chairmanship under the aegis of the Citizens Committee political faction, which had steamrolled Mingledorff into office.

Lee Mingledorff spearheaded all of the changes that became so necessary in a reform movement that turned Savannah politics upside down, including the correction of mismanagement that had driven city government to the brink of bankruptcy. Some of the changes and improvements were so basic, it was hard to grasp that they hadn't been accomplished in earlier administrations. For example, the Mingledorff administration built Savannah's very first sewage disposal plant in the late 1950's, beginning what would become a comprehensive, yet highly costly, countywide pollution-abatement program, ultimately negating the years of unhealthy environmental damage resulting from the simple expedient of having dumped raw sewage into the Savannah River and other tidal streams. The administration also installed urban renewal, and instituted the extension of the city's water and sewerage systems into the unincorporated areas of the county, enhancing and expediting the growth of suburban development.

Mingledorff resigned as mayor in 1962 to head a slate of

candidates for the county commission, continuing the slow but steady routing of machine politics. In the machine's counter-attack against the Mingledorff-led challengers, it made Mingle-dorff the main target while virtually ignoring his running mates. When the votes were counted, six of Mingledorff's ticket (including the aforementioned William Lynes) were elected, but Mingledorff was one of two losers in the challenge. His political career ended there, but its effects didn't. One of the prices he paid for public service was the breakup of his marriage to the former Mary Louise Budreau. He later married the widowed Huldah Cail Lorimer, owner of the multiacre Millhaven Plantation in Screven County, some sixty miles north. But after settling down as a gentleman farmer, with sideline involvement in Screven County's civic activities, he began to experience health problems, which became so severe that he chose to end his own life. Savannah remembers him as one of its best and most dedicated public servants.

Malcolm Maclean. When Lee Mingledorff resigned as mayor to run for the county commission, Savannah's aldermen chose one of their own, Mayor Pro Tem Malcolm Roderick Maclean, to serve out the balance of Mingledorff's term. Maclean then won the office in his own right, in two succeeding elections, but lost it on his bid for a third term in 1966, a casualty in the racial revolution.

Maclean, a Phi Beta Kappa graduate of Yale Law School, and a "charter member" of the Citizens Committee reform move-ment, joined the city's legal staff when Mingledorff took office, and later became an alderman. Maclean moved into the mayor's office as if it had been designed for him, built upon Mingle-dorff's achievements, and instituted some of his own. It was his administration that started planning for the Civic Center, and which advanced progress toward pollution abatement. Urban renewal projects went forward, and suburbia continued to expand. Computerization began. It might not have been exactly a golden era, but by no means was it tarnished brass. Then came the sit-ins, the kneel-ins, the wade-ins, and their accompanying uproar as the push across the United States for desegregation gained momentum. By the Grace of God, Maclean happened to be mayor at the time.

Savannah didn't experience nearly the turmoil that many other Southern (also Northern) cities did, yet turmoil enough. Window-smashings, fire-bombings, and other forms of violent outbursts occurred in some parts of town. Marches formed every night, and some during daylight hours. It was not a happy time, but citizens appreciated that there were responsible leaders within Savannah's black community who enjoyed respect and held appreciable control over their peers. What happened in Birmingham, Detroit, Harlem, and Rochester would not happen in Savannah.

What did happen, however, set up sufficient discontent to create among a large number of whites a backlash just waiting to manifest itself next election day. Through Maclean's reasonable and rational approach to problem-solving, a biracial committee that he appointed and often met with charted a course of compromise between the black leadership on the one hand and, on the other hand, those whites who didn't want to desegregate. Restaurant, lunch counter, and hotel owners would have preferred things as they had always been; so would theater operators. But Maclean and his biracial committee persuaded and prodded; and change occurred, initially almost ceremoniously, with reporters and photographers present, recording blacks sitting down with impunity in restaurants, registering at local hotels, buying tickets, and entering theaters. One theater manager proclaimed loudly to anyone who'd listen that he personally hadn't wanted to integrate, "but the mayor made me do it." Maclean later admitted that he had granted anyone wanting a scapegoat permission to name him.

Maclean insisted he never intended to be a social engineer, only to do what was right. He went further by meeting personally with black leaders and city officials, and by promising to create better opportunities for blacks to work in the public sector—which he did. To confidants Maclean conceded that he probably had committed political hara-kiri by doing what he deemed to be right because whoever might oppose him would be getting the backlash as well as the out-and-out redneck vote. The out-and-out rednecks made no bones about their displeasure at the turn of events. Some in ordinary garb and some wearing Ku Klux Klan sheets and pointy-head hats picketed theaters and accosted white patrons, trying to shame them from "going to the show with niggers." They threw the "n" word around with reckless abandon, directing it straight at the blacks who were buying movie tickets.

By the time Maclean stood for reelection, the overt counter-demonstrations by whites had ceased, and they never had been much, not nearly as large or as danger-prone as the black demonstrations had been. But Democrat Maclean's challenger, Republican J. Curtis Lewis, Jr., rode into office with backlash support augmenting the votes that came from his own personal popularity. Ironically, Lewis wasn't then, and still isn't, a racist. As a wealthy second-generation owner of the Ford franchise and with financial involvement in other enterprises, Lewis was known for his benevolence, for his leadership in many community endeavors, and for his prominence as a Baptist, a Shriner, and as a member of other organizations in Freemasonry. Once in office Lewis broadened the city-initiated opportunities for black citizens by establishing the federally sponsored Model Cities program, offering new jobs, and rehabilitating blighted neighborhoods. Savannah won the All-American City award for its one-on-one help of minorities through attacking problems in the ghettos.

Malcolm Maclean had sacrificed himself on the political altar, simply by doing what "was right" while under tremendous pressure to maintain the status quo. Truly, he was a Savannahian who made a lasting impression.

The Adlers. The custom of Orthodox Jews in designating namesake-sons is to honor a forebear—grandfather or uncle—but not a son's father. So among the Orthodox, you do not find "Juniors." It's different with Reform Jews, and the late Sam G. Adler named one of his two sons Sam Junior. The other, Lee Adler, is a namesake of his grandfather, the late Leopold Adler, founder of what for decades was Savannah's leading department store, located at the southeast corner of Bull and Broughton, where a federal building now stands.

The elder Sam Adler became one of Savannah's leading citizens, imbued with a civic spirit that ran deep. He was in the forefront of many movements that boded economic benefits for the community. With an eye upon building future good leadership, he became a cofounder of the Savannah Leadership Seminar, a six-month, in-depth course of training for younger Savannahians who were chosen by their employers to devote an afternoon a month, listening to lectures by experts on topics exploring all aspects and facets of community life. The present Leadership Savannah program is an outgrowth of that initial civic project.

Lee Adler, the elder of the sons, has become noted nation-wide as a preservationist, not only for his leadership in the Historic Savannah Foundation, the privately financed agency responsible for restoration of the Historic District, but also for his personal involvement in turning run-down houses in the Victorian District (which abuts the Historic District) into decent abodes for lower-income families. He is deeply involved in the National Trust for Historic Preservation, and lectures frequently in forums elsewhere.

Sam Adler, Jr., unlike his brother who opted for stock-brokering, stayed with the family retail business. After the downtown store burned, and the late Leopold Adler's estate was settled through a court battle with the elder Sam's sister, Olga, the two Sams opened a women's apparel store in a southside shopping center, and later moved into a mammoth expanse of floor space in the then-new Oglethorpe Mall. They kept the Adler logo, which had been familiar to downtown shoppers for generations. As his father aged and later was sidelined by illness, the younger Sam became the sole operator of the business. Finally, when he decided to retire from business, he chose to close the store rather than sell it, saying "the Adler name" meant too much to the family for him to abide someone else's opera-tion of the business and perhaps the dilution of its reputation and its accent on quality retailing. Reputedly he became even wealthier as he negotiated Oglethorpe Mall's purchase of the remaining years of his ninety-nine-year lease.

Ever a strong presence on the local scene, outspoken and sharply critical on matters ranging from government to the community's solicitation of new business and industry, Sam, Jr., was sometimes called "The Mouth of the South," a sobriquet he seemed to relish. He announced in 1985 that he intended to leave Savannah, but not for another year, and he would devote that year to "clean air." Now, Sam Adler, Jr., on a kick is an experience for those around him, and especially for those he might target as the polluters of the air—Union Camp Corporation in particular. Union Camp manufactures kraft paper, a process from which sulfuric emissions permeate the atmosphere. Over the years the company has invested millions in emission control, and even the company's sternest critics will concede that Savannah doesn't "smell as bad" as it used to. Still, Adler maintained that Union Camp wasn't doing enough or spending enough. He found forums hither and yon for airing his concern for clean air—civic clubs, television interviews, statements to the newspapers. He compiled figures and statistics. Engage him in conversation, he'd immediately pull from his pocket a set of index cards on which he had noted all those figures and statistics, as well as quotations from medical and environmental spokespersons on the impact of sulfuric emissions upon the populace. He chided the media for not doing what he regarded as enough to arouse the public.

The year ended, and Adler announced that he had created the awareness he intended in Savannah and that he was off to the far west. He settled in Twin Falls, Idaho, where he raises horses and enjoys life away from industrial emissions. But he revisits Savannah occasionally and usually exacts an interview in which he sounds off on his updated impressions of his hometown. Sam Adler, Jr., his brother Lee, and their late father definitely made impressions on Savannah.

William Murphey. One of Savannah's "old school" bankers was William Murphey, who was chairman of the board of the Citizens & Southern National Bank when he retired in the early 1950's as Mills B. Lane, Jr., namesake son of the bank's late founder, was coming to the fore to head the institution and revolutionize banking in Georgia. To everyone, he was Mr. Murphey—never on a first-name basis, not even with his successor, the young Mills.

Mr. Murphey had been a reporter for the *Macon Telegraph* in his college days at Mercer University. His early employment was as secretary to the president of the Central of Georgia Railway, and from there he gravitated into money business, working his way up the ladder, finally becoming head of C & S (now NationsBank). I met him as a reporter covering the bank beat, and he was a steady source of tips on changes and developments in the realm of finance and business. He was a director of the Seaboard Air Line Railroad and once called me to interview the railroad's president in his office. It was an in-depth interview, Mr. Murphey himself posing most of the questions on the Southland's overall economy and prospects for the future. I merely sat there, taking notes and occasionally getting in a question of my own. The visiting executive marveled at the turn the interview took, and Mr. Murphey, as modestly as he could, told him "I used to be the head reporter of the Macon paper."

William Murphey insisted that whenever I wrote anything about his bank I must capitalize the word "The" because it was a part of the bank's title. I had already been reminded of that, many times, by city editor Jack Cook: "Remember, it's capital 'T,' Tom." I would remember. Mr. Murphey tolerated boss politics in Savannah, saying that reform movements could be "too radical," and he was generally conceded as the money-brains of local politics. He also was the money-brains behind many of the businesses in Savannah because his bank held the notes on them. Gentle, civic-minded, philanthropic—Mr. Murphey was all of that. But, business-wise, he was firm and stern, and he injected fear into many an entrepreneur. I always felt flattered that he seemed to like me. When I wed in 1946, he was the only bank official on my beat to send a wedding present, and he gave me father-like advice on how two could live as cheaply as one—ironic, coming from a confirmed bachelor, but appreciated nevertheless.

Any other Savannahian named Murphy spelled his surname without an "e." And most such Murphys are Roman Catholics. William Murphey was a Protestant, and I often wondered whether, as a youth, he merely inserted the "e" to emphasize the distinction. I never dared to ask him, so commanding a regal-like presence did he exude as the soul of dignity and self-assuredness. Later, after I had become assistant city editor of the *Evening Press*, a new reporter named Ray Dilley was assigned to the bank beat, and he was promptly apprised of the spelling of Mr. Murphey's name as well as the capitalization of the article in the C & S's title. Coming in one day with his first story on the C & S, Dilley wanted to write things just right and asked whether Mr. Murphey had a middle initial. City editor Cook, whose desk was beside mine, piped up: "His middle initial is in his last name. Remember that."

Hansell Hillyer. In the late 1940's the South Atlantic Gas Company, based in Florida, acquired Savannah Gas; and coming to Savannah to operate it was Haywood Hansell Hillyer, originally from St. Louis, and by way of Louisiana and Florida. A large man, on the rotund side, Hillyer adapted to his new environment with a suddenness that nearly swept Savannah off its feet. His was a commanding presence. He was eloquent and articulate. He was forward-thinking. He viewed Savannah as a sleepy town needing an awakening, and he set out to sound the wake-up call.

Hillyer joined the Chamber of Commerce and soon became its president. He deemed the Chamber among the sleepiest of the local institutions. He persuaded the board to hire a dynamic executive director in the person of Cliff Davenport, whose work with chambers and other business organizations had earned him a reputation for getting things done. With Hillyer at the head, and Davenport running things, the Savannah Chamber of Commerce sprang into action, figuratively juggling six or seven balls in the air simultaneously. More staff was added. Responsibilities were categorized.. Slower-moving Savannahians sometimes called Hillyer "Hitler," but they soon perceived that he not only meant well, he also imparted a can-do attitude to even the slowest-moving. The Chamber's impact on Savannah became immense.

Hillyer was a visionary in every sense. He did everything with a flair, and once proposed bringing to Savannah as a tourist attraction the decommissioned USS *Missouri*, aboard which General MacArthur accepted Japan's surrender. Missouri, after all, had been Hillyer's home state. Hillyer also rejuvenated the old Community Chest and steered it into a broader charitable organization under the new name of United Community Services, the forerunner of the present United Way. He enlisted the community's top executives to fill key roles in UCS as many agencies abandoned their separate campaigns to come under the umbrella of centralized fund-raising with allocations to the agencies. Harben Daniel, a radio executive who would bring Savannah's second television station (WSAV) on the air in 1956, became a strong ally of Hillyer and concocted the "One Big Package" slogan that UCS used for years.

Natural gas came to Savannah via pipeline from Texas, rendering obsolete the gas works on the old Fort Wayne property at Bay and East Broad streets. Hillyer persuaded his wife, Mary, to oversee the renovation of the old gas works property, unsightly and soot-blackened. Mrs. Hillyer thus launched a miraculous transformation of the buildings where gas had been manufactured from coal, as well as the near-slum (also soot-blackened) residential units, alongside the old gas works and fronting onto East Broad Street. She converted them into classy apartments and one-family residences for sale or rental. The old gas-works structures now house shops and luxury apartments, as well as the headquarters offices of the Episcopal Diocese of Georgia in a building the gas company donated to the diocese. All of that restoration, which provided an inspiration to other downtown preservationists, greatly enhanced the premises of the Pirates' House, one of Savannah's best-known restaurants, by providing attractive surroundings and a huge parking lot.

Hansell Hillyer and associates later sold the Savannah Gas Company to the Atlanta Gas Light Company, and there remains just north of the Pirates' House the huge above-ground pipes that Hillyer installed when natural gas came to Savannah. Above the pipes is a sign, a reminder of Hillyer's flair, reading: "My Other End's in Texas." A less flamboyant soul wouldn't think to place such a sign, thus leaving viewers to wonder "just what in hell are those big pipes?"

Curtis Lewis. Not every heir to a substantial estate possesses the ability to parlay an inheritance into a larger fortune and, at the same time, maintain a reputation for kindness, honesty, and philanthropic outreach. Not every such heir fritters away what Daddy has left, but many of them do. Julius Curtis Lewis, Jr., however, is not numbered among such irresponsible wastrels. He has built well upon the J. C. Lewis Motor Company,

Savannah's first and still-only Ford dealership, which his late father left a good job with the Packard agency to found. Those familiar with automotive history know that there's no such thing now as a Packard automobile, and that Ford cars will be on roadways forever.

Curtis Lewis was still in college when his father died. Instead of dropping out and returning home to operate the automobile agency and manage his dad's extensive property holdings, he relied upon the car agency's longtime officials to carry on the business until he earned his diploma. Finally, upon returning, he kept intact the agency's reliable staff and began to run things himself, with their loyal support. He has expanded the car dealership, opened other dealerships in other cities, built Savannah's third television station, acquired TV stations elsewhere, and otherwise enhanced his position as one of Savannah's wealthiest men.

Curtis Lewis, however, is more than just a successful businessman. As a philanthropist, he has been one of the strong supporters of the YMCA, which has become a large and excellent family center, on land he donated. He has contributed and solicited many dollars for the Shriners' free hospitals for crippled and burned children. Countless charities have benefitted from Lewis' benevolence. He is a pillar of the First Baptist Church. He has lent his talents and expertise to business and industrial solicitation. And, in spite of his busy schedule, he has served a four-year term as mayor of Savannah, the first of only two Republicans to hold that office.

Noted earlier is the fact that Lewis unseated Malcolm Maclean partly with the aid of a white backlash, due to the latter's having been mayor at the time destiny brought the city to the point of desegregation of public facilities and institutions.

Lewis was not then, and still isn't, a racist. He did not charge into office by rousing the rabble the way some Georgia politicians had done in the past. The white backlash simply was there, and it was not the only factor contributing to the Lewis victory. The chief factor was Lewis himself—he enjoyed many friendships, had a solid reputation as upright and God-fearing, and particularly a reputation for being honest in his business dealings. He is what Southerners regard highly—"a family man." And while Malcolm Maclean also can fit that mold, it was time for the political pendulum to swing anyway; indeed, the Citizens Committee, born as a reform faction, had enjoyed more than a decade of political success.

In other words, it was "time for a change," and it was at a point where the Republican Party was becoming a presence. Lewis went into City Hall with a six-man aldermanic board, more conservative than the Maclean administration, and none of them too sold on the council-manager form of government. Soon the administration and City Manager Arthur A. "Don" Mendonsa came to a parting of the ways. Native-son Picot Floyd, with prior experience in city government in both Savannah and Alexandria, Virginia, was hired as Mendonsa's replacement from the faculty of the University of Georgia's Institute of Government. The new mayor and aldermen found Floyd not to be as malleable as they would have liked, but, generally, the professional and political sides of government worked well together. The Lewis administration instituted the then-popular Model Cities program, financed by the federal government, which instituted many improvements in a blighted neighborhood. That program's progress, as well as a sweeping cleanup campaign throughout all of Savannah's blighted areas, won an "All-American City" award for Savannah. And while former Mayor Maclean's administration had been slightly more liberal and had engineered the lowering of racial barriers, it was during the Lewis administration that the city hired its first black department head, retired Army Lieutenant Colonel Tom Sears, to be in charge of Model Cities.

In spite of the record of the Lewis administration in uplifting the quality of life for the minority population, former county commissioner John P. Rousakis and his slate, including Bowles C. Ford, Savannah's first black candidate for an aldermanic seat, unseated the Republicans in 1970. Rousakis, in his campaigning, won over the minority bloc, and he exploited the fact that internal wrangling by some of the Lewis aldermen had inhibited a smooth-running city government. Although Lewis was one of the most conciliatory mayors that Savannah had ever had, public statements on issues by him and some of his aldermen sometimes would differ. If the public occasionally was confused, it was understandable. And near the end of the Lewis administration, differences with City Manager Floyd began to surface, becoming more pronounced during the interregnum between the election of the Rousakis slate in July and the swearing-in the following October.

During Lewis' term as mayor, there was talk of his running for Congress, and he seemed at one point receptive to the notion, but he decided against it. In retrospect, Curtis Lewis never truly seemed to enjoy being Savannah's mayor. He didn't run for the office the first time friends approached him, but thought out the prospect for a full four years before finally yielding to urgings. A modest man, he exuded a mild disdain for all that politics demanded. When he finally ran, against Maclean, he expressed shock that a certain self-anointed spokesman for the minority population approached him with a request for four thousand dollars as a "guarantee" for obtaining the minority bloc of votes. In telling the story Lewis said that he was told he could put up the money and "no one would have to know." To which, he related, his reply was, "But I would know, and it would be wrong to buy votes." Also in retrospect, there was no "guarantee" that the person who approached Lewis held any appreciable sway over the minority bloc.

Curtis Lewis left office with a record of a number of achievements, including a lower crime rate that he partly attributed to an expanded, and brighter, street-lighting program within the poorer neighborhoods. He also had declared all-out war on the drug trade by setting up a specialized police unit. His Model Cities program, which in the succeeding Rousakis administration would become a broadened community-development program, provided an excellent head start toward curing decades of neglect. Lewis went back to his business empire, which he has expanded greatly. He continues somewhat as a political activist, mainly through support of various candidates. Yet, in spite of the fact that he remains a Republican, he has contributed also to the campaigns of some Democrats, even to those of John Rousakis, the man who defeated him. Well, I noted earlier that his is a conciliatory nature. Definitely, it is. And Curtis Lewis definitely has made a positive impression upon Savannah, in many ways.

John P. Rousakis. Five four-year terms in City Hall made John Paul Rousakis Savannah's mayor with the longest tenure. Actually, he served an extra year beyond the twenty to which he was elected, the twelve-month holdover due to a revision of Georgia law requiring municipalities' elections to be held in November. Until that law passed, cities, towns, and hamlets were holding elections willy-nilly throughout the year; Savannah's were in July, with winners taking office the following October. Alas, the extra year did Democrat Rousakis little good because, when he went for his sixth term in November 1991, Republican Susan Weiner defeated him.

A lot happened, however, to change Savannah before voters decided it was time for a change, and a lot happened to him. Rousakis, a first-generation Greek-American, began to make friends early in life, when he was growing up and working in his immigrant father's Paul's Soda Shop. Paul Rousakis' place was popular with the high-school crowd. They hung out there during after-school hours, and Paul's was a favorite stop for a soda or milkshake as teenagers took their dates home after a dance or movie. Little Johnny became everyone's favorite. He became a star athlete in Savannah High School, and the team he captained as a senior won the state basketball championship. He earned a basketball scholarship to the University of Kentucky, was sidelined by an injury, was drafted into the Army during the Korean War, and returned to finish his higher education at the University of Georgia. His political career began when he helped an older friend, Carl Griffin, successfully campaign for Chatham County sheriff. Later, after a successful start in the insurance business, he ran for a county commission seat and won as an "outsider" going up against an established political organization.

It was not simply a case of defeating a single opponent when Rousakis won that race. In those days county commissioners were elected at large and not in separate districts. He ran independently, in effect against the entire commission, so he definitely was in a loyal-opposition position when he took his seat. Nevertheless, Rousakis became effective as a commissioner, advanced ideas the others sometimes would accept, and gained much public exposure by pressing his proposals. Most Savannahians knew him anyway, but he now became familiar to those who didn't. In 1970, with a lot of urging—but, being politically ambitious, needing not much encouragement—he resigned from the county governing body in order to oppose Republican Mayor Curtis Lewis' bid for a second term. And to court the minority bloc of voters, Rousakis chose a respected black insurance executive, Bowles C. Ford, to be a member of his ticket—Savannah's first black aldermanic candidate since Reconstruction. The Rousakis team won by attracting younger Savannahians as well as older ones who had either opposed Lewis four years previous or who felt the GOP administration had not done enough.

Once in office Rousakis demonstrated a keen grasp of municipal government, backed with an enthusiasm that prompted observers to say he had been born to be mayor. He really did fit the office, and over the years that he served, Rousakis was undeniably Savannah's foremost spokesman. 'Twas said that Rousakis would fly to the upper reaches of Lower Slobbovia to promote Savannah, and he virtually did. On legislation affecting cities, Rousakis became an invited adviser to Presidents Nixon, Ford, Carter, and Reagan. He became president of the Georgia Municipal Association, and later president of the National League of Cities. On forums across the country Rousakis was a champion of cities. He made trade trips to foreign countries, including his father's native Greece; and he designated Patras, Greece, as Savannah's sister city. He once thought of seeking the governorship, but that thought was only fleeting. Savannah, he said, was where he belonged.

Some projects started under previous mayors came to fruition under Rousakis, and he started many of his own. The Savannah

Civic Center was completed, and the pollution-abatement program, still ongoing, became a reality when Rousakis cut the ribbon opening the city's huge sewage-treatment plant. He grabbed hold and ran with the street-lighting project Lewis had started. The Rousakis administration accomplished more paving of Savannah's many miles of dirt streets, particularly in poorer neighborhoods, than any previous. Recreational opportunities were expanded, and new facilities were built, including the Paulson softball complex, to which Rousakis persuaded aircraft manufacturer Allen Paulson to donate many of his dollars. Affirmative action became a guideline in City Hall. The list of achievements could go on. Rousakis' only big failure was his effort to bring about consolidation of county and city governments, an idea whose time hasn't yet come in Savannah, but one day shall.

The Lewis administration and Arthur A. "Don" Mendonsa, who later would become one of America's top city managers, came to the parting of the ways. When Rousakis took office, Picot Floyd was city manager, and he worked compatibly with the elected officials. But Floyd left in 1972 for a job in Washington, and Rousakis promptly lured Mendonsa back to Savannah from Decatur, where he was DeKalb County's chief administrator. Mendonsa took up where he had left off; and until his retirement in 1995, during the Weiner administration, he applied his knowledge and expertise to not only running the city efficiently, but also to going after federal grant money to help get new programs started, one of which was a much-expanded police communication and dispatch system. Computerization, which Floyd had started, came to full bloom under Rousakis and Mendonsa.

John Rousakis stayed five terms in office with the solid

support of the black community, as well as good support of the middle- and upper-income whites. But as the Republican Party became stronger, Rousakis finally faced a GOP opponent, Susan Weiner, who drew heavily from his white support and who also cut significantly into the black precincts. When Mrs. Weiner defeated him in 1991, Rousakis carried every predominantly black precinct, but not nearly by his margins of the past. He returned full-time to his insurance business, and in 1995 he made an unsuccessful bid to regain his old office. In the city's first nonpartisan election, which eliminated the need for party primaries, Rousakis ran third in a four-candidate race, leaving Mayor Weiner and Alderman Floyd Adams to compete in a runoff, required by law whenever no candidate receives a majority of the votes cast. Adams won the runoff to become Savannah's first black mayor. Rousakis declared his retirement from politics, which of course meant he did not intend to seek office in the future. But it's a foregone conclusion that he will continue his political activism in other ways. He may stay a sideliner, but it's not his nature to stay quiet. Not anyone who has made such an impression on the community could do so.

Andy Calhoun. Such a quiet and meditative person as Andrew Pickens Calhoun does not impress others as a political type, and certainly not as one who could endure very much adversity and the acrimony that adversity breeds. But the real Andy belies all first-blush assessments. A banker by profession, and now retired, Calhoun headed the Board of Education during its most hectic period as the school system was making its transition into becoming fully racially integrated. Fate decreed that he would be president of the board the last two years of his six-year term, and as the head man he spent nearly as many hours in federal court as he did as a vice-president of Trust Company Bank. By then the desegregation suit against the school system reached the nitty-gritty, showdown stage. It required someone of stamina, with a very thick skin and with strong dedication to the community, to endure the ordeal of day-after-day testimony and cross-examination on the witness stand.

During that period Calhoun received hundreds of threatening telephone calls at his home, not to mention scathing letters, and a couple of threats that he would be bombed. At the core was the complaint of blacks that the schools were not being integrated with the "deliberate speed" that federal edicts had demanded, and never mind the costs to the taxpayers that busing and other accommodations required. Also, never mind the ongoing shifting of demographics occasioned by the integration of neighborhoods. "Right now" was the demand, and the litigants had the federal government on their side.

After leaving the school board, Calhoun became chairman of the county's board of registrars, responsible for registering voters and keeping the voting lists current. While chief registrar, compensated by the token salary of $300 a month, had been more a civic job, and an easy one, in the past, it became quite demanding during Calhoun's time in the post. Again, black demands bore heavily. He was accused of not making registration accessible, and never mind that the registrar's office operated eight hours a day at the Courthouse. Calhoun and his board decided to set up substations for voter registration in various parts of the county. But complaints arose that there weren't enough remote registration locations, and he then yielded to those. Someone of less stamina would have wilted, but Calhoun survived that ongoing crisis as he had during his school board service, and the community benefitted from such endurance. Truly, one of Savannah's unsung heroes.

Ruth Healy. For years it was said that without Ruth Healy no ship could sail into or out of the port of Savannah—an exaggeration, of course, but a tribute to the Lady of the Waterfront. Mrs. Healy was the executive secretary of Atlantic Towing Company, for years the only towboat company on the Savannah River. In her role Mrs. Healy recorded the arrivals and departures of ships from all over the world, communicated with them by radio as they approached the bar off Tybee Island, knew most of the sea captains by name, and was a fountain of knowledge on such matters as the kinds of ships, how much water they drew, what their cargoes were.

She was the reporter's friend, at least the reporters who covered the waterfront. She received twice-daily telephone calls, sometimes more, from scribes trying to keep abreast of shipping activity. Sometimes she'd offer a tip that someone of prominence was aboard an approaching vessel (most cargo ships carry a limited number of passengers), and in the year after World War II she would advise the newspapers whenever ships were bringing in repatriates—that is, American nationals who had been stranded in foreign lands when the war started. Good subjects for dockside interviews. If a ship was in distress offshore, Mrs. Healy would know about it.

Ruth Healy also was one of the several prime movers in the Altrusa Club's project to place a statue of the legendary Waving Girl on the riverfront. The Altrusans collected the money through public solicitation and hired the sculptor, the famed Felix deWeldon. Providentially and coincidentally, the city assigned Morel Park, a small plot of green space, as the location of the statue. Morel Park happened to be right beside

Atlantic Towing's riverside property. Until her retirement, Mrs. Healy could view the impressive statue from her office window —every day.

Catherine Charlton. There is no such thing now as a Society section in the *Savannah Morning News*. On Sundays the paper still carries articles on Society with a capital "S," but not in such abundance as in former days. Wedding and engagement announcements, debutante activities (now, both white and black debs), feature articles on some social events. But there was a time when daily Society pages ran, and when Miss Catherine Charlton, the society editor, was definitely Savannah's social arbiter.

Catherine was a member of an established Savannah family, a Vassar graduate, and the consummate soul of propriety. She was one of the founders of the Junior League; in fact, she was the one who suggested in the first place that Savannah organize a Junior League after visiting a city where such an organization already existed. The Junior League is an organization of socialites, of course, but it's also one of the most benevolent groups in town. Its members raise thousands of dollars annually through thrift sales, and now and then sponsor the Junior League Follies, featuring themselves, spouses, and boyfriends— an amateur show, but by no means amateurish. Tickets are priced high, and the profit goes to charities.

Miss Charlton knew and practiced all the social amenities, and she also was one of Savannah's best newspaperwomen. She was a taskmaster who insisted that the quality of her staff's writing match and surpass that of the more serious writers on the newspapers. No story made print without her personal editing. Standing alongside printers in the composing room and occasionally picking up ink stains on her clothing and hands, she daily supervised the makeup of her pages. She also had the knack of dealing tactfully with mothers of brides, each of whom felt her daughter's announcement should rate top billing on the page layout. Someone of lesser patience would have made enemies of readers, but, even if her decision disappointed a mother, the mother would leave smiling. We male editors who also had to deal daily with disappointed and sometimes irate readers envied Miss Charlton's style of interpersonal relations, but we never could quite emulate it.

When Catherine Charlton died, she did so with the satisfaction that she had impressed the newspapers' constituency, for it was a sure bet that in the days of the Society pages most Savannahians, inside or outside the main social circle, were readers of those pages.

Westley W. Law. Long before Dr. Martin Luther King and others became nationally prominent in the civil rights movement, W. W. Law was in the forefront for black people. His vocation was letter carrier for the Postal Service; his avocation was, and still is, civil rights. He was a veteran one-man "marcher" (figuratively in earlier days, of course) when, finally, the daily and nightly marches for civil rights began in the 1960's. In many forums his had been the lone voice crying in the wilderness, but suddenly there were thousands of other voices singing "We Shall Overcome." The success of the civil rights movement is now a part of our history, past and contemporary, so there's no need to recap it here. But Westley Law's accomplishments have gone far beyond merely serving many terms as president of Savannah's chapter of the National Association for the Advancement of Colored People, as well as heading the Georgia NAACP.

Of poor upbringing, Law was never formally schooled in the

science of historical research, but on his own he has become Savannah's foremost historian in and for the black community. Through his leadership, "black heritage" has become more than a mere phrase in Savannah. He has researched records, and supplemented documented material by sifting grain from chaff in the area's black folklore. He also promotes public programs commemorating the significant contributions of black citizens (and noncitizens when blacks were in slavery) to the growth and advancement of our area. Many who have gone ignored in history books are now known, and revered, and spotlighted in Savannah's Black Heritage center; and the latest project into which Law made significant input is the development of an NAACP museum in a historic building on Martin Luther King, Jr., Boulevard, a principal north-south street formerly named West Broad. Savannah's westside, and particularly West Broad Street, are interwoven into the history of the city's black population.

Not easily did Westley Law achieve his accomplishments and attain his goals. He faced an uphill struggle most of the way. Not always has he been addressed as Mr. Law, the longtime custom in old Savannah having been to address blacks by either their first names or their surnames, without the courtesy title. He is now, and has been for years, Mr. Law, and if ever anyone earned the courtesy title, it is he. And few have made such an impression on Savannah. His legacy is already in place—an inspiration of self-assuredness to those of his race who may have thought that their lot in life was one of hopelessness.

Eugene H. Gadsden. The son of a respected black educator who made significant contributions to schooling in Jim Crow days, Gene Gadsden became a lawyer ... and a politician. Mostly, though, he stayed in the background, dispensing advice

256

and good counsel to blacks on the way up. Like his father, for whom Chatham County's school board named the Robert W. Gadsden Elementary School, Gene Gadsden has been the soul of dignity, seldom if ever raising his voice in anger, his projected air of purpose and wisdom rendering the need for outbursts unnecessary.

During the racial revolution, when things were not always calm and collected, Gadsden demonstrated a knack of settling things down, brushing aside acrimony, and getting to the heart of whatever matter was in dispute. Often his was a calming voice over disturbed waters. No white politician would think of courting support from the black community without, usually first but by all means eventually, touching base with Gene Gadsden. "I'll always be involved in the politics," he once said to me, stressing that he regarded the political arena as the place for blacks to look in order to better themselves.

He became a law judge for the Workers' Compensation Board and built a reputation for even-handedness and fairness. Then, when a Superior Court judgeship opened in Chatham County at a time when governors across the United States were becoming more determined to place black lawyers into judicial seats, Gene Gadsden became the choice of the governor of Georgia. It was an appointment widely hailed by members of the bar, both white and black, and Judge Gadsden served until retirement with the same fairness he had demonstrated earlier. Until recently, as his hearing became impaired, he still heard cases as a "senior judge," a title accorded retirees from the bench who, though no longer "active," are needed nevertheless to deal with the heavy caseloads in Superior Court.

Varnedoe L. Hancock. Long before anyone ever heard of United Way—in fact, long before United Way was ever invented—Varnie Hancock ran Savannah's Community Chest. It was a scaled-down version of what United Way is now, an umbrella agency for several charitable organizations, appealing once a year for public contributions and then parceling out monthly distributions to the organizations.

Savannah couldn't have found a more even-handed executive for such an agency. Hancock had grown up in Savannah and knew everybody who was anybody. He could communicate well with heads of business and industry as well as with those who ran the charitable organizations. He knew them all by first name. He earlier had been a staff member of the YMCA, one of the Community Chest's beneficiaries. He utilized the Y's gym and swimming pool, and thus stayed in top physical shape. With the movers and shakers of Savannah he played handball at the "Y" and got to know them well. Well into his seventies he still played handball.

Hancock's Community Chest became the nucleus of a broadened umbrella agency for charities, called United Community Services for several years, then United Way. The biggest agency to come under the umbrella was the Red Cross, which had been holding a separate fund-raising drive each year. And in that merger of human services, Varnie Hancock became the manager of the Red Cross chapter, a post he held until a well-earned retirement.

Hancock involved himself in many civic activities and was Rotary's secretary seemingly forever. If there was a good cause, he would be one of its advocates and supporters, and likely a board member. He also was the most visible layman of St. John's Episcopal Church, there every Sunday as a greeter at the door, there for practically every funeral, a member of the vestry, a Sunday school teacher, involved deeply in the Men's Club, and often a delegate to diocesan conventions. Savannahians called him "Mr. St. John's," yet at his funeral in 1986 the plain Burial Office was read from the Book of Common Prayer, with no homily in which his life of devoted service, not only to the church but also to the community, could be acknowledged. It is customary in some parishes to "bury everyone alike" and not to extol the departed soul. Still, that absence of special recognition disappointed many of Hancock's friends, who had to be content with the fact that the acknowledgment of this good churchman and citizen was embodied in the outward and visible gathering of his numerous friends who packed the church.

Darnell Brawner. It was said that Darnell Brawner had delivered half of Savannah's baby boomers, and that he could recognize more women by their bottoms than by their pretty faces. An exaggeration, of course; if the truth be known, it was more like three-quarters of the babies he delivered, and he contended that he did so know women by their faces because most of the bottoms look alike. There were other OB-GYN physicians in Savannah during the post–World War II period, but Brawner certainly delivered more than one doctor's share of the babies. Yet, with that reputation for bringing so many children into the world, Darnell Brawner became just as well known for his other contributions to Savannah and vicinity.

Brawner grows roses as a hobby. He is very much into roses, more than someone who just buys a rosebush at a nursery and sets it out in the garden. He simply knows roses. He has crossbred roses and produced hybrid varieties, entered blooms in shows, and won ribbons. When Memorial Medical Center was developing its entranceway from Waters Avenue, Brawner virtually took command of the landscaping, bringing in volunteers from the Savannah Rose Society and personally directing as they planted roses into a bed that he designed beneath an array of flags representing the thirteen original states. Afterwards, he and other volunteers were back at least once a week, pruning and preening. Memorial's garden, however, is not the only spot where Brawner has spread roses. He has given away thousands of rose bushes to friends and to institutions. When the roses grow in Savannah, it's a good bet that many of those you see have some kind of relationship to the good doctor, and many are next-generation hybrids from plants he initially gave to friends.

Brawner also became a writer, authoring several books reminiscing on his own experiences as well as recollections related to him by others of older generations. One of his books, a "fictional" account of a capricious, screwball college student named Clarence, didn't fool many of Brawner's Savannah friends. Indeed, after reading the book they agreed that it was patently obvious—Brawner and Clarence were one and the same. Brawner does not to this day deny contentions that his account of Clarence is autobiographical. Nor does he confirm it, but everyone knows, or strongly suspects.

Darnell Brawner served six years on the school board, his last two as president, visited every school in the Chatham County system at least a half-dozen times, and sometimes came to board meetings wearing surgical clothes, having just left a woman in the early stages of labor so he could at least call the meeting to order and get things started. He would conduct such a meeting until he received a call to report immediately to a hospital's delivery room. Off he would scoot, leaving the meeting in the capable hands of the vice-president. If things at the hospital ran smoothly, he'd sometimes be back before meeting's end, retrieving the gavel and announcing sex and weight of the offspring he had just delivered.

A Baptist by faith, Dr. Brawner has studied extensively the religious history of Georgia. Information he gleaned from old records inspired him to construct a replica of the earliest rural Baptist church in these parts, on its original site in nearby Effingham County. The original church, merely a log cabin, was long gone when Brawner found the location and with his own hands (he had help, of course) built the tiny log structure, complete with hand-hewn pews.

In retirement, Dr. Brawner operates a farm near Savannah, but returns to Savannah so much that only his closest friends realize he has moved out of town. He continues a whirlwind kind of involvement in civic matters, though now on a lesser scale. People such as he, who have been so deeply involved in community service even while carrying a work load that would cause lesser souls to cringe, do not slow down very much. And get this—he continues to play tennis at least twice a week.

Tony Mathews. The Mathews family has been in the fish business ever since the first of the first of the Mateo clan came over from Italy and Americanized their surname. Every Mathews fish market bore the names of its individual owners, in large letters on the outside walls of each store. And every Mathews had the same middle initial—"C" for Cannarella, a part of the old-country Mateo family.

The Mathews, individually and together, were successes in the fish business; and most of them adopted avocations beneficial to the community they so very much appreciated as a place where their immigrant family found not only fortune and success, but also acceptance. Because not in every community are those of foreign birth and extraction assimilated into the warp and woof as in Savannah. Tony Mathews decided he'd be a political activist and thus help to better his community. He carried out his intentions with an inspiring display of courage in the face of physical pain and handicap.

Antonio Cannarella Mathews was born here to immigrant parents in the early 1930's. Like his older brother, Joseph "Dedi" Mathews, Tony wanted to become a boxer, although he perhaps never envisioned such Golden Gloves titles and other honors as reaped by Dedi (pronounced "dee-dye"). He simply was satisfied to become a fair amateur fighter, boxing for Benedictine Military School and later for the Catholic Young People's Association. By and by, Tony married his childhood sweetheart, Joan Morel, and they started a family.

But one day, while working in his father's retail fish house, Tony complained of a bad headache. He was running a fever and passed out. At St. Joseph's Hospital he was diagnosed with polio, and he would live out his life in a wheelchair, carrying a portable breathing apparatus. His malady, however, did not deter Tony Mathews from carrying on. After he had recovered, he and Joan operated an Italian sausage company, which also sold seafood specialties. He seldom if ever missed Mass at Blessed Sacrament Church. And he never missed an election. He became devoted to the cause of the Democratic Party, intensifying his involvement when a Georgian named Jimmy Carter jumped into the presidential derby in 1976. But before Carter, Tony had served on the Chatham County Democratic Executive Committee, and after Carter he became the party's county chairman. Before his death from a seizure in early 1996, he would earn the Democrats' top national and local awards for leadership.

Yet, as deeply committed as Tony Mathews was to the cause

of Democrats, he never spoke ill of local Republicans, nor they of him. Indeed, he had too many friends who also happened to be Republicans. Tony merely fought them along party-line differences. He relished being called a "yellow-dog Democrat," which is a Georgia expression for someone who would vote for a yellow dog rather than for a Republican. "Yellow dog and proud of it," he would say, puffing on the mouthpiece that came from his breathing machine, sometimes wheezing a little as he spoke, but always smiling, with a twinkle to convey a tweak of his GOP friends. Friends estimated that for Tony Mathews' wake and funeral the combined crowd of friends who packed Blessed Sacrament Church rivaled in size the turnout a few months earlier for the consecration of Bishop Kevin Boland at the downtown cathedral.

Kathy Haeberle. In *Only in Savannah* I started to record Katherine Beatson Haeberle as Savannah's best female reporter ever, but I hesitated because there have been some very good ones. Upon reflection, I say Kathy was among the very best, male or female. She was instinctive and intuitive, and those assets will help a reporter track down news. Kathy had another asset to go with those—curiosity. She seemed always to sense that something else was behind the couch, so she would look, and more than not, she'd find.

Kathy did not attend college. Right out of high school, she came to the *Evening Press* newsroom to be copygirl, a job that happened to be open the day she approached me after church and allowed that she'd be interested in newspaper work. The fact that I told her about the job, and introduced her to the boss when she came down the next day, branded her as my protégée, and I still brag about it. She soon graduated from the copygirl job, and took on duties as religion editor in addition to her chief responsibility as a reporter. Doing religion spare time, she won several awards in such categories as Best Religion Page, Best Religion Feature, and Best Layout. She also was perfecting her knack at getting the scoop. She could outdo both the print and electronic newsgatherers in getting the story first. She used guile and cunning in making scoops, sometimes diverting rival reporters down blind alleys while she, meanwhile, made her way straight to where the news was.

There was one occasion in particular when Kathy, arriving at City Hall shortly after lunch, about the time all the TV reporters would drop by, noted that one after another of the city aldermen was arriving and taking the elevator to the fourth floor. Usually the aldermen go to the second floor, where they get their mail and where the mayor's office is. The city manager abides on the fourth floor, so Kathy reasoned that some important meeting was about to take place. The other reporters might have reasoned similarly at first, until Kathy cornered one of the aldermen and, loud enough to be overheard, asked him a question about a project he was interested in. The TV reporters, listening to his comments, then asked him to say on videotape what he had just said to Kathy. The alderman uttered, after which the TV people packed their gear and left the city manager's outer office, Kathy leaving with them.

Kathy walked out of the building to the sidewalk, indulged in some small talk with the TV reporters, watched them drive off, and then she ran back inside City Hall and took the elevator to the fourth floor. By golly, something was going on inside the city manager's office, and she was determined to find out what it was. She simply walked to the city manager's office door, knocked politely, entered, and took a chair. She knew that under the sunshine law the city fathers would not ask her to leave. She sat there and took notes as the mayor and aldermen discussed with the city manager a big departmental shakeup and restructuring. She got the story, then went to her office and wrote it for the next morning's editions—while her peers in television, content with that innocuous little quotation from an alderman, were riding around hoping for a good fire, or murder, or some other kind of tragedy.

That was typical of Kathy Haeberle's style and dedication. She could cover anything, from a concert of classical music to a killing. Her forte was politics, and she knew every local officeholder by name, as well as many across the state. She covered two Georgia gubernatorial campaigns, and learned something about inside politics the year she took a leave while her husband, Marine Corps Master Sergeant Lee Haeberle, was stationed in the nation's capital. Kathy went to work for Congressman Elliott Hagan, who represented Georgia's First District, which includes Savannah. Kathy Haeberle became the first female city editor of the Savannah dailies, and when she retired in 1993 she was second in command on the central copy desk. In retirement, she serves as a tour guide for visitors. With her experience probing behind the scenes, it's reasonable to conclude that the tourists she takes around learn a whole lot more about Savannah than the other visitors. Not every tour guide knows where the skeletons abide.

Bill Owen. He lived past eighty and may well have been Savannah's counterpart of Bernarr McFadden, the nationally known publisher of *Physical Health* magazine who in his senior years was in better physical shape than many men his junior. C. William Owen was an excellent specimen of manhood. He stayed in shape two ways—by working out daily at the YMCA, and by playing the chimes daily in the steeple of historic St.

John's Episcopal Church. He was not a chimer by profession, nor was he a physical therapist; those were his avocations. He was employed by the insurance industry as an adviser for fire underwriters. He could adjust his job hours to afford his other outlets.

The chimes of St. John's now are a full carillon of forty-three bells, and they are played electronically from the keyboard of the church's magnificent organ. In Bill Owen's day, St. John's had only fifteen bells in its belfry, played manually by pulling levers, attached by steel rods to the bells above the chimer. Pulling those levers demanded strength, dexterity, and agility. For example, the chimer would pull levers at the far end of his console and then would be required by the hymn music to make a sidewise jump to the opposite end of the console to pull the lever for the next-needed note. Bill Owen, therefore, offered to observers the picture of a veritable jumping-jack. In a fifteen-minute concert he would work up a soaking sweat inside his gym suit.

Most of his concerts ran that length—fifteen minutes. He played for fifteen minutes before each Sunday service, and another fifteen as church was letting out. Weekdays he would climb into the steeple and play quarter-hour concerts each afternoon. Also, he was available usually to play after weddings, serenading happy couples as they left the church. Bill Owen indeed made an impression on Savannah and her visitors, pealing forth beautiful religious music, prompting strollers to pause in Madison Square and listen in awesome enjoyment. The legendary "Chimes of St. John's" add a lovely tuneful dimension to the ambience of downtown Savannah.

Tom Coleman. One rightly could call Joseph Thomas Coleman, Jr., Savannah's All-American boy, although he hasn't been a boy for years. But while growing up, Tom Coleman seemed to do everything right. As a student in Benedictine Military School, he commanded the cadet corps. He excelled in football at Benedictine—sturdy lineman, team captain; and he played other sports. He also was an elocutionist, invited while a student to speak and recite before civic clubs, his foremost recitation being a dramatic "Casey at the Bat." He earned a football scholarship to Georgia Tech and captained the Yellow Jackets of Coach Bobby Dodd as a senior. He earned a reserve Army commission at Tech, served as a combat officer in the Korean War, and came out a captain. He entered the construction business in his native Savannah, and became head of the local branch of a regional company. He entered politics as a city alderman with the Citizens Committee reform faction; later won the chairmanship of the Chatham County Commission; and then after laying out of politics for a year (business reasons), he won a seat in the Georgia Senate and served ten two-year terms before retiring again from politics, a retirement that has held up. He now is on the university system's Board of Regents, theoretically nonpolitical.

In the state Senate Coleman held leadership posts on several committees, including Highways and Roads, and shepherded through the upper house many important pieces of legislation. Because of his excellent record as head of Highways and Roads, the state named a section of Interstate 95, approaching the new Savannah International Airport, in Coleman's honor.

The affable Tom Coleman, an Irish-Catholic, holds a record of public service matched by very few politicians, and through his whole political career there was never any hint of scandal or conflict of interest. He ventured into politics as collective Savannah's "That's my boy!" and he emerged holding the same

267

high esteem of his community. He bore the Democrat label in his political career, but operated as an evenhanded officeholder, squarely facing the issues, irrespective of partisan sponsorship. Ironically, after winning most of his elections unopposed, he faced his first big challenge at the polls as the Republican Party began to grow stronger in Georgia and fielded an opponent for his First District seat in the Senate. Nothing personal, Republicans said, but the national party, targeting grass roots as well as gubernatorial and congressional offices, decided to go after a senior Democrat in Georgia; and what better seat to target than "Georgia-One." Coleman warded off two challenges by the GOP, and he won the second of those races by only a slim margin. In politics, sometimes, a centrist in the opposite party becomes as fair game as an extremist, and never mind whether that centrist has been cordial to the opposition in the past. After those two challenges, Coleman opted to quit the Senate a winner, although his supporters felt he again could withstand another GOP challenge.

Attestation to Tom Coleman as a statesman rather than a partisan politician came as he faced the first of those last two Republican challenges. Coleman never had paid much attention to his own political record in the sense of setting down his achievements and failures (of which there were few) for future reference. But when he and his supporters realized that the GOP was serious about ousting him, Coleman decided, for the first time in his career, to hire a public-relations specialist to boost his campaign. He chose Betty Platt, a longtime activist who had never PR'd for a Republican, and never would because she was a dyed-in-the-wool Democrat.

Ms. Platt set about gathering material on Coleman's record in order to produce campaign literature for distribution to the populace. She asked Coleman for his scrapbook, and he told her that he had never kept one. "No loose newspaper clippings?" Ms. Platt pursued. No, he replied, because he had never felt that to be necessary, and seldom had he even read articles about himself. "Strangest dadgum politician I ever saw," Ms. Platt lamented, as she dropped by the newspaper office one day asking to view Coleman's clip file in the library. "Would you believe, we've got a real statesman out there, and the Republicans want to get rid of him, f' Lord's sake." Coleman's publicist turned to his wife, Mary, thinking perhaps she had a scrapbook. Yes, she did, and it ended with a story about his last football game for Georgia Tech, plus a few articles from the Army's hometown news service, printed in the local press when her husband was in Korea.

Tom Coleman's personal modesty—the fact that he never felt the necessity for preserving proof of his political service for fanny-covering purposes—is rare among politicians, most of whom, after being first elected, start developing the paranoia syndrome. Coleman simply performed his duties, as best he saw them and as best he could, and let the chips fall. He remains Savannah's All-American boy, even in his sixties.

Mac Bell. The civic contributions by Malcolm Bell, Jr., to Savannah are many and varied. In his career as a banker he chaired or served on just about every board, commission, and committee whose purposes were to enhance the quality of life in Savannah—Red Cross, United Way, Board of Education, Savannah Port Authority—the list runs much longer.

Bell was born into a newspaper family, and he proved that there must be something to the contention that printer's ink in one's veins is inbred. His grandfather, Frank G. Bell, was publisher of the *Savannah Morning News* in the 1920's; his father, Malcolm Senior, was an official of the newspaper company until his retirement; and his brother, Frank, was a reporter until deciding to opt for a career as a pilot in the Air Force. Mac Bell wrote several books on aspects of Savannah's history, including *Savannah, Ahoy!* about the S. S. *Savannah*, the first steam-powered vessel to sail the Atlantic (or any ocean), which departed this city for Liverpool in May 1819 and revolutionized commercial shipping. He wrote articles for the *Georgia Historical Quarterly*, the official organ of the Georgia Historical Society, a statewide organization headquartered in the Mother City, which he once headed.

Mac Bell also was an excellent photographer, collaborating often with his wife, Muriel Barrow Bell, to record on film many of Savannah's landmarks, some of which fell victim to the wrecking ball before preservationists came to the fore. Indeed, he was one of the preservationists, and lived in a magnificent townhouse in the Historic District. His photographs were, mostly, classic black-and-white studies of the urban environment of his hometown, and many are preserved by the Georgia Historical Society.

The demeanor of Mac Bell was in marked contrast to his dynamic personality. No more laid-back mover and shaker ever lived. He was what I regarded as an uptown good ol' boy, friendly to everyone, never ruffled, calm as the waters on a windless day, yet a bundle of energy. I often wondered how he managed time enough to run the Savannah Bank & Trust Company, for years a home-owned commercial bank that merged with North Carolina–headquartered First Union. He left Merrill Lynch a year or two after joining that brokerage firm following World War II, advanced to the bank's presidency, and was board chairman when he retired and decided to move to the

North Carolina mountains. Malcolm Bell, Jr., definitely left his mark on Savannah, and the mark was long and broad.

Others, of Course. It would be impossible to set down names and reminiscent sketches of all Savannahians who have made impressions on our community. These have been only a few who have become indelible in the mind of the author. A companion listing would include Raymond Demere, the oil industrialist who won trophies sailing his *Ocean Queen* yawl in ocean races; Robert C. Roebling, grandson of the man who built the Brooklyn Bridge, who settled on nearby Skidaway Island and, after retiring as a cattle baron, donated most of his property on Skidaway for the Ocean Science Center; Robert W. Groves, the multifaceted business tycoon who was active in civic and philanthropic endeavors; Emanuel Lewis, one of Savannah's best, most interesting, as well as entertaining, lawyers, who also served in judicial posts; Don Harwood, who was general manager of the newspapers, Chamber of Commerce president, and Airport Commission chairman as plans were initiated and building started on Savannah's fine new airport; Donald Rosenblum, three-star general who came to the area to command the Twenty-fourth Infantry Division at Fort Stewart, moved back after retirement, and is much involved in community life; Nola Roos, a pioneer in women's involvement in local politics; Jesse Dixon Sayler and Marion Faircloth Baker, who served successively as Savannah's first and second female customs collectors; Esther Garrison, a wonderful lady, an educator who before her death would serve several terms on the school board, and for whom a school is named in tribute to her community service; Katherine Redmond, longtime clerk of council who worked compatibly and efficiently through all the administrations she served, irrespective of political party; Diane

Reese, Savannah's first black clerk of council; Barbara Kiley, our first female tax commissioner; the Reverend L. Scott Stell, Chatham's County's first black commissioner, whose lawsuit led to school desegregation; the Dyer and Hogan families, whose members, both male and female, have for generations secured the mooring lines of every ship docking in Savannah Harbor; Jack Cay, an insurance mogul whose volunteer time as a civic leader set a sterling example for others to emulate; Dwight James Bruce, a superior organist who directed the First Baptist choir for years, and who was the founding president of the Savannah Symphony Society, and a radio executive who helped to lead WTOC, Savannah's first station, into the age of television; Boykin Paschal, general manager of the local dailies and a creative pioneer in advertising techniques; the Fred Wessels, father and namesake son, the former of whom started a local insurance firm on a shoestring and whose legacy to the latter was a multimillion-dollar business; Mr. and Mrs. Fred Weis, who successfully operated the Savannah Theatre as uphill competitors against one of Georgia's largest film-exhibiting chains; Arthur Lucas, head of the aforementioned Lucas & Jenkins chain, whose namesake opulent movie palace in downtown Savannah is being restored at this writing to serve as a community theater. The list could be endless, and Savannah is better because these fine people and countless others not mentioned here (because I failed to preserve notes) passed this way, paused, and served.

Epilogue

I questioned my judgment when I began this sequel to *Only in Savannah*. I asked myself a thousand times whether I could recollect, glean up through research, and set down in words sufficient additional anecdotes and assorted trivia and important stories to do another book. That word "do" is a Savannah idiom; whatever one is about, he or she "does." The First Book was the result of being urged to do a book; newspaper readers over the years have suggested that I do a column on one subject or another; in school we did our homework (and there's a story floating around about one college student who asks another: "Has you did your Greek yet?"). Well, I've done it, for better or for worse, and with much gratitude for the encouragement offered by readers of the First Book that I do a sequel.

I doubt that there will be a third such book because I've always wanted to venture into fiction, and intend to try fulfilling that desire. In fact, before beginning this book I had written several chapters of a mystery, with a Savannah setting. It was a nice exercise, but not exactly what I want, so I'll likely start over, but with the same hero whose name I cannot allow to stay out of print because of the way that name came to me.

But let me say this about my beloved Savannah, the city I lived in as a baby and returned to with my parents and sister Nancy in 1935: This is a city that is full of good stories. Many books have been written about the Mother City of Georgia. It's an exciting city, thus inspirational. It's historic, thus inspirational. It's beautiful, thus inspirational. Savannah has changed, it's in the process of more change, and it shall change in the future. Yet, it remains Savannah, with a basic charm and ambience transcending change. That's what makes Savannah special. You can't say that about Atlanta, which once was every

Georgian's special kind of grown-up country town. Atlanta has a new kind of ambience, though some of the old remains in some of the neighborhoods—if you can figure how to leave the many expressways and find those neighborhoods. You get lost in Atlanta, and that's a pity because Atlanta has become the South's hub. Trouble is, those who come from the hinterlands to the hub never knew the old Atlanta.

You can't get lost in Savannah. We're a shipping hub in our part of the world, a business hub on the Atlantic Coast, a something-to-see hub for thousands of tourists. But, first, foremost, and always—we're Savannah. And Savannah is the city I love.